*"If you want to get the results that winners get,
you must first think like a winner thinks!"*

So how does a winner think? Here is a list of the ten core beliefs that are unique to all peak performing men and women. Consider each one carefully, and imagine what your world would begin to look like if you held the same beliefs and made them a part of your life today.

One: Winners are not born, they are made.

Two: The dominant force in your existence is the thinking you engage in.

Three: You are empowered to create your own reality.

Four: There is some benefit to be had from every adversity.

Five: Each one of your beliefs is a choice.

Six: You are never defeated until you accept defeat as a reality, and decide to stop trying.

Seven: You already possess the ability to excel in at least one key area of your life.

Eight: The only real limitations on what you can accomplish in your life are those you impose on yourself.

Nine: There can be no great success without great commitment.

Ten: You need the support and cooperation of other people to achieve any worthwhile goal.

So turn the page, and start to think like a winner!

THINK LIKE A WINNER!

THINK
LIKE A
WINNER!

Dr. Walter Doyle Staples

WILSHIRE BOOK COMPANY
9731 VARIEL AVENUE
CHATSWORTH, CALIFORNIA 91311

Library of Congress Cataloging-in-Publication Data

Staples, Walter Doyle.
    Think like a winner! / Walter Doyle Staples.
        p.   cm.
    Includes bibliographical references and index.
    ISBN 0-88289-833-7
    1. Success.   I. Title.
BJ1611.2.S67   1991
158'.1—dc20   90-19985
                                                              CIP

Cover design by David Visel and Associates, Torrance, CA

Manufactured in the United States of America

Published by Pelican Publishing Company, Inc.
1101 Monroe Street, Gretna, Louisiana 70053

Contents

Preface

"To change the world, you need only perceive it
in a different light."
—The Author

Everyone wants to be a winner.

Nobody could ever deny the truth in this statement. Subconsciously, deep down, everyone wants to be successful—to "win" at life. Many people fervently believe they are worthy of it and deserve it. All the while, most are confused and disappointed that true success hasn't yet come their way.

It's a curious fact that many people don't realize there is a process to become successful. They readily accept the fact that to become a successful doctor, engineer, or lawyer, there is a process to this end— several years of serious study and effort. Why should it be any different to become successful at life?

It should be self-evident that if all you harbor are "failure" thoughts, then all of your endeavors will result in failure. It follows you need to harbor "success" thoughts if you want to be successful. You must first *think like a winner* if you want to become a winner. You need to acquire the empowering beliefs of the world's super achievers!

And that's why you need this book. In fact, if you read only one self-help book in your lifetime, make it this one! It represents a complete manual for personal and professional development based on practical, proven advice.

Its primary objective is to convince average people that they can become exceptional in one or more key areas of their lives, regardless of their upbringing, education, or previous level of accomplishment. Its message is universally applicable to managers, teachers, salespeople, administrators, engineers, nurses, entrepreneurs, secretaries, and students alike—to anyone willing to put more into life in order to get more out of it.

It also contains more relevant quotes—from over one hundred famous people throughout history—to support key points in the text than any other book of its kind. This translates into more than *five thousand years* of collective wisdom, assuming each of these individuals lived an average of fifty years.

Obviously, *thinking like a winner* has been practiced for a very long time by some of the most successful people who have ever lived. It is not a new concept or fad that will soon go away. You should make a serious attempt to learn from the hard-earned wisdom of other successful people who have gone before you, rather than simply from your own mistakes. In this way, you'll progress farther much, much faster. Time, after all, is your scarcest asset.

This book demystifies the meaning of the word "success." There are no magic powers at work that make people successful. Average people are average only to the extent they have average "picture-images" dominating their subconscious reality. Likewise, exceptional people are exceptional only to the extent they have exceptional "picture-images" dominating their subconscious reality. What you "see" in your mind is what you expect. What you expect, then, is what you get. This is the principal difference between people who achieve only average results in their lives and those who achieve exceptional results.

One of the most effective tools to create new picture-images, and in turn a new reality, is a process called *reframing*. Reframing involves changing the way you represent ideas and experiences in your mind. It is always more effective to represent experiences as positive and fulfilling rather than as negative and defeating. In this way, you are empowered to move ahead in your life and accomplish great things for yourself and others, things you otherwise would not have done. Remember this: the only people who do not change their mind are stubborn people who won't and dead people who can't. Some realities are permanent—but most are not.

Here are a few of the questions that inspired the quest for knowledge that ultimately led to this book:

- Why are some people more successful than others?

- How can you gain control over your thoughts and actions?

• What are the unique characteristics of high achievers?

The rewards you receive in life come as a result of your *performance*, not your *potential*. This book puts your current performance in relation to your full potential into clearer focus for rational assessment. It puts these two factors into better perspective in light of information not made available to you before.

Before embarking upon any great endeavor, Thomas Edison (1847–1931), the prolific American inventor, gave this advice: "The first thing is to find out everything everybody else knows, and then begin where they left off."

The information in this book attempts to represent what "everybody else knows" concerning human potential and personal growth. It provides you with a meaningful starting point, a new beginning to a richer, more fulfilling life.

To quote Thomas Mann (1875–1955), the German novelist in America who received the Nobel prize in literature in 1929: "Order and simplification are the first step toward mastery of a subject; the actual enemy is the unknown."

The subject you want mastery over is the process of how and why you think the way you do, for *when you change your thinking, you change your life.*

Acknowledgments

No author writes a book without enormous help from others. I have drawn insights and ideas from many sources including magazines, books, tapes, seminars, and lectures. Drawing on my own twenty-five years of business experience and lecture work, I have built upon these ideas to present as original an approach as possible to support my thesis: *To be a winner, you must first think like a winner!*

My understanding of this subject has been affected most significantly by the following individuals:

Kenneth Blanchard	Wayne Dyer
Napoleon Hill	Maxwell Maltz
James Newman	Norman Vincent Peale
Tom Peters	Anthony Robbins
Robert Schuller	Brian Tracy
Denis Waitley	Zig Ziglar

I trust this book advances the cause they all so unselfishly serve: the development of human potential.

Finally, a special word of thanks to Kenneth Blanchard, Art Linkletter, James Newman, Norman Vincent Peale, Anthony Robbins, Robert Schuller, Brian Tracy, and Denis Waitley for their kind testimonials and interest in my work; to Joan Price Winser, former Consul General of Canada in Los Angeles, who thinks like a winner every day of her life; to Betty Westbury, who typed the first draft; and to my editors, Claudette Wassil-Grimm, Faren Bachelis, and Barbara Marinacci, who added greatly to the original manuscript.

Introduction

"Man is what he believes."
> —Anton Chekhov (1860-1904)
> Russian novelist and dramatist

Psychology is the scientific study of human behavior and mental thought processes. It is involved in all aspects of your life including your happiness and sadness, and your relationships, either good or bad, with family, friends, business associates, and society in general. No endeavor—from building a marriage, raising children, communicating your ideas to others, selling a product, or establishing a new business — is ever entirely separate from psychological purview.

During the past thirty-five years, major breakthroughs have been made in the field of behavioral psychology. Among the most significant are theories about the nature of the self-image, the power of positive thinking, and the cybernetic or goal-seeking nature of the human success mechanism. All of these approaches are combined in an exciting, new methodology called *Neuro-Linguistic Programming* (NLP). The term Neuro-Linguistic comes from "neuro" meaning brain and "linguistic" which refers to language. "Programming" is the inputting of an idea or concept into the mind. NLP, then, is the study of how people communicate both verbally and nonverbally with their brain, and how this affects their central nervous system and behavior.

Despite these breakthroughs, the public retains a certain skepticism about any approach that claims to effect meaningful and predictable change in individual behavior. This is not because these theories do not work. Indeed, when applied individually or collectively with diligence and determination, they have proven tremendously effective in helping many thousands of people develop higher levels of self-confidence, increased energy and enthusiasm, and a new sense of purpose and direction in their lives.

There may be a pragmatic explanation for the public's resistance to applying self-improvement techniques. Collecting, studying, assimilating, and applying all of the relevant information is simply too burdensome a task for the average person. Few can afford the luxury of taking five years out of their lives to carry out all of the above activities. Most people are too preoccupied with their daily routines to make a major commitment to personal growth and professional development. Instead, they continue to follow in their familiar rut — and try to survive at least one more day.

This book aims to help busy people overcome the time constraints in their lives that severely limit self-improvement. It concentrates on the one most significant causal factor that determines all self-directed, purposeful behavior: namely, the personal beliefs and their associated images that people hold about themselves and their abilities, and the expectations these beliefs in turn generate.

Expectation Theory

I call this approach *expectation theory*. Expectation theory holds that your fundamental beliefs about yourself and your world are the principal determinants of your success in life. In fact, it is through your beliefs that you create the very world you live in.

The practical application of the theory works in this way:

- The beliefs you hold are the direct result of all the thinking you have, or have not, engaged in. Beliefs are latent but powerful forces buried deep in the confines of your mind.

- Your beliefs, in turn, create your expectations about results and future outcomes. Expectations are active forces at work in your mind.

- Your expectations, in turn, determine your attitude. Your attitude, once expressed, determines your behavior.

Consider the following cause-and-effect relationship to see how personal beliefs represent the very foundation of your life:

WHEN YOU CHANGE YOUR THINKING,
you change your beliefs;

When you change your beliefs,
you change your expectations;
When you change your expectations,
you change your attitude;
When you change your attitude,
you change your behavior;
When you change your behavior,
you change your performance;
When you change your performance,
YOU CHANGE YOUR LIFE!

Note that you cannot change your life by trying to change your life; you cannot change your performance by trying to change your performance; you cannot change your behavior by trying to change your behavior; you cannot change your attitude by trying to change your attitude; you cannot change your expectations by trying to change your expectations; you cannot change your beliefs by trying to change your beliefs. *But you can change the picture-images or internal representations you hold in your mind that represent your ingrained thinking.* This will bring about change in all the other areas of your life that are important to you.

Your beliefs represent conscious decisions you have made in the past about yourself and what you expect or do not expect to accomplish. These decisions are now repeated unconsciously as you go through life. They continuously control your thinking, direct your behavior, and determine your relative level of performance. How you perform in any given area of your life is only partly a function of your potential in that area. In fact, it is largely a function of your *deep-seated beliefs.*

Of all your beliefs, the most important are your *core beliefs*, for they are absolutely critical to your future. You possess thousands upon thousands of beliefs about every aspect of life. You have an opinion or belief about tennis, air pollution, sports cars, politicians, sailboats, pasta, antique furniture, flowers, rock music, snakes, airplanes, camping . . . and on and on. But none of these particular beliefs has a major impact on your life. The same cannot be said about the core beliefs listed at the beginning of the book. *For core beliefs are basic to your very being,* and are primary determinants concerning the direction your life takes.

Your mind is the dynamic force behind the marvelous success system within you. Whatever you believe, picture in your mind, and think about most of the time, you eventually will bring into reality.

In its simplest form, expectation theory says that you generally get what you expect. Positive expectations are the single, most outwardly identifiable characteristic all successful, winning personalities demonstrate. Such people naturally radiate high levels of confidence, enthusiasm, and optimism while going about achieving their goals.

Consider for a moment some of the successful people you have met — the teachers, coaches, and business and community leaders you have admired. What aspects of their behavior stand out most in your mind as being unique? Aren't they all generally very confident, enthusiastic, and optimistic? If they have become successful by being this way, then you can as well. You need only perceive the world as they perceive it, and in this way allow yourself to perform as they are able to perform.

Self-Limiting Beliefs Equate to Self-Defeating Behavior

The total accumulation of data involving everything that has ever happened to you in your life is referred to as your personal belief system, your reality, or the truth as you know, understand, and accept it to be. It serves as your frame of reference as you continue to experience new things in life and represents the total "programming" your mind has been subjected to, voluntarily or involuntarily, up to now.

For example, who you are at this very moment, sitting and reading this page, is *what your mind believes you are.* Your abilities to solve a problem, perform a task, or reach a specific goal all depend on your mind's stored beliefs about your strengths and weaknesses in each of these areas.

The breakthrough comes when you realize that the belief system you now possess is generally unreliable, since it is based on information that is often inaccurate, insufficient, or irrational. Few of us really "know" that much about anything, even in this modern age, especially about our own inherent talents and abilities that rarely have been fully and properly tested.

People acquire their beliefs from their prior experiences — or, more correctly, from their interpretation of these prior experiences. Therefore, any particular belief you may now hold is more of a subjective opinion than an objective fact. Only by the critical reassessment of long-standing beliefs can you change them and move ahead with your life. This necessarily involves doing some . . . deep, concentrated *thinking!*

When You Change Your Thinking, You Change Your Life

There is a process whereby you can change your life. You can flush out all the old, tired, I-used-them-before thoughts and fill your mind with new, challenging, I-am-in-charge thoughts.

Did you know you are in charge? *Yes, you are!* You need only recognize it and exercise your authority. This book will show you how to change your current thought processes and particular manner of thinking in order to bring about dramatic change in your life. The object is always high-performance human behavior to help you get what you want rather than what you now have.

You have what you've got by doing what you've been doing — thinking in the particular manner you have become accustomed to. It's simple enough. If what you want in the future is different from what you've got in the present, *you have to change what you've been doing!*

The rewards you receive in life do not come because of your potential. They come as a result of your *performance*. It is your performance, then, that you must focus on and ultimately improve upon.

There is a high road and a low road through life. The high road allows you to focus your efforts and concentrate your energy on accomplishing your goal. The low road diverts your attention and dissipates your energy resources. It is always more productive to focus on what you perceive as challenges or opportunities rather than on what you perceive as problems or set-backs; to focus on reasons why you can achieve your goal rather than on reasons why you cannot; to focus on solutions rather than on excuses. There will always be impediments between what you want and what you've got. Your attitude toward these temporary obstacles, rather than the obstacles themselves, will determine in the end whether you succeed or fail.

Your life is not determined so much by your outward conditions and circumstances as it is by the way you perceive these factors to be. Your world is basically what your thoughts make of it. American psychiatrist Dr. Karl Menninger once remarked: "Attitudes are more important than facts." All success is "self"-centered. As you will see, it must begin and be brought about *from within*.

The Challenge in Positive Thinking

The body follows the path most illuminated by the mind, whether it be rocky or smooth. In this way, you can enter the depths of despair and confusion or reach the heights of enlightenment. By looking out your window on the world, you can see problems or opportunities. They are in fact two sides of the same coin and both are present in great abundance. What you choose to focus on in the end is what you dwell upon. This entity then grows in your consciousness to become bigger than life, your world as you accept it and make it to be. It is the way you have decided to interpret all the faces of the things that reflect in the "eye" of your mind, and makes either a hell or a heaven of your life here on earth.

This paragraph describes the very real challenge we all face. A positive approach to life has not been widely embraced and put into everyday use by the average person. *Positive thinking is practical living*. Of all the choices available to you, it is the most productive and the most fulfilling.

Positive thinking is not a cop-out, an excuse to avoid reality. Instead it helps create its own reality, one that is more consistent with effective behavior and high performance. It helps keep all the pessimism so prevalent in our society at an appropriate distance and in proper perspective. It does not allow the 10 percent that is not perfect in your life to influence and control 100 percent of your thinking and day-to-day existence. *Your reality is what you make it to be.* In the end, it is your perception of reality that will make all the difference in the way you think, the way you behave, and the way you perform.

As individuals, we are all different, yet in many ways, we are also the same. We are all made from the same mold and blessed with life and the potential for high achievement. We all have a unique mix of talents and abilities that usually go undeveloped and underutilized. We all have twenty-four hours each day and seven days each week to live out our lives in whatever way we choose. Life is really a series of choices. They are your right as well as your responsibility. In fact, the only thing you don't have a choice about is making choices, for to avoid them is to make them. This book deals with the most important choice in your life: *your particular manner of thinking.*

The process of positive thinking is more simple than most people realize. Positive thinking primarily involves focusing your attention on *positive subjects* or on the positive side of a particular situation, and using positive words, images, and actions to express yourself. You can train yourself to think more positively by training yourself to choose what you pay attention to and what you say about it, both to yourself and others. You can learn to find the good even in the bad, thereby making the bad not so bad anymore.

This approach invariably increases the amount of happiness in your life. Happiness is a state of mind, a decision to adopt a mental strategy that leads to a more effective and satisfying life. Of course, you cannot expect to achieve everything in life you want just because you want it. But you can achieve more than you ever thought possible if only you take the time to develop the talents and abilities you already possess. "We know what we are but know not what we may be," was the keen observation of William Shakespeare (1564-1616), the famous English poet and dramatist.

Such purposeful action puts you in control. It frees you from having accidental circumstances, good luck, or other people determine your level of happiness. *You should never, ever surrender control to external forces.*

So I invite you to read on, and begin to discover who you really are and what you are capable of achieving. Try to identify the major role expectations play in the many examples presented in the text. The learning experience will be all the more meaningful if you are able to discover and determine for yourself what makes you the person you are today. You can hope to participate in the evolution and growth of the human race only to the extent you discover and bring into reality your full potential as a human being.

Where Are We Headed?

Many new and brilliant discoveries are being made every day that reflect human progress, our steady march toward a better understanding and control over our environment. From the secrets of the atom to the exploration of outer space, great achievements are being recorded, many not considered within the realm of possibility only a few years ago.

But ask yourself this vital question: *Do you have adequate knowledge of yourself?* Do you understand the way you think, and why you respond and behave the way you do? Do you fully appreciate the potential you possess, the true power of your mind? Many in our society do not—the alcoholic does not, the drug addict does not, and the school dropout does not. In fact, the average person does not. I believe we would be better served if we first tried to better understand our own physical, mental, and spiritual nature, the workings of our mind, before trying to discover all the mysteries of the universe.

The greatest mystery in the world involves the essence of Man. We have learned how to manage and control many facets of our environment. Yet one thing still eludes us: we have yet to gain mastery over ourselves, over our thinking, and over our lives. The words of Alexander Pope (1688–1744), the English poet, written more than two hundred and fifty years ago are as timely today as they were then: "Know then thyself . . . the proper study of mankind is Man."

NEURO-LINGUISTIC PROGRAMMING
Reframing Exercise #1
"THE CONFIDENCE BUILDER"

Stand in a quiet room and imagine yourself feeling supremely confident, and totally at ease with yourself and your surroundings. This should represent a peak experience or mental "high," something you probably have experienced only a few times in your life. You can do this by recalling an occasion from the past when you felt this way or by simply imagining how you would feel if you were in such a marvelous state.

Now consider how you would stand, breathe, and look in this heightened state of well-being. As you become aware of your posture — back straight, shoulders set, and head high—form a fist with one hand and smash it into the palm of the other several times with great vigor and intensity, each time shouting, "Yes, I can!" out loud in your most confident voice. As you become aware of your breathing in this state of absolute confidence — slow, deep, and from the abdomen—repeat the same gesture and affirmation. Do this sequence over again as you become aware of your facial expression: eyes, jaw, and teeth all set in a confident, comfortable manner. For a few moments, consider your whole physiology as you stand and experience this enhanced state of awareness.

Do this exercise ten times each day for one week. After this time, you will have anchored this desirable mental state into your subconscious reality, and can recall it on demand before or during any anxious moment by merely forming a fist and repeating the affirmation to yourself, even in a soft whisper. Always remember this as your *"think like a winner!"* feeling. It is your door to a new reality and an exciting future.

PART I

The Argument
for Expectation Theory

CHAPTER 1

What Makes People Successful?

"Change your thoughts and you change your world."
—Norman Vincent Peale

Have you ever wondered what distinguishes a successful person from somebody who is not, the reason why one person is able to achieve more success than another? Thousands of studies have been conducted over the years in search of the answer.

Many leading thinkers and writers have spent their entire lives addressing this very question: Why are some people consistently more successful than others in all aspects of their lives? Some people seem to "have it all." They have more friends, enjoy better health, perform at higher levels, make more money, and benefit from more effective and loving relationships than others do.

A common belief held by many is that success in life is the result of either heredity, your childhood environment, good luck, or some combination of all these things. At first glance, there appears to be some logical basis for such a point of view. After all, you don't have any choice regarding the parents you end up with, the city or town you are born in, or your particular nationality. Nor are you generally consulted on how many brothers or sisters you have, what language you speak, or who your neighbors are. Hence your parents' genetic makeup and environment automatically become a major part of your life, whether you like it or not.

First, what are the facts that relate to the theory that successful people, solely because of heredity, are destined for success?

No one set of genes is common to all successful people. Successful people come in a wide variety of sizes, shapes, and colors, and with different physical and mental attributes. No two are exactly alike. There are examples of identical twins with exactly the same genetic code where one goes on to success and the other does not. Also, we all know of people who were not successful at one point in their lives and later went on to achieve great success, with their genetic code staying exactly the same in the process.

The other argument, that people are successful solely as a result of their upbringing, has more validity. Researchers have discovered that certain environments tend to produce certain behavioral characteristics, positive leading to positive and negative leading to negative. Children raised in a ghetto environment have a higher incidence of failure in school and crime, for example, than children raised in middle- and upper-class neighborhoods. But it works both ways. Families raised in poverty have produced a good number of successful offspring, and middle- and upper-class families have produced their fair share of failures. Success, then, is not guaranteed by environmental factors alone.

On the other hand, there is overwhelming evidence to support the premise that success results more from certain mental traits and personality characteristics known as *attitudes* than from any other single factor. Attitudes are the result of choices you make — decisions to *believe or not believe* in particular aspects of your life. For example, some people choose to adopt firm beliefs in honesty, integrity, resourcefulness, effort, and respect for their fellow human beings. Others do not. You tend to adopt such beliefs from the thinking of those around you, those you have associated with and who acted as your role models during your formative years. To this extent, you are a product of the wide range of suggestive elements in your environment.

However, positive attitudes and beliefs are not peculiar to any one environment. They are simply present everywhere, to a greater or lesser extent, and you choose to make them a part of your life or not. *Clearly, winners are not born, they are made—a key core belief of all peak performing men and women.*

Consider the following statements that demonstrate particular mental traits characteristic of all high achievers:

- Yes, what will be will be, but instead of doing nothing about it, I intend to do something about it.

- Yes, I believe my fate is ultimately in my hands, that if it is to be, it's up to me.
- Yes, luck will play some role in my life, but only as I make happen what I have decided will happen.

Such people believe they are in control of their lives, and are willing to accept full responsibility for their behavior and the results it brings.

Now to dispel the last argument, that luck is a main factor, let me share with you an ancient Chinese legend that clearly illustrates that luck has little to do with success in life.

The story is told of an old man who seemed to have everything. He had a beloved son, a prized horse, and many of the material things that most people want. But one day his most valuable possession, his horse, broke out of the corral and ran away into the nearby mountains. In one catastrophic moment, he lost this priceless asset.

On hearing of this calamity, his neighbors came to offer their profound sympathy. They all said to him, "Your horse is gone, what bad luck!" Then they cried and attempted to console him. But he answered back, "How do you know it's bad luck?"

Sure enough, a few days later, the horse returned home where he knew there would be ample food and water. Along with him, he brought back twelve beautiful wild stallions. When all the townspeople heard the good news, they came over and congratulated the man, saying, "What good luck, thirteen horses!" And the wise old man replied, "How do you know it's good luck?"

They remembered his words the next day when his son, his only child, tried to ride one of the wild stallions. He was thrown off, broke his leg, and was left with a permanent limp. When his neighbors heard about the accident, they came to him again and said, "Your son, forever a cripple. What bad luck!" But the wise old man again asked, "How do you know it's bad luck?"

Sure enough, about a year later, a warlord came to town, conscripted every able-bodied young man, and took them off to battle. The battle was lost and all the warriors were killed. The only young man left in the village was the old man's crippled son, for he had not been conscripted due to his handicap.

The moral of the story is this: ***You don't know when something is good luck or bad luck, so don't count on it to get you where you want to go.***

The Key to Success

Back to our question: Why are some people more successful than others?

In its simplest form, the answer is this: *the key to success lies in your particular manner of thinking.* When you change how you think about yourself, your relationships, your goals, and your world, your life will change. If you change the quality of your thinking, you necessarily will change the quality of your life.

You'll see in subsequent chapters that you can control your thinking. For example, you can do only two things with your conscious mind. You can (a) initiate a thought of your own choosing, or (b) respond with a thought to a particular external stimulus. These are the only two types of conscious thinking you ever have to cope with in life. *And you can control them both!*

This ability to control what you think about from minute to minute and day to day is *the first great wonder of the mind.* For in it lies your individual freedom.

Ralph Waldo Emerson (1803–1882), the noted American essayist, philosopher, and poet, once commented, "So far as a man thinks, he is free."

You are what you think.

One of the most insightful discoveries that history's great teachers have given us this century is what the late Earl Nightingale, the famous broadcaster and educator, calls the strangest secret. He said, "You are what you think" or "You become what you think about." As it says in the Bible, "As a man thinketh in his heart, so is he." The power, then, is *within you.* Your ability to change your life lies in your capacity to think, and to think differently if you choose.

Successful people, whether they are consciously aware of it or not, are constantly demonstrating this truth in everything they say and do. For our purposes, we will define successful people as those individuals who purposely set bigger and bigger goals in their lives, who work progressively toward the attainment of these goals, and who enjoy a dynamic, well-balanced life in the process.

Consider this example. A planning session was convened in a large office products company to set new sales objectives for the upcoming year. Tom, the director of marketing, wanted to set the tone for the discussions by introducing Mike, the year's top salesperson, to all the sales agents present. He asked Mike to come to the podium to be recognized by his peers for his significant accomplishment—earning commissions that were five times higher than the group average.

After a round of applause, Tom challenged the group by asking several questions. "I want you to take a good look at Mike. What is there about him that is different? What has Mike got that the rest of you haven't, that enabled him to earn so much more?" He continued. "Is Mike five times smarter? No. Records show he has average intelligence. Is he better educated? No. He has a Bachelor's degree in business administration from the local college. It took him several years of night school, but he persevered. Did Mike work longer hours or skip annual vacation? No, his attendance reports show he took the same amount of time off as most others. Is his territory larger or more concentrated with key accounts? No, his territory is average. His five years of experience with the firm is average. In fact, almost everything about Mike seems to be average."

Tom went on. "Mike, we're really stumped. What is it that allowed you to perform at a far higher level than all the others here? Did luck or fate have anything to do with it?"

"No, I don't think so," Mike replied. "It wasn't luck that I kept every sales appointment I made the past year or that I followed up each call precisely one week later. It wasn't luck that I made sure every order I received was serviced properly and the merchandise was delivered on time. It wasn't luck that I attended evening classes for six years to complete my degree. It wasn't luck that I read ten books in the past year on effective sales techniques and time management. No, I don't believe it was good luck or fate that made me the top performer in the company last year. But I think my positive mental attitude and the expectations it produced had a lot to do with it. I set my goals high, five times higher than the average, and I firmly believed I could achieve them. I planned my work, then worked my plan in order to reach my goals. I simply did each day what my plan indicated would get me where I wanted to go."

"There's the difference!" Tom exclaimed. "That's what sets Mike apart. The difference is in the quality of Mike's thinking. He thinks five times bigger, and I suggest, five times smarter. We must understand this fact: *the quality of the thinking that guides your intelligence is far more important than the amount of intelligence you actually have.*"

The Process of Thinking

Since our central theme revolves around mental thought processes we call "thinking," it is important at the outset to define this word in detail. *Webster's Ninth New Collegiate Dictionary* defines the verb "to think" in its transitive form as follows:

> 1: to form or have in mind 2: to have as an intention 3 a: to have as an opinion b: to regard as: CONSIDER 4 a: to reflect on: PONDER b: to determine by reflecting 5: to call to mind: REMEMBER 6: to devise by thinking 7: to have as an expectation: ANTICIPATE 8 a: to center one's thoughts on b: to form a mental picture 9: to subject to the processes of logical thought

As an intransitive verb, it is defined as:

> 1 a: to exercise the powers of judgment, conception, or inference: REASON b: to have in or call to mind a thought 2 a: to have the mind engaged in reflection: MEDITATE b: to consider the suitability 3: to have a view or opinion 4: to have concern 5: to consider something likely: SUSPECT[1]

Daniel Webster (1782-1852), the American statesman and orator, said, "Mind is the great lever of all things; human thought is the process by which human ends are ultimately answered."

Three general categories of thinking may be derived from these definitions: (1) to turn over in the mind; meditate; ponder; reason; to give continued thought to, as in order to reach a decision; to understand or solve. This thinking about the present primarily involves creating solutions and determining meaning from conflicting pieces of information, adopting an opinion or belief about a particular subject, or reaffirming adopted opinions and beliefs; (2) to have in mind, recollect or remember by recalling the past; and (3) to anticipate or expect a given result based on historical data by thinking about the future and what it may bring.

Conscious thinking is carried out more or less with your full knowledge of the process taking place. You are aware of the act and it often involves your inner voice talking to yourself. You then proceed to answer yourself. This internal, two-way conversation takes place continuously during all of your waking hours. Its direction and intensity are determined by current dominant themes or patterns of thought you have decided to entertain at a particular point in time. On the other hand, *subconscious thinking*, as described in this book, takes place without your full knowledge, although you are often aware of how your body is reacting to it.

To live is to think. You are basically a mind with a physical body. Your flesh, bones, and muscles can be reduced to 80 percent water, plus a few chemicals of little value. But it is your mind and what you think that determine who and what you are. Even when you are asleep, you are thinking up a storm at the subconscious level. When you stop thinking, you stop living. You are "brain dead."

Every action you take—to eat, talk, go for a walk, or read a newspaper—is preceded by a thought impulse. While you may consider all of these activities to be more or less automatic, they are the result of a message originating in your brain being sent through your nervous system to your muscles to act or not to act. A thought, that powerful, formidable force, is behind it all. Thus you are a product of your thinking in all you say and do. "Great men," Emerson wrote, "are those who see that thoughts rule the world."

Thought is the original source of all success, prosperity, and happiness in the world. All of history's great discoveries and inventions are the result of ideas and thoughts. Thought is also the source of all failure, poverty, and unhappiness in the world. Those thoughts that predominate in your mind determine your character, career, and all aspects, both positive and negative, of your life. As John Milton (1608–1674), the English poet, observed, "The mind is its own place, and in itself can make a heaven of Hell, a hell of Heaven."

Thinking is the highest form of activity humans are capable of performing, yet few people really think. Too often you trick yourself into believing you are thinking because you are aware of some mental activity going on in your mind. Most of the time you are simply exercising the mental faculty known as recall by which you replay your past experiences, much like music on a tape, in the form of *mental pictures or images* that have been previously recorded in your subconscious mind. You revert to previous programming—your internal memory files, if you wish—and the result is habitual behavior. Previous programming is your only basis for comparison and you necessarily act in a preconceived way or expect a similar outcome to repeat itself. In such cases, the law of belief applies.

Henry Ford (1863-1947), the famous American industrialist, commented on the subject in this way: "Thinking is the hardest work there is, which is the probable reason why so few engage in it."

This ability to formulate images and hold pictures in your mind is unique to the human species, and it is this faculty that raises you above all other living things. You are the director, producer, scriptwriter, and principal actor of all the images played on the motion picture screen of your mind. To a very large extent, *all that you accomplish or fail to accomplish in life is a direct result of the images you hold in your mind.*

Did you know you actually think in images and not in words? Images are simply mental pictures that originate from thoughts representing ideas and experiences. Primitive humans communicated their ideas and experiences to others for thousands of years by drawing pictures in the sand or on the walls of their caves. Only recently have humans created various languages and alphabets to symbolize these "picture" messages. Your mind has yet to adapt to this relatively new development. An image has a much greater impact on your brain than words, reflecting the fact that the nerves from the eye to the brain are twenty-five times larger than the nerves from the ear to the brain. You often remember a person's face but not his or her name, for example. The old saying, "A picture is worth a thousand words," is true.

You think in a three-dimensional format.

It is also important to realize that you think in a three-dimensional format, a concept first developed by James Newman in his excellent book *Release Your Brakes!* Every thought you have has an "idea" or verbal component, an "image" or conceptual component, and an "emotional" or feeling component. Each plays a specific role.

Consider the word *beach* as an example. The idea component that creates initial awareness is simply "beach." The image component is whatever picture you conjure up in your mind at the sound of the word. All the meaning lies in the image. For most, it will include large expanses of clear, white sand, waves breaking on the shore, and people sunbathing or throwing Frisbees. The emotional component, which represents the mind-body connection, is what you feel or sense as a result of the image. It could be the warmth of the sun on your body or the soft sand between your toes. Others may imagine an isolated beach stretching off in the distance for several miles without a person in sight. Their emotional reaction would probably include feelings of peace, solitude, and tranquility. All of the feelings you evoke are dependent on the particular image you conceive. If you were knocked unconscious by a massive tidal wave as a child, for example, your feelings about a beach may well be radically different. It probably is a place you prefer to avoid.

In the same way, you record information in your mind about all of your experiences in a three-dimensional format: verbal, conceptual, and emotional. This information is collected through your five senses to form the basis for your personal belief system or your understanding of the world in aggregate form as you know it. Scientists estimate that there are about one hundred billion cells known as neurons in the average human cerebral cortex. They are capable of storing more than one hundred trillion bits of information. All of your memory elements are recorded in three dimensions, the three components of everything you have ever thought or experienced. This way that you think, in images and in three dimensions, will be important later on when we discuss the self-concept, the self-image, and self-esteem.

What Are You Telling Your Mind?

I credit one simple concept with getting me started on my journey into self-discovery. After a great deal of study and contemplation, I came to the conclusion that *people have in their lives today exactly what they keep telling their mind they want.* At first, I found this statement more than a bit disarming. I knew what I had and I thought

I knew who I was at that point in time, although I didn't own very much and I didn't amount to very much either. Yet to admit to myself that what I had and who I was emanated from what I kept telling my mind I wanted, was asking too much. How could it be that I was responsible for my own relative lack of success when there were so many other factors conveniently all around me that I was so sure were the cause? Impossible, I thought.

Fortunately, this concept stayed with me. The challenge it forced me to face would not go away. So I continued to study my own behavior and that of many others in great detail to further verify its validity. Having done this study and knowing what I know now, I am prepared to repeat this statement to you: *you have in your life today exactly what you keep telling your mind you want.*

Your physical world today basically reflects all of the thinking you have or have not engaged in up to now. There are principles that exist for you and for me. They represent universal law. By explaining these principles, I will demonstrate that you have today exactly what you keep telling your mind you want . . . *by way of mental images.*

Self-Study

Some psychologists say that if you spend an hour a day completely immersed in any one subject for a period of five years, at the end of that time you would be considered somewhat of an expert in that particular field.

In my own case, I knew there was room for me to grow and change for the better. I wanted to find out how I could bring about constructive change in my life. So I took five years to travel down this long, difficult road seeking the answer and I believe I have found it. *I discovered that the dominant force in my existence was the thinking I engaged in—a key core belief.* So I resolved to take control over this process, for by doing so, I knew I would be taking control over my life.

I spent the next twenty-four months never watching a television program, never listening to a radio broadcast, and never reading a newspaper or magazine. And I was careful to avoid any negative conversations that I became exposed to because I knew they would have a negative impact—on me!

As I talk about the terms *positive* and *negative*, I want you to think of positive as being creative and constructive, and negative as being despairing and destructive. One implies progress and improvement, while the other implies retreat and defeat. I want you to keep this important distinction in mind, for by using the terms positive and negative, we are talking about creative forces and destructive forces at work in your mind.

To better understand the different effects of positive and negative habit patterns of thought, consider from your own experience the effect the following feelings, the "activating process" of thought-images, have on you and other people in your life: joy, pride, love, excitement, optimism, and enthusiasm. Now compare their effect to that of fear, anger, guilt, resentment, jealousy, despair, and hatred. All of the former characteristics have a creative, constructive influence on a person and those he or she comes into contact with, whereas all of the latter have exactly the opposite effect. Positive and negative effects follow from positive and negative feelings, which are created by positive and negative thoughts, or more correctly, by positive and negative thought-images.

Each of us has the choice to think and act either positively or negatively, constructively or destructively. "If so," you may say, "why on earth would anyone choose the negative?" The point is that no one consciously makes such a choice each time he or she thinks. You simply have allowed yourself to become conditioned to think in what has become an habitual way, and it just repeats itself. *Almost all of your thinking as an adult is done habitually, at the subconscious level.*

Unfortunately, most of us have developed a multitude of negative habit patterns of thought. As Samuel Johnson (1709–1784), the English lexicographer, noted, "The chains of habit are generally too small to be felt until they are too strong to be broken." We all have become locked into using certain patterns of thought that are engraved on the engrams of our mind.

Habits are a significant influence in your life. They can be the best of servants, and help you reach new heights; equally, they can be the worst of masters, and freeze you in your tracks. *Habit is simply the result of thinking in an habitual way.* The vast majority of your behavior, in fact over 99 percent, is reflexive since it is based on information that is buried deep in the caverns of your subconscious mind. Almost all of your thoughts are echoes of your past perceptions and programming. This is why you must learn to become a *thinker*, or better yet, an *original thinker*, for this is the only way to allow reason to triumph over reflex.

To illustrate the powerful influence habitual patterns of thought have on you, take the example of looking both ways before crossing a street. If you were born in North America, you were automatically conditioned to look left first, then right. If you were born in Great Britain, you were automatically conditioned to look right first, then left, since cars there travel on the left-hand side of the road. There is nothing so comical as watching American tourists in London trying to undo what they have become so accustomed to doing. They first learned their response at an early age by conscious effort based on the particular circumstances prevalent in their environment. Through repetition, this response became habitual, a sort of stored program requiring almost no thinking at all, at least not at the conscious level.

In the very same way, certain thought patterns or mind-sets have been programmed into your subconscious, and they make you the particular person you are today. These patterns can be changed by re-learning different, more effective thought patterns. It involves increasing your level of awareness of what you want to change, and consciously repeating the new learning experience you desire over and over again in your imagination. New thought-images produce new life experiences.

Consider how important thoughts are in your life from the following poem titled "Thoughts Are Things":[2]

> I hold it true that thoughts are things;
> They're endowed with bodies and breath
> and wings:
> And that we send them forth to fill
> The world with good results, or ill.
> That which we call our secret thought
> Speeds forth to earth's remotest spot,
> Leaving its blessings or its woes
> Like tracks behind it as it goes.
>
> We build our future, thought by thought,
> For good or ill, yet know it not.
> Yet so the universe was wrought.
> Thought is another name for fate;

Choose then thy destiny and wait,
For love brings love and hate brings hate.

—Henry Van Dyke

CHAPTER 2

Principal Influences
in Your Upbringing

"Whether you believe you can do a thing or not, you are right."
—Henry Ford

We have seen an enormous change in American society since World War II. With the introduction of modern technology and the proliferation of consumer products, people now enjoy a new option, one that wasn't available to them to the same extent before. Increasingly, they can deal with their environment in a less active and purposeful way. Hence people can avoid more mental challenges today than they ever could before.

There is instant gratification of almost every human need. The explosion in fast-food restaurants probably epitomizes best the American obsession with making things both easier and faster. People don't have to do things anymore. They don't have to cook, sew, read, write, or repair the lawn mower. There is always an expert or machine available somewhere that solves all of their problems.

Television in particular has been all too effective in separating viewers from their brains—from their ability to think and be creative as individuals. TV addicts prefer to have someone else do their thinking for them. This can only mean that they watch TV in order to escape from their own thoughts.

Television has made a majority of Americans habitual consumers of "canned" experiences, contrived fantasies of an unrealistic world that simply pass the time and rape the mind of its own creative nature.

Television has been called chewing gum for the mind. In fact, it is much worse. It is a cancer that attacks the creativity, independence, initiative, and energy of the general population.

At the present time, more than 96 percent of American homes have one TV set, 59 percent have two or more, and 20 percent have three or more. Twenty-two percent have fifteen or more channels to watch. At the same time, less than 10 percent of the population read books on a regular basis.

Whether we like it or not, television is a major factor in determining society's role models — and, through them, society's values and priorities. Human problems in most television programs are reduced to simplistic solutions, usually involving violence as the process most acceptable and effective. There is also an emphasis on sex and sexual gratification as a primary human obsession. Lust, hate, greed, revenge, and adulterous relationships are all depicted as virtuous and vital, and are carefully woven into most plots and story-lines.

Television conditions the mind in a major way by creating a false, unrealistic world. It makes you believe that the world of the soap operas or the world of crime and violence is the only one there is. You then end up accepting this distorted perception of your environment, and it necessarily affects your thinking and behavior.

A study of scholastic achievement levels from 1960 to 1975 shows a marked decline in verbal and mathematical skills during this period, coinciding with the same time TV was emerging as a significant cultural phenomenon in the United States. TV wastes valuable learning time and brings viewers down to the lowest common denominator. Seldom are people challenged to rise up to a higher standard that is portrayed as achievable and worthwhile.

Psychologists tell us that children have about five or six years to establish their basic values and beliefs, and to develop their incredibly vast and rich genetic heritage. Children are born with a wide variety of talents and abilities. These talents may be scientific, artistic, scholastic, athletic, or musical, for example. Children need only a receptive and stimulating environment to tap and exploit them. The proper environment encourages exploration, and develops enthusiasm for growing and excelling. Seldom does television encourage the development of human potential. It is basically a time-killer. It wastes precious, scarce, irretrievable time.

The Role of Education

It is interesting to note how young people perceive the role of modern education as they contemplate life's many challenges. Many believe that if they go to school and become expert in their chosen field, everything will fall neatly into place and bring about the coveted success they so desperately desire. Aspiring professionals spend considerable time weighing the merits of which school is more reputable to attend or which company is more prestigious to join. Few consider the importance of their particular manner of thinking as part of their overall education. Superior intelligence may avail nothing along the path to success. Dedication and hard work alone are not the answer. Education or talent will not guarantee it. There are many people in the world who are well educated, highly intelligent, and talented, yet are unemployable. At least they cannot hold on to any one job.

It seems that *thinking* as a skill has received limited attention in our modern society in general and in our educational system in particular. This situation is beginning to change. Progressive educators have shown increased interest in the "art" of thinking. Thinking is a subject in itself. It is capable of being organized, analyzed, improved upon, learned, and taught. Thinking as a separate subject is worthy of serious, practical study and may well represent the greatest educational innovation in this century.

Educators must acknowledge accelerating change in our environment and the relative explosion in new information. We are told that the world's information base is doubling about every five years. Therefore the imparting of information can no longer be the primary objective. For one thing, it is all readily available in libraries and on floppy discs for the asking. Also there is too much of it around for any one person to become familiar with it all. In fact, no one needs to know that much about everything.

H. Ross Perot, former chairman of Electronic Data Systems and one of the richest men in America, made an interesting comment about mechanical computers versus human competence. He said, "We can grind out enormous amounts of accurate data, but people must always look at it, analyze it, and decide if this data is relevant. It's terribly important we never confuse data with wisdom as we enter the age of information. More than ever, we need people who are capable of *original thought*" [emphasis added].

I believe we should stop confusing education with instruction. Education should devote itself more to the exercise of rational judgment and common sense where the individual contributes significantly to problem-solving. Instruction, on the other hand, can continue to transfer basic knowledge in the traditional way.

These views are corroborated in a U.S. Department of Education report released in San Diego in July, 1986.

"Specialization in undergraduate education has become a source of weakness," wrote Thomas Kean, governor of New Jersey and head of the commission. "The U.S.A.'s colleges are turning out specialists when employers really need well-rounded graduates. Employers are now telling us that the workplace needs strong critical thinking and interpersonal skills in people who can be trained in specialties on the job. We've got to reward risk-taking and creativity," Kean said. "Creativity exists on every campus but it's being stifled."

Other findings of the report:

- Too many students enter college without the knowledge, skills, and attitudes needed for success.
- Too many colleges don't allow students active involvement in their education.
- College graduation rates, especially for minorities, are dropping when they should be climbing. Only 30 to 40 percent of students graduate in four years from the school they first entered as freshmen.

We must continue learning throughout our lives in order to remain competitive, competent, and productive people.

Only today is it being accepted that education should be a lifelong, ongoing activity. We must continue learning throughout our lives in order to remain competitive, competent, and productive people, and to keep growing as human beings. Adult education courses abound, with evening and weekend programs featuring gourmet cooking, diet, exercise, stress reduction, and attitude development.

Corporate America also is taking a much more active role in education, advising and assisting educators in designing courses that better meet their specific needs.

Donald Petersen, chairman of Ford Motor Company, put the problem in perspective when he recently commented, "By the year 2000, *75 percent* of all employees in the United States will need to be retrained or taught fresh skills as our volatile economy continually redefines our jobs"[emphasis added].

Regarding reading ability, Petersen goes on to say that "while 96 percent of young Americans read well enough to select a movie from TV listings, fewer than 40 percent are able to interpret an article by a newspaper columnist."

A U.S. Education Department report confirms how serious this problem is. It found that the average adult reads at about the seventh- or eighth-grade level, that 20 percent of young adults between the ages of twenty-one and twenty-five read below the eighth-grade level, and that 5 percent read below the fourth-grade level. More than twenty-seven million Americans are functionally illiterate. Half of the nation's one hundred million workers read below the ninth-grade level. The resulting cost in lost productivity to American business is millions of dollars a day, according to San Diego literacy expert Dr. Thomas G. Sticht.

In all probability, you didn't learn anything in school about how to accumulate great wealth, how to develop a positive mental attitude, or how to make your dreams come true. While our education system fails to teach people these things so they can live better, more fulfilling lives, there is still a means to this end.

The great Scottish philosopher, Thomas Carlyle (1795-1881), explained it this way:

> If we think about it, all that a university or final highest school can do for us, is still but what the first school began doing—teach us to read. We learn to read in various languages, in various sciences; we learn the alphabet and letters of all manner of books. But the place where we are to get knowledge, even theoretic knowledge, is the books themselves. It depends on what we read, after all manners of professors have done for us. The true University of these days is a collection of books.

In other words, his message is that we first need to learn to read, then we need to read to learn!

It has been found by experts studying personal growth and high performance human behavior that people change mainly as a result of the books they read and the people they meet, since these two factors have the most influence on a person's particular manner of thinking. This begs an important question: What kind of books are you reading and what kind of people are you meeting and associating with?

What Are Your Beliefs?

Many people ask me if one book or seminar can change their lives. I believe it can if only one, powerful, mind-expanding concept takes root and grows in your consciousness. As the American writer, Oliver Wendell Holmes (1809–1894), once noted, "Man's mind, stretched to a new idea, never goes back to its original dimension." A great deal of common sense is inherent in our being, although the process of living buries it under a heavy blanket of false impressions. We allow ourselves to be conditioned to a remarkable extent by our environment and upbringing to believe many things about ourselves and our world that are simply not true.

For example, most of us believe that the oceans are a vast system, and that there is and always will be an abundance of clean water in the world. The truth is that water is in relatively short supply. Note that the distance from the surface of the earth to its center is about three thousand miles, and the average depth of the oceans is only two miles. That is not a lot of water to support five billion people.

There is also the notion that the oceans are a major source of food for the world, if properly managed. But the efficiency of food production in the sea is magnitudes lower than on land. In the sea, it takes one thousand tons of grass to produce one ton of tuna. On land, it takes only ten tons of grass to produce one ton of beef.

John Marks Templeton, one of the most successful mutual-fund managers in the world, was recently asked in an interview what he considered to be the single, most important factor contributing to his success. His reply:

> ***Probably my concept of reality.*** Over the years, I've been convinced of a higher power, that nothing exists except

God. There is no other reality. What people in the past called reality is temporary and often misleading. For example, take the concept that you are sitting still. The truth is, because the earth is rotating, you are going eastward at more than one thousand miles an hour. Because the earth is revolving around the sun, you are going in another direction at two thousand miles an hour. And because we think the sun is rotating in a milky-way galaxy, you are flying away at fifteen thousand miles an hour. All these directions are realities. Therefore the appearance that you are sitting still is very misleading [emphasis added].[1]

Now consider this: If you have been so wrong about such a simple thing as "sitting still," just think how wrong you may be about your potential for high achievement! It is a sad but true fact that the information you use to formulate your basic beliefs about yourself is almost always inaccurate, insufficient, or simply irrational. It cannot pass a common-sense test.

I advocate a practice I call **original thinking**. Original thinking is the critical reassessment of the basis for long-standing beliefs, especially beliefs you have made and continue to accept about yourself. Often you will find that the basis for a previous belief is weak, that under scrutiny it just doesn't stand up. For example, you may think you cannot speak in front of a large audience. But if you are able to change this belief, you can move on to greater things in your life.

Unfortunately, most of what is called **thinking** consists of finding reasons why you should continue believing as you already do. This only leads to more habitual behavior.

A key skill associated with adopting realistic beliefs is to learn to separate rational, reliable information from that which is not. Primarily this involves critical observation, listening, and reasoning. This process is called **crap detecting** — a term coined by Ernest Hemingway (1899–1961), the famous American novelist and short-story writer. It is necessary to counter the progressive mental manipulation of our consumer society so prevalent today.

It is all too easy to be deceived by faulty thinking. Take the following story-line for a commercial as an example of the way you are manipulated to act in a way that is not consistent with sound logic:

Bobby Bigtime is a very good athlete.
Bobby Bigtime drinks Brand X beer.
You should drink Brand X beer.

On examining this scenario, there is no logical basis to assume that Bobby Bigtime is a good judge of beer just because he is a good athlete. His criteria for deciding what constitutes good beer are probably radically different from your own. Your qualifications in this area are just as relevant and valid as his. It should be your own experience that determines what you like in a beer.

In this way, typical middle-class Americans are thoroughly brainwashed and don't even know it. More than fifty thousand advertising messages a year tell them how to dress, what to eat and drink, which car to drive, where to live, what to believe, and which values, wants, and aspirations to have. All are directed at predisposing them to think and act in a specific way. They are encouraged to consume for the simple reason that consumption is good for them, and necessary to maintain their particular life-style and image of themselves.

Atypical Americans are more discerning. They sift through the mass of commercial advertising looking for its true meaning and relevance to them as thinking, intelligent people. They become not so much a product of their environment as they do a product of their thinking.

Crap detecting is a key survival skill if you want to be master of your life and in control of your behavior. You have to evaluate at face value everything you experience or have experienced in the past, especially what you have been told about yourself and your potential for high achievement.

For example, you were likely told as a youngster that if you didn't do well in school, you would never do well in life. So if you were a poor student, you probably resigned yourself to a life of mediocrity, believing you could never aspire to anything significant. But all research shows there is no direct correlation between academic achievement and lifetime earnings.

Ironically, success in school may preclude success in life as well. Many top students grow up believing that if they do well in school, they will also do well in life. They therefore become complacent and overconfident, and assume they no longer have to work hard as adults to continue succeeding. They too are trapped by a false belief. Both groups, then—those who perform poorly in school and those who perform well—often find themselves on opposite ends of the same problem; namely, an addiction to a false belief that often precludes success in life.

Consider the following poem about beliefs and the profound effect they can have on your life:[2]

> Doubt can stop you in your tracks
> It can drain away desire,
> Believing, on the other hand,
> Can set your world afire.
>
> When you hold the opinion that
> You can reach that special dream,
> You have the edge needed to make
> Achieving much easier than it may seem.
>
> Believing in your ability
> Affects the way you act,
> And produces an air of confidence
> Which influences how others will react.
>
> When you believe you can achieve
> And believe it with all your soul,
> You possess a powerful asset
> You most likely will reach your goal.
>
> —Anonymous

Abundance Is Everywhere

Your personal belief system creates your reality. This is an immutable law of the universe. Personal beliefs are the very foundation of your life. And as we have discussed, many of your current beliefs are mistaken. Mistaken beliefs are seldom nurturing, for they cut you off from seeing opportunities in life and the abundance that is all around you.

A belief in scarcity—for example, that there isn't much abundance in the world—is a fatal error. A person who holds this belief sees life as a pie with just so many pieces. If you get a piece of the pie, this means there is one less piece for someone else. Or if others have the slice that you have set your eyes on . . . too bad, it is already taken!

A logical extension of such thinking is to believe that if you succeed, another must fail. If you are prosperous, someone else must be poor.

After all, there isn't enough of everything to go around. There isn't enough love, there isn't enough creativity, there isn't enough money, and there isn't enough success. This also means that you can't have more of what you now want unless you take it away from someone else.

Another mistaken belief is that you must be careful to protect what you already have because others are surely after it. The safe approach, then, is simply to trade. Give a little to others of what they want in return for receiving a little of what you want. But at all costs, *never give first!* You may never get repaid! By using this cold, calculating approach, you end up living in a prison of your own making, and the prison bars represent mistaken beliefs.

I explained how I eliminated all the negatives I could from my life for a period of twenty-four months. I stopped watching the six o'clock evening news on TV, stopped reading the daily newspaper, and stopped listening to the late news on TV again at 11:00 p.m. You know, it really isn't "news" at all since you've heard it all before. So-called news is simply destructive, negative programming disguised as news-worthy occurrences. It is biased reporting—all the crimes, disasters, and calamities of the day that people then associate with being the normal state of affairs. When all the negative aspects of life—those which are bleak, bad, or bloody get most of the publicity—they take on an aura of greater importance in your mind than they deserve. And you readily identify with them because they reinforce what you already believe reflects reality.

By focusing repeatedly on life's negative events, you tend to adopt a more negative outlook on everything. Negative news will always bring you down to its destructive level. It can never bring you up to a more creative level. You simply cannot afford to wallow around in the depths of negativity. If you do, you will continue to formulate thought patterns in similar terms, and all is lost.

Consider this "BAD NEWS/GOOD NEWS" scenario:

1a.   Unemployment has inched up to 5 percent.

1b.   Employment is holding firm at 95 percent.

2a.   A plane crashed today at L.A.'s International Airport.

2b.   Five hundred and forty-nine out of five hundred and fifty planes landed safely today at L.A.'s International Airport.

3a.   Mr. Jones died today at age eighty-four.

3b.   Mr. Jones' life involving eighty-four long, productive years came to a fitting end today.

4a.   Joe Barnes lost a finger in an industrial accident today.

4b.   Joe Barnes still has seven fingers and two thumbs, not to mention a healthy mind, to keep doing what he does so well.

5a.   One out of three marriages today crumbles and ends in divorce.

5b.   Two out of three marriages today flourish and last a lifetime.

Which news is more accurate?
Which news is more positive?
Which news is reported more often?

Your mind is the force behind the marvelous success system within you. Whatever you believe, picture in your mind, and think about most of the time, you eventually will bring into reality. If you say to yourself, "I can't," "I am not worthy," or "It will never happen to me," then this is what you will tend to bring about. By believing in scarcity, you will "see" scarcity, you will experience scarcity, and for you, there will be scarcity.

Scarcity is the mother of selfishness, jealousy, aggressiveness, and resentment. All of its effects are negative.

Abundance is the mother of prosperity, creativity, kindness, and love. All of its effects are positive.

Whenever you experience a negative emotion, first stop and take a minute to examine the underlying belief that supports it. Ask yourself, "Why do I feel this way? What is the belief I have that causes it? Is this belief realistic, logical, and an accurate reflection of the real world?"

If the answer is no, change the belief into a positive affirmation that will lead to more positive emotions and constructive behavior. Ridding yourself of negative beliefs and rigid, illogical thinking sets you free and on the road to increased prosperity and personal fulfillment.

Can One Idea Change Your Life?

Many people who have taken seminars and read self-help books have been able to develop higher levels of self-confidence. They have changed their personalities to become more patient, kind, and loving, and have transformed their personal relationships, especially with spouses and children. They now enjoy increased energy and determination, more fulfilling careers, and a greater sense of purpose and direction in their lives. The experience can be a little like being reborn, like being able to begin life again armed with powerful new concepts and knowledge. Anyone can achieve at higher levels than he or she ever thought possible.

There was a time when researchers estimated that people used about 20 percent of their full potential or inherent intellectual powers. Today, however, knowing so much more about the complex human machine, experts claim we are using only 1 or 2 percent at the most. In fact, there is no real limit experts can place on human potential, on what you can achieve in your life. It is limited only by the unlimited capabilities of the creative powers of your mind.

Napoleon Hill (1883–1970), author of the classic work *Think and Grow Rich*, is probably best remembered for this profound statement: "Whatever the mind of man can conceive and believe, he can achieve."

We all live in a very structured, orderly world. Nothing happens by accident. There are principles and laws which have universal application. They govern our existence. Consider this observation of Dr. Wernher Von Braun, the late German space scientist, often called the father of space exploration:

> After years of probing spectacular mysteries of the universe, I have been led to a firm belief in the existence of some superior power. The grandeur of the cosmos serves only to confirm my belief in the certainty of a Creator. I just cannot envision this whole universe coming into being without something like Divine will. The natural laws of the universe are so precise that we have no difficulty building a spaceship to fly to the moon and can time the flight with the precision of a fraction of a second. These laws must have been set by somebody.

As you'll soon see, just like the laws of physics, chemistry, or astronomy, there are mental laws as well that are infallible. The law of belief is just as valid and meaningful as the law of gravity or the law that says light travels at 186,000 miles per second. So success in your physical world, such as sending a spaceship to the moon, is not unlike success in your mental world, reaching your full potential. Both are predictable and a direct result of doing specific things in a specific way.

The price of a book or seminar is relatively small. But it can only be a beginning. The price you must pay to meet the challenge we all face — how to get the most out of yourself — is much higher. You must first learn the rules of the game, the mental laws that exist for everyone, and then work diligently at putting them into practice.

There is also a price to pay for continued failure or living in mediocrity. Can one idea change your life? Of course it can. If you take what you are going to learn in this book and put it to practical use, it can totally change your life. You'll never be quite the same person again, if you keep an open mind and delay final judgment until you have taken the time to assimilate and reflect on what you have learned.

As we go along, do not decide that yes, you agree with this point but no, you don't agree with that one. Try not to prejudge each point as it is being presented based on your current manner of thinking. Take the contents of the book as a whole first, as a new, enlightening experience that at least is worthy of your consideration. Just *think* (there is that word again), what if the *five thousand years* of collective wisdom presented in this book is right about you, and you have been selling yourself short?

The world cannot change you for the better,
even if it wanted to.

The world is impersonal. It really doesn't care if you succeed or fail. That is up to you. The world cannot change you for the better, even if it wanted to. Only you can do that. *But first you must begin to perceive yourself and your world in a different light.*

Most people don't realize that the joy from growing comes more from the journey than from the destination itself. There is an ancient Chinese proverb that says a walk of a thousand miles must begin with a single step. And each step brings its own reward. Are you prepared to take this first step, to admit that maybe, just maybe, what you are going to hear about you is more in line with reality than what you previously thought?

Selling you on yourself is the hardest "sell" in the world, since by the time most people are being sold to, they have experienced enough of life that their preprogramming quickly rejects any new information that is inconsistent with their firmly established beliefs. People remain convinced of their inadequacies mainly because they have experienced a good deal of mediocrity and failure in their lives, and it is only natural that they identify more with what they "know" and have experienced than with what they have not. Most people haven't experienced a great deal of success in their lives, and if they have, they discount it as an aberration.

Risk and Change

All change involves an element of risk — risk of the unknown and risk of failure. But change, whether you like it or not, is inevitable. A look at yourself in the mirror will tell you that. Your thinking will change as well as a result of any new experiences you are subjected to or you initiate to take place yourself.

Hence you can choose by default or by design. You can regulate this process if you decide to do so. You can regulate its direction and its intensity. You can control this process because you can control your thinking from minute to minute, from "picture to picture" in your mind. You have the choice to think positively or negatively, constructively or destructively. And your built-in success system is designed to work faithfully. It will always succeed in ensuring that you get whatever you keep telling your mind you want. It will create and bring about constructive outcomes or create and bring about destructive outcomes. All this will happen by law, not by circumstance. Success is not an accident.

So the course I am asking you to embark on does involve some risk. But consider which is worse: to risk change that you can control or to risk change that you cannot? Do you think that enough good things will happen to you by chance (twelve wild stallions turning up in your corral) such that you will get all the rewards you want in your life?

I say these things will not happen. In fact, even if you were to win a million dollars in the lottery next week, it couldn't buy you all the good things you really want. I don't know of any meaningful friendships that are for sale, for example. You could have asked Howard Hughes. He had all the money in the world anyone could ever want, yet he died abandoned and in total misery at the height of his wealth and fame.

To bring about change in yourself is not the easiest thing in the world to do. It takes a great deal of desire, self-discipline, concentration, and effort (read "thinking" for all of these)—which is why so few people actually change significantly in their lifetime.

Recall your high school reunion ten or fifteen years after graduation. Did you notice much change in your former classmates? Or in your parents as they are now compared with how you remember them when you were growing up? Or consider yourself. Are you today a more outgoing person, a better listener, more tolerant, more venturesome, and more goal-oriented than you were five years ago? What new interests have you developed? Have you fostered new friendships, become a better parent, or improved your interpersonal skills? Do any or all of these personality traits interest you?

If you have changed, it only means you have changed your particular manner of thinking. If you have not, it only means you have not changed your particular manner of thinking. This is your choice, a choice available to each of us. It is never too late to begin living a more satisfying and more fulfilling life.

I hope as you begin to discover who it is you truly are and what it is you really want to be, that you will fall completely, unequivocally in love with yourself. And I hope at some point you'll be able to look in the mirror each day and say, "Boy, I sure love you! I'm high, high as a kite in love with you, scars, flaws, and all!"

Now you may say all this self-love is egotistical, that you are being selfish. But as you'll soon see, you must love yourself before you can express love convincingly to others. And you must express love convincingly to others to receive love in return. It's the law of cause and effect, the principal, overriding law of the universe. You must always give in order to receive.

A healthy, positive self-image is your greatest asset, if you can learn to develop one. According to recent polls, four out of five Americans have a low self-image—that's 80 percent of the general population! And even the other 20 percent could use a boost. The results show up everywhere: in low productivity, academic underachievement, self-induced illness, depression, and violent crime. The most widespread and debilitating disease in the world today is not cancer, it's not heart disease, and it's not AIDS. It's low self-esteem brought on by a poor self-image. People suffer from it at all ages, at all socio-economic levels, and in every country in the world.

Many people try to block out the reality they have created for themselves. They resort to overworking, overeating, smoking, or addiction to television, alcohol, or drugs. To withdraw and try to escape from life is one means of coping, but it is neither very satisfying nor very productive. Also, it is not necessary. *You can create a new reality,* one that meets all your needs and satisfies all your desires. But first, it involves thinking. In fact, it involves *changing your thinking.* Remember, if you keep doing what you've always done, you'll keep getting what you've already got.

If you are becoming the person you know you are capable of being, life will be a dynamic, thrilling experience. It will come about as you begin to broaden your basic beliefs, especially your beliefs about yourself and what you can accomplish in your life. Nothing is more exciting than the realization that you can accomplish anything you really want that is consistent with your unique mix of natural talents and abilities. *In fact, you must confer the right to succeed upon yourself!* You have only to decide who it is you really want to be and what it is you really want to do, and be willing to pay the price to earn these things.

To conclude, I'd like to repeat the story of a man who fell into a deep hole and yelled repeatedly for someone to help pull him out. When it finally became apparent to him that no help was forthcoming, he grew tired of waiting and proceeded to get out by himself.

From this we see the same power that traps you can also free you. It all depends on *your particular manner of thinking.*

CHAPTER 3

A Model of Human Behavior

"Man is not the sum of what he is but the totality
of what he might be."
— Anonymous

In this chapter, we'll consider a formula intended to represent a model of human behavior. It attempts to explain how you function as a dynamic, goal-oriented mechanism in terms of a natural cause-and-effect relationship.

Humans Versus Animals

What is involved in the process we call *thinking?* We can only contemplate how we contemplate—since we must use our own thought processes to understand our own thought processes. When we ask our internal mechanism to turn in on itself for analysis and understanding, it's a little like asking the right hand to hold the right hand. This is, necessarily, a difficult and inaccurate process.

If we look around us in nature, we find that animals can communicate with one another, and many of them have senses of sight, smell, and hearing much more highly developed than our own. But probably even the most intelligent of creatures doesn't know it is alive. Animals cannot deal in concepts, abstractions, or theories, and they have no choice in the goals they set or in the way they go about achieving them.

Witness the annual migration of Canada geese thousands of miles south each fall to warmer climates. They have never received formal training in navigation, geography, or seasonal weather patterns. Yet somehow they know just when to begin their journey and exactly where to go. In the same way, beavers don't go to engineering school to learn how to build dams. They know how to do it instinctively. But they always build the same kind of dam, using the same basic materials and technique. You don't see a particularly gifted beaver designing an improved dam, then teaching his new prototype to others.

What makes the mind of humans superior to the brains of animals? By physical appearance, human brains and animal brains look very much alike. They have the same general shape, structure, and composition. As to size, the brain of a chimpanzee, one of the most intelligent of animals, is smaller than man's, but the brains of elephants and dolphins are much larger. If size and shape don't account for the difference, then what does?

Human behavior is vastly different from animal behavior. We function by using free choice rather than rote instinct. Our range of possibilities has no limit. We are free to learn, grow, experiment, and create. We have more than just a brain. We have a mind with a spark of intellect. We know we are alive and that someday we will die. We know we have choices, and that a particular choice will result in a particular consequence. We can contemplate our existence on this earth and what may be in store for us in the hereafter.

The Formula

Although we don't know a great deal about why the human mind is superior to the brain of animals, we do know that instincts help animals cope successfully with their environment. Rather than selecting their own goals, animals have goals that are preset into their consciousness to ensure their procreation and survival. In this sense, animals can be said to operate with the aid of "success" instincts.

In the very same way, we also have been engineered for success. We also possess a goal-striving success mechanism that always works faithfully. However, in our case, we are key participants in the process. By way of our mental faculties, we are co-creators of our existence, key determinants of our behavior, and in turn the results we achieve.

The following formula is presented to help explain human behavior. Although it is an immense oversimplification, it still represents a useful tool to predict with some precision the outcome or performance of operating the human machine based on certain key inputs. The operating formula for the human machine is this:

YOUR PERFORMANCE (P)

equals

YOUR SELF-IMAGE FACTOR (SIF)

times

YOUR MENTAL INPUT FACTOR (MIF)

Your *self-image factor* (SIF) is the person you "see" yourself to be, with the abilities you believe yourself to have. Your self-image is the most dominant factor that affects everything you attempt to do.

Your *mental input factor* (MIF) is made up of your HARDWARE (HW), namely your physical mind and body, plus your SOFTWARE, representing various *key factors of success* (FOS) that are common to all peak performers and essential to success.

So our equation now becomes:

$$P = SIF \times (HW + FOS)$$

or

$$P_n = SIF_n \times (HW + FOS_n),$$
$$\text{where } n = 1,2,3...$$

P_n is a particular level of *performance* for a specific activity you may perform as part of your personal, social, or professional life. It could be driving a car, building a flower garden, or playing tennis. Consider some of the activities an office manager, engineer, or teacher must perform. All probably have to write a report, do a presentation, make recommendations, and deal cooperatively with other people as part of their regular responsibilities. There are hundreds, even thousands, of performance indicators and an equal number of matching self-image factors for a wide variety of activities such as these for every person.

The single *constant factor* in this equation for a given person is your *hardware* (HW) or basic equipment comprising your physical mind and body. Your mind and body are directly linked through your central nervous system, which results in certain physical actions being generated as a result of specific mental inputs. This neurophysiological system is common to all humans and operates in exactly the same way.

The two *variable factors* you contribute to the process are (a) your *self-image factor* (SIF), the person you see yourself to be, and (b) your *software* or various *key factors of success* (FOS), representing your beliefs, knowledge, and ability to adopt and apply certain success principles that are essential to all peak performance. These success principles include such factors as a positive mental attitude and the ability to set goals, manage your time effectively, be creative, and work effectively with other people.

The two factors, SIF and FOS, are personal and unique to you and represent *your particular manner of thinking* when processed through your physical assets. A person's particular manner of thinking is the critical factor affecting all human performance. As William James (1842–1910), the noted American psychologist and philosopher, wrote, "Human beings, by changing the inner aspects of their minds, can change the outer aspects of their lives."

All of this takes into account the mind-body connection, the fact that your physical actions are simply the outward manifestation of your inner thoughts. This recognizes the universal truth in the statement that you are and will become that which you think about most of the time.

In brief, your self-image acts as either a multiplying factor or a dividing factor, and combines with other key factors of success you possess in varying degrees to produce an output called *performance.* Clearly your performance is related to your actual potential to perform at a given level, but equally important, it has a lot to do with your knowledge, beliefs, and mental attitude.

You can see that if you raise or lower either of the two key variable inputs, which are both mind-centered, you necessarily raise or lower your performance. Your level of performance at any given activity is largely dependent on your particular manner of thinking about that activity.

In the pages that follow, we will consider these components in the human equation: (1) your basic hardware (the physical mind and body), (2) the self-image (the person you see yourself to be), and (3) twelve key factors of success that are common to all high-performance human behavior.

You Are Greater Than
the Sum of Your Parts

You should know several basic truths about yourself. They will help you better understand the full potential you possess. Many of these truths are self-evident, yet you may not be acting in a way that takes each one fully into account.

The vast majority of people are born as complete persons. There is probably nothing significant missing from your basic equipment. You were built to the highest of specifications, able to program and reprogram yourself at will, and even repair used or damaged parts as necessary. Scientists tell us that every single cell in your body is replaced at least *once every seven years*, and that you manufacture twenty-one billion new red blood cells *every minute* of your life to replace those that are destroyed.

You were designed to be creative and to explore your possibilities. But you always create according to the basic beliefs you hold about yourself, your abilities, and your world.

These beliefs are based on conscious decisions you have made in the past about yourself and what you are capable of achieving. These decisions are now repeated unconsciously as you go through life, and they continue to affect your thinking, direct your behavior, and determine your relative level of performance.

How you perform in any given area of your life is only partly a function of your potential and largely a function of the person you "see" yourself to be. What you see in yourself is what you get out of yourself. What you present yourself to be, in the end, is what is drawn out of you.

Your subconscious is totally cooperative and supportive regarding whatever you choose to think and believe. It has duly collected and recorded all previous conscious interpretations you have made during your lifetime, and has never sat in judgment on the merits of your choice. It has always said yes to your ideas and beliefs about yourself and your world, and faithfully continues to act on them to ensure that the results you achieve are always consistent with *what you keep telling your mind you want*.

In the same way, your subconscious always says yes to your potential. But you must decide what your potential is, then tell your mind that this is what you want. In other words, you must first develop high, positive expectations for yourself, then set your sights firmly on these as worthy, achievable goals.

You can exercise complete control over your mental thought processes. The key is what you decide to think consciously, which then directly affects how you think subconsciously. Remember, your self-image is buried deep in your subconscious mind. You can bring about predictable change in your behavior by managing your thoughts more effectively. You can, to the degree you choose, develop new, more effective habit patterns of thought that will release your full potential.

Unfortunately, most of us are held back by destructive feelings generated by negative habit patterns of thought. Most of your fears result from negative thinking and preprogramming. You will always experience fear when you contemplate failing, being embarrassed, or being rejected, for example. But you cannot rid yourself of the fear you feel by sheer willpower alone. You can *change the feeling only by changing the thought-image you hold in your mind*, a process known as reframing.

All in all, you are greater than the sum of your parts. You inhabit a physical body that is the vehicle through which you act, but the greatest part of your being is non-physical in nature.

There is infinite thought power within you.

Many of the great discoveries in history prove that our stored information is not limited to our own memories of past experiences or acquired facts. Edison believed he received many of his greatest ideas from a source outside himself. This ability to pick ideas "from the air," to acquire knowledge that transcends the known sensory functions, is available to anyone who consciously seeks to exploit it. Emerson compared individual minds to inlets in an ocean of universal mind. This is the reason there is so much abundance contained in thought. Since you can tap into universal wisdom, reputedly the source of all knowledge of the past, present, and future, there is infinite thought power within you. You need only learn how to access it.

As Langmann observed, "Everyone has his or her frontier of the mind. On one side of it, everything is tried, known. On the other side is that part of yourself that hasn't been explored. All of life's great adventures are on that other side."

In fact, research shows that about 88 percent of the brain is dedicated to subconscious thought activity. Like an iceberg, the largest part of your being is "submerged." Yet you are aware neither of its presence nor of its power.

Total Success

Total success strives for a high level of accomplishment in both your personal and professional life, including family, social, and business aspects. It also requires necessary attention to your physical, mental, and spiritual health. Many people accept the presence of a superior power in their life, and often it plays a major role in determining the values and beliefs they hold. The objective must always be to achieve a balance, a just proportioning of emphasis so that you are complete as an individual. Recall that successful people are those individuals who purposely set bigger and bigger goals in their lives, who progressively work toward the attainment of these goals, and who enjoy a dynamic, well-balanced life in the process.

Most of us are familiar with people who have achieved significant success in one particular area of their lives, yet have failed miserably in other areas. Some are sports celebrities, movie stars, and political figures, while others are friends, neighbors, and relatives. In many tragic instances, people equate happiness with the pursuit of material wealth. Consider the case of the ambitious young surgeon who worked frantically for five years to build up a lucrative practice, only to be sued in divorce court by his wife for everything he owned. Or the man who at age twenty-seven was the world's highest paid hockey player, but by age thirty-five was crippled and penniless due to drug and alcohol abuse.

There have been many instances of severe depression, incapacitation, and even suicide by those who achieved great success in terms of fame and fortune but were unable to cope with the glitter, glamour, and public adoration. When fame and fortune are firmly in their grasp, they falter and self-destruct.

Certainly a balance in priorities goes a long way toward maintaining a proper perspective and sense of proportion. For example, family priorities should include common interests, common activities, and common goals; social priorities should include exposure to new people, new ideas, and new directions; business priorities should include shared values, shared effort, and shared reward; and spiritual priorities should include a sense of gratitude, a sense of reverence, and a sense of glory.

In the end, each person must decide what success means. Although success will always mean different things to different people, most people expect in the end that success will bring happiness and a sense of fulfillment to their lives. Happiness must be pursued and found in the many facets of life that are available to you.

Here are some common denominators most people equate with happiness and success:

Health. You need a high level of physical and mental health and energy to do the things you really want to do and to receive the satisfaction you need to persevere. Unfortunately, most people are greatly limited in this area as the following recent survey from the U.S. Department of Health and Human Services shows. It found that 58 percent of Americans do not exercise regularly, 31 percent smoke, 29 percent drink to excess, 28 percent are at least 20 percent above their ideal weight, 25 percent skip breakfast, and 22 percent get insufficient sleep.

Financial freedom. Financial freedom means learning to live within your means and not on your credit cards. Most people overspend, hence are always in debt or barely breaking even, with nothing being reinvested. The average American spends 105 percent of his or her disposable income; the government spends even more. Financial freedom requires financial responsibility, knowing you can afford the possessions and life-style you are enjoying. One person may be able to enjoy financial freedom at $20,000 a year, while another may not be able to do so at $50,000 a year.

Benjamin Franklin (1706-1790), the famous American statesman, inventor, and writer, offered this advice regarding personal finances: "There are two ways of being happy: we may either diminish our wants or augment our means — either will do — the result is the same; and it is for each man to decide for himself, and do that which happens to be easiest. But if you are wise, you will do both at the same time."

Worthy goals and ideals. All high achievers have worthy goals they are striving for and worthy ideals they are living by. Many people have not taken the time to set personal goals in their lives. Others lack ideals and honesty in their dealings with other people.

Personal relationships. People crave warm, loving, personal relationships. The ability to enter into and maintain intimate, loving relationships is indicative of having a well-balanced, fully functioning personality. Meaningful relationships represent an outward reach to satisfy an inner need for belonging, acceptance, and love in its many forms.

Peace of mind. Everyone wants peace of mind, to have a sense of inner peace and contentment with who you are and what you represent. All of the great works in psychology and philosophy aim at helping people achieve higher levels of peace of mind. Without it, we know nothing else really matters. If you are always preoccupied with negative feelings such as fear, anger, or guilt, they will sap your energy and command your attention, thereby preventing you from functioning at your very best.

Self-actualization. The final factor most people equate with total success is what Abraham Maslow calls self-actualization, meaning "to bring into reality through action." It is the inherent need to demonstrate high achievement, competence, creativity, and a degree of personal autonomy. It is the knowledge and feeling that you are becoming everything you are capable of becoming, that you are realizing your full potential as a human being as you go through life.

We see that high performance in all of the key areas of life leads to total success. Let's proceed now to analyze each component in the performance equation to see how this is brought about. We shall begin with your basic hardware involving your physical mind and body, proceed to the self-image, then conclude with various key factors of success.

Your Basic Hardware:
The Mind/Body Connection

Few people fully comprehend the magnificence of their minds. You are in possession of something both powerful and priceless. No amount of human effort or money could create the mind of a six-year-old child in terms of size, speed, efficiency, and reprogrammability. It is truly a miracle of miniaturization.

It is no coincidence that today's personal computer operates very much like the human mind, since it was humans who conceived and designed it. But no one has been able to design and build a mind better than the one you already possess.

Paul Thomas provides this description of the brain in his excellent book *Advanced Psycho Cybernetics and Psychofeedback*:

> The human brain is remarkably compact. It weighs only about 50 ounces in the average adult male and about 5 ounces less in the average woman. It requires only about 1/10 volt of electricity to perform efficiently, yet it is composed of literally tens of billions of nerve cells. Although the brain operates both less rapidly and less accurately than a computer, it leaves even the most advanced computer far behind in its truly staggering capacity. The network of interconnections (called synapses) between the billions of nerve cells (neurons) in the brain is potentially able to process information bits in ways whose number is equivalent to 2 to the 10^{13}. This is a number considerably greater than the total of all the atoms in the universe! Yet so neatly packaged is the human brain that in order even to approach such a capacity, a modern computer would have to be at least 10,000 times larger than the average brain.[1]

It has been estimated by experts that it would take *ten million years* to count the number of nerve connections in the brain if they were counted at the speed at which a clock ticks.

The human brain is acknowledged to be the most complex biological structure known to exist anywhere on earth. Nestled inside your cranium, it is the best protected organ in your entire body and enjoys the highest priority concerning the distribution of blood, oxygen, and nutrients. Your brain is suspended in a circulating fluid medium and actually "floats" inside a shock-resistant shell.

The preeminent role played by the brain in controlling all bodily functions is evident in the design of the body itself. The lower part of the structure, known as the brain stem, merges with the spinal cord to form the central nervous system, which is in touch with all parts of your body. Any activity that goes on in your brain affects every single cell in your body, directly or indirectly, through the extensive network of nerves that are present in all body tissue.

The conscious and subconscious parts of the mind have totally different roles, yet they work in close harmony with one another.

The *conscious part* is the rational, objective, discriminating faculty of the brain. Its role is to take in information from the environment, compare it with previous experiences, determine whether it is relevant or not, then finally make a decision. The conscious part is always making a decision that is either yes or no in the sense of accepting or rejecting incoming information. Every single piece of information that the conscious mind accepts is then accepted by the subconscious as well. It is accepted as being true, as a fact that may or may not reflect reality accurately.

We know two objects cannot occupy the same space at the same time. Likewise, the conscious mind can hold only one thought at a time. You cannot imagine both catching and dropping a ball at the exact same time, for example. Therefore, the thought can only be positive or negative. It can only accept or reject an idea. Whenever the conscious mind says, "Yes, this is what I believe," the subconscious accepts it instantly and reacts on it through the central nervous system.

Let us return to the simple example of crossing the street. If you suddenly hear the horn of a car as you are about to begin, you'll look in the direction of the sound and see an approaching automobile. You next compare its location and rate of speed with similar experiences in the past, and make an assessment whether you can safely complete your walk or not. If you decide you cannot, that you must make a hasty retreat back to the curb, then the subconscious instantly activates the leg muscles and you step back out of the way. Most of us are not particularly concerned about how we go about doing this, which leg to move first and which second. The motor activity is so well ingrained that our success system is simply activated, and it moves us out of harm's way.

But consider what the subconscious message might be to the leg muscles of a healthy, fit person who "knows" he or she can easily get out of the way, as compared with another person who believes he or she is not particularly fit, is a bit clumsy, and cannot easily get out of the way. *In either case, whatever is stored in memory applies.* If what is stored is a belief that you cannot get out of the way, then you are likely to freeze on the spot and get run over. It is the same with all thoughts. If you accept the idea that you are going to fail, get run over, for example, then the subconscious will agree with the belief and proceed to bring it about.

The *subconscious part* is like a large data bank and functions similarly to a mechanical computer. It stores and retrieves all the data pertaining to every experience, thought, image, or idea you have ever entertained. The subconscious always works to make all of your words and actions fit a pattern consistent with your previous conscious programming. It ensures that you remain true to the image you hold of yourself. You always walk, talk, think, behave, and perform in a manner consistent with the information your conscious mind has already accepted as representing the real you.

The key to success is to control what you think about, for you always get what you keep telling your mind you want. If you keep your conscious mind focused on what you *desire* rather than on what you *fear*, on the person you want to become with the attributes you want to have, then this is what will evolve in your experience. Success can result only when you take systematic control of the thoughts you allow to occupy your conscious mind from minute to minute, from day to day. Positive thinking requires a comprehensive thought management program. Positive thinking works when you focus on positive thoughts and use positive words and actions to express yourself.

The Story of Helen Keller

Helen Keller was born June 27, 1880, in a small town in Alabama. In February, 1882, when she was one and a half years old, Helen was struck with an unknown illness, experiencing a very high fever and severe pain. When she finally recovered, she was both deaf and blind.

When Helen was seven, her father arranged for a tutor, Anne Sullivan, to move in with the family. Anne eventually taught Helen how to communicate using finger movements, how to read by Braille, and eventually how to speak. Helen was among the very first with her severe sight and hearing impediments to master these particular skills. Anne Sullivan was her constant companion for the next fifty years.

What did Helen Keller do with her life, despite her seemingly insurmountable handicaps? She graduated from Radcliffe College with honors in 1904, alongside some of the most brilliant young women of her time. She became an accomplished public speaker and social critic, passionately dedicated to helping disadvantaged groups such as the handicapped, the poor, and the oppressed. She wrote five books, and claimed as close friends many notables of the day including Alexander Graham Bell, Mark Twain, Albert Einstein, and Charlie Chaplin. She met with the kings and queens of Europe, and every U.S. president of her lifetime. At age seventy-five, she was the first woman to receive an honorary degree from Harvard University. Three films were made about her life.

Helen Keller died on June 1, 1968, at the age of eighty-seven. She remains to this day a shining example to millions of people that so much can be accomplished in life regardless of what handicaps, real or imagined, may exist. It is a matter of application and dedication, having a cause you believe in, and unswerving determination to make a difference.

Helen Keller is revered as a genius. Yet she only accomplished more than most other people — while beginning with far less. Essentially, she did not allow her limitations to hold her back.

The Genius in Creativity

With the mind you now possess, you too have the potential to be a genius — if only you begin to put its incredible powers of thought to better use. As William James pointed out, "Genius means little more than the faculty of perceiving in an unhabitual way." As we have already noted, you have 2 to the 10^{13} different ways of processing information!

When you pry open a closed mind, creativity and imagination tend to be sucked in like air into a vacuum. When Sir Isaac Newton (1642–1727), the great English mathematician, was asked how he went about discovering the law of gravity, he answered, "By thinking about it." This, of course, is what he did, but obviously it is a gross oversimplification. Many people before Newton had witnessed an apple falling to the ground. But Newton gave serious *thought* to it and reacted differently to its occurrence. He asked himself, "Why did the apple fall down and not up?" He removed his thinking out of its traditional groove and searched for an answer by approaching the problem from several different angles.

In thinking about anything creatively, you must learn to get out of well-worn grooves. Consider for a moment how you can quickly change a *FIVE* into a *FOUR*? You may find this to be an intriguing problem, and at first you may have trouble knowing how to begin. The answer: remove the "F" and "E" from either end of the written word FIVE, and you are left with the Roman numeral IV, the symbol for FOUR. In this instance, the suggestion was to think only in terms of written words, not Roman numerals. This surprising answer will not be discovered by people who think in similar patterns, down familiar paths that are well known and non-threatening to them.

Most "facts" are pure fiction in disguise,
especially those you have adopted about yourself.

Similarly, your current thinking is being directed, or more accurately, is being *MISdirected*, down certain paths that are more comfortable for you. It is vastly more convenient to accept the fact that you could never speak in front of a large audience than to realize that you are merely forming an opinion about your ability in this particular area. Of course, it is not a fact that you cannot perform this activity until you adopt the belief that then makes it so. Most "facts" are pure fiction in disguise, especially those you have adopted about yourself. Until you learn to think along different grooves, you will not be able to travel down new avenues or explore new possibilities to reach your full potential.

Consider the ability to remember names. Some people have developed this skill to a fantastic level, to a level the average person considers impossible. I have heard about a public speaker who met seven hundred members of his audience at the front door and asked each of them their first name, their last name, where they lived, and what they did for a living. A little while later, he invited everyone to stand up, then proceeded to go up and down each row, and repeated each piece of information exactly as he had first heard it. All this after being exposed to it only once! Yet this man, Harry Lorayne, author of *The Memory Book*, claims that anyone can develop this same ability by removing his or her thinking out of traditional grooves.

Or consider reading ability. The average person reads about 250 to 300 words per minute and remembers only about 10 percent ten minutes later. Yet with proper instruction involving coordinated hand-eye movements and keen concentration, you can learn to input several thousand words per minute into your brain much like a decoder reads prices on goods at a supermarket. It is not uncommon for people completing a fifteen hour speed-reading course to read 4,000 to 7,500 words per minute, with up to 85 percent comprehension.

How many latent skills are waiting within you to be developed? You can develop your strength; a weightlifter will tell you that. You can develop your sense of touch; a blind person will tell you that. You can learn a variety of foreign languages; a linguist will tell you that. And you can develop your sense of taste; a wine connoisseur will tell you that. You have all this potential, all these abilities, but you have never tried to develop them beyond what your current thinking has decided is normal and acceptable for you.

To conclude this chapter, consider the wisdom contained in this delightful poem by Edgar Guest titled "Equipment":[2]

> Figure it out for yourself, my lad,
> You've all that the greatest of men have had,
> Two arms, two hands, two legs, two eyes,
> And a brain to use if you would be wise
> With this equipment they all began,
> Do start from the top and say, "I can."
>
> Look them over, the wise and the great,
> They take their food from a common plate,
> And similar knives and forks they use,
> With similar laces they tie their shoes,
> The world considers them brave and smart,
> But you've all they had when they made their start.
>
> You can triumph and come to skill,
> You can be great if you only will.

You're well equipped for what fight you choose,
You have arms and legs and a brain to use,
And the man who has risen great deeds to do,
Began his life with no more than you.

You are the handicap you must face,
You are the one who must choose his place,
You must say where you want to go,
How much you will study, the truth to know.
God has equipped you for life, but He
Lets you decide what you want to be.

Courage must come from the soul within,
The man must furnish the will to win.
So figure it out for yourself, my lad,
You were born with all that the great have had,
With your equipment they all began.
Get hold of yourself, and say: "I can."

CHAPTER 4

The Power of Perception

"Nothing has any power over me other than that which I give it through my conscious thoughts."

—Anthony Robbins
Author of the best-seller
Unlimited Power

Let's explore in some detail the process of perception, for it is this faculty that gives meaning to everything you experience. We are indebted to James Newman, creator of the PACE seminars, for this comprehensive and very useful model of conscious and subconscious thought processes.

Conscious Thought Processes

You are more aware of some activities going on in your mind than others, and these represent conscious thought processes over which you can exercise control. Conscious thought is actually a slower, more limited form of thought than most subconscious mental activities. Conscious thought involves four steps: (1) sensory perception, (2) association, (3) evaluation, and (4) decision. All of these processes take place in a fraction of a second.

Sensory perception is the fraction of all the data you input that you are aware of. It tells you what is going on both inside and outside your body. Through your sight, sound, smell, taste, and touch sensors, you pick up some of what is going on in your external environment. There are a multitude of other sensors inside your body that provide information regarding internal conditions such as pain, temperature, hunger, thirst, and so on. The quantity of information you receive is so great that your mind is forced to develop a series of filters or "discriminators" to screen out unimportant data, and to allow in only information that you deem is important or relevant to you as a unique person. For example, you become more aware of the toes on your left foot when someone proceeds to step on them. Likewise, an artist would draw more information out of a painting on display than would a person who has no knowledge of this craft.

The way you perceive the world and how you react to it is particularly relevant. You develop your own personalized screening mechanism based on the relative importance you assign to various inputs that are consistent with your accumulated values and belief system. To the degree that you are now absorbed reading this paragraph, for example, you will not perceive countless other things going on all around you. The radio or TV may be playing in the house, the neighbor may be cutting his lawn, or a plane may be flying overhead. Through the process of selective perception, you are able to ignore all of these coincidental occurrences, and instead direct your full attention to what you have decided is most important to you at this time.

The second conscious thought activity you undertake is *association*. As you perceive a given stimulus, you check to see whether anything comparable has happened to you before. If nothing exactly the same has been recorded, you will proceed to compare the event with any similar experiences to try to find some meaning. If your memory files are completely blank, you will find no meaning at all in the event.

Immediately following the association phase, you undertake an *evaluation* of the perception. This involves making judgments about the importance, validity, and implications of the message or event being perceived based on data already stored in memory from previous similar experiences.

The final conscious thought activity is *decision*. It is the output or action that follows the previous three-step sequence, and is the basis for initiating a specific behavioral response. Based on what is perceived and available in memory to compare it with, you can decide to respond in any one of a variety of ways: you can do nothing, wait for more information, begin to act with caution, or leap into action. Your response to someone shouting "FIRE!" is certain to be different from your response to someone softly whispering, "It's time to wake up, sleepyhead."

It is important to note from this series of conscious mental processes that your behavior is not simply a function of what is now happening. It is primarily dependent on (1) the particular stimuli you allow to enter your consciousness, and (2) the specific data you have collected previously to compare them with. If a similar experience in the past resulted in a particular decision, you will respond in a similar fashion on this occasion, all other things being equal. Your previous interpretations, decisions, and actions from the past are primary determinants of your current behavior.

We have noted that this total accumulation of data from the past involving everything that has ever happened to you is referred to as your personal belief system, your reality, or the truth as you know, understand, and accept it to be. It serves as your frame of reference as you continue to experience new things in life and represents the total programming your mind has been subjected to, voluntarily or involuntarily, up to now.

The next important consideration is to realize that your belief system is almost always incomplete and, therefore, is unreliable. We are all a bit ignorant in that no one can hope to know everything, or even everything about a single subject, whether it is something as small as an atom or as large as the universe. As Thomas Edison once quipped, "We don't know one millionth of one percent about anything."

The belief system you now have is generally unreliable.

So it is only natural that there are major distortions in the perception process. Through selective perception, you seldom perceive reality as it actually exists. You only perceive what your screening system decides is important. Two witnesses to the same crime never see exactly the same thing, since they focus their mental spotlight on different visual aspects. Each witness then associates and evaluates each aspect in light of his or her own personal belief system, which is never the same for any two people. It should be no surprise, then, that individual interpretations and conclusions about what actually occurred are usually different. Therefore you must accept the fact that the belief system you now have is generally unreliable, based as it is on faulty information.

The ability to see and accept new possibilities in life has a lot to do with moving ahead rather than falling behind. Your notions and perceptions, which have become your biases about yourself and your environment, are affected constantly by signals from a wide variety of external sources. Collectively, they form a mosaic and ultimate basis for your attitude "profile," reflecting your personal belief system. Therefore to see yourself differently, you have to change as many of these outside signals as possible so that the world begins to look different to you.

Individual perception is all-encompassing and all-powerful. How you perceive the world defines for you the environment you live in. It defines your hopes and your fears, and sets upper limits on your expectations in life.

We know people like to hold on to old ideas and beliefs as though they were valued personal possessions. Why is this? In part, to reconsider adopted points of view involves thinking. In fact, it involves original thinking, which questions a previous assumption or the original basis for a previous assumption. All such thinking "hurts" since it requires considerable effort and self-analysis. As well, it involves some risk. People will not throw away an old hat until they have acquired a new one to replace it. It is the same with ideas. You first have to make room for the new idea, then discard the old one. People will not accept a new idea unless they believe to do so is in their own self-interest. In other words, the new idea or belief has to have a better "fit and feel" than the old one in the total context of a person's new reality structure, the new way you are seeing yourself.

Unfortunately, people who do not rethink their past are condemned to repeat it. Habitual thinking can only lead to habitual behavior. It can be compared to treading water or marking time as the world passes you by. The only people who can change their mind are those who use it.

The process of sensory perception is even more complicated than this brief explanation suggests. There are also significantly different abilities from person to person in their physical capacity to perceive accurately. Consider this detailed description from *The Art of Thinking* of how you physically "see" your world:

The human eye is an amazingly complex mechanism. It is made up of cells, rods, pigments, nerve connectors, fluids, and an incredible number of moving parts. The normal human eye is capable of perceiving *several million* variations of color when it is functioning properly. The range of color discrimination between different sets of eyes is tremendous. Some people see little or no variation in color. Other eyes have discriminating ability to almost see an infinite number of gradations. There are enormous variations in depth perception, in the ability to differentiate among textures, in peripheral vision, in perception of movement, in distant vision, in the ability to see patterns, in the discrimination of close-up details, in variations within and between areas of light and dark. No two pairs of human eyes are the same, mechanically or anatomically. No two pairs of eyes see things in the same way. Our differences in perception begin with this basic and astonishing fact [emphasis added].[1]

Thus even before the brain and the conscious thought processes just discussed can begin to take place, we are confronted with this important fact of life: the world is a different place for each pair of eyes. It is also a different place for each pair of ears, each nose, and all the other sense organs.

You are destined to be misinformed forever about many aspects of your world. You now accept many things that are not true, such as the idea you are sitting still, yet you still manage to live your life and function reasonably well in spite of this handicap. Some people are not content to live with all this misinformation. They actively seek out opportunities to correct false beliefs. They search for new information to update their mental model of reality—*then they decide what they want it to be!* In this way, these people arm themselves with a more realistic and powerful set of beliefs and hence are able to move ahead in their lives.

We all live in a mental domain. Perception ultimately takes place in the brain, not in the sense organs. Therefore what we "see" is only *our mind's interpretation of what is actually there*. In fact, *we don't know what is actually there!* It is totally an "assumptive" world that we create and come to know, according to Adelbert Ames, an early investigator of perceptual psychology.

In *Beyond Biofeedback,* Elmer and Alyce Green make this comment on human perception:

> *No one has ever seen the outside world.* All that we can be aware of are our interpretations of the electrical patterns in the brain. Our only view of the world is on our own living internal television screen. The occipital (visual) cortex is essentially the screen and the eyes are two cameras that give us information about the frequencies and intensities of light. When the eyes are open we say we are looking at the world, but it is the occipital cortex that we actually "look" at. What we "see" are millions of brain cells firing in appropriate ways to display the retinal activity [emphasis added].[2]

Testing Your Perception

Each of us even has a visual blind spot, a small area in the field of view of each eye where *you cannot see anything.* At about fifteen degrees to the outside of each eye's point of focus is the angle at which the optic nerves going to the brain merge with the sensory nerve cells inside the eye. This spot on your retina has no receptor cells and any visual image that falls at this point is lost. Most people never notice this deficiency because the eyes move about so quickly, they allow your brain's short-term visual memory to fill in the gap.

The scale below will allow you to find the blind spot in your right eye. Invert the picture, and the same applies to the left eye.

First, focus directly on the number 10 at the left end of the scale with the book about six inches from your face. Close your left eye, and notice the large black dot at the extreme right of the scale out of the peripheral vision of your right eye. As you continue to focus on the number 10, slowly move the book away from you. You'll find that at a distance of about fifteen inches, the black dot will disappear.

Figure 1

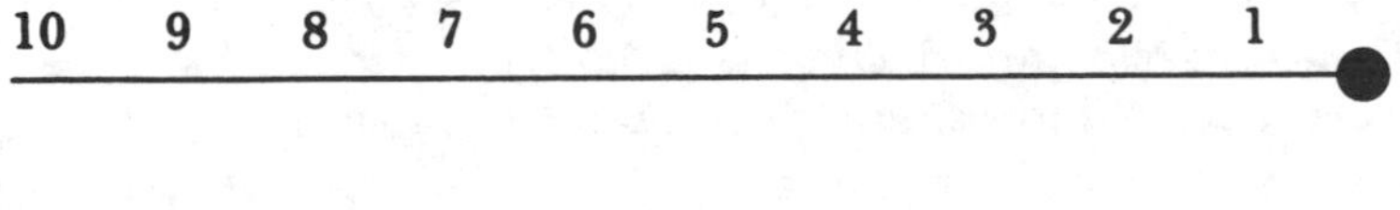

10   9   8   7   6   5   4   3   2   1   ●

Another example of perceptual confusion is the fact that the way you package a concept often causes you to reject the idea. Compare the two figures below and judge which line is longer, A or B.

Figure 2

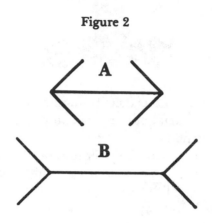

This is the famous Müller-Lyer illusion and it has intrigued researchers for years. The line in Figure B appears to be longer than the one in Figure A. Both are exactly the same. Perception seems to be affected by the way pictures are organized, in this case whether the arrowheads at the end of each line are pointing inward or outward.

Can it also be that the way you "package" your self-image, by superimposing meaningless additions or baggage onto it, also changes who you think you are? Is all of what your parents, teachers, or employers may have said very relevant to who you are and what you are capable of achieving? No, of course not. Much of it is irrelevant and must simply be cast off. When you eliminate the unnecessary "arrowheads" from your past, you'll find that what remains is the real you. At least it is a more realistic view of yourself that you can study and assess on its own merits.

Consider the familiar picture below for a moment. What do you see?

Figure 3

Some see the outline of a classic Roman table. Blink once or twice, and you may see the facial outlines of two people facing each other. Blink again, and you may see a funnel stuck into the top of a bottle whose cap has been removed. Another may say it shows reverse gravity, that if you invert the picture, it shows a liquid being poured from a bottle something like polish from a jar.

Do the two lines below "appear" parallel or not to you? Now look along their length by rotating the page ninety degrees to confirm your view.

Figure 4

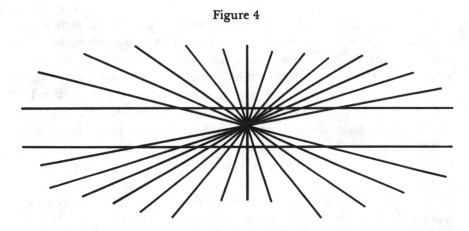

As a final example, consider how your perception process can limit what you actually "see" by counting the number of squares in the figure below. Assume for a moment that each square represents an exciting new opportunity waiting to be exploited by you:

Figure 5

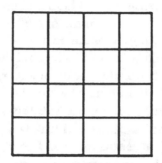

Some will see sixteen squares. Others will see twenty-six. With a great deal of persistence, you'll discover that there are thirty squares in all. But you'll have to push yourself to see this many. Few of us perceive all that is available to us. Isn't it interesting that much of what we need to "see" in order to be successful in life is invisible to the human eye?

The point of these exercises is this: *You are empowered to create your own reality—a key core belief if you want to turn your life around.* You can look in the mirror and see a *lower* self or a *higher* self. Both of these reflections are there, *but you need to see the one you want,* and in the process, activate the subconscious to accept it on your behalf. When you are able to connect with your higher self in this way, you'll reach the heights consistent with your full potential. It's like the glass of water that one person says is half empty and another says is half full. Of course, both answers are correct. But one has a more positive connotation attached to it.

You need to create your own reality. Keep in mind that in each of the above exercises, your perception process failed you. Therefore, since you don't know how things really are, isn't it only prudent to represent them in a way that empowers you to move ahead in your life with more confidence, more energy, and more determination?

As the Jesuit philosopher Pierre Teilhard de Chardin (1881–1955) once said, "It is our duty as men and women to proceed as though limits to our abilities do not exist. We are collaborators in creation."

False beliefs about yourself can be fatal. At best, they lead to mediocrity. False beliefs rob you of your energy, your desires, and your future. *You must believe in yourself,* in your ability to succeed before you can succeed. Self-belief leads to high self-esteem and high expectations, the two cornerstones of all high achievement.

Take the example of the elephant, one of the strongest animals in the world. When a young elephant in the wild is first captured, its handlers fit an iron clamp around its leg and attach it with a chain to a nearby banyan tree. Naturally, the elephant tries over and over again to pull itself free. But despite its considerable strength, it is not successful. Only after struggling for several days and hurting itself does it realize the futility of its efforts and finally give up. From this point on, the elephant never attempts to break free again, even when a small chain and wooden stake are used. For the rest of its adult life, the elephant succumbs to a self-limiting, false belief about its ability to perform in this particular area. In other words, it has accepted an *internal representation* of itself as a captive animal incapable of breaking free. Naturally, it continues to reflect this belief in its behavior.

Researchers have discovered a similar tendency toward behavioral rigidity in a species of fish commonly known as a pike. Usually a pike will attack any minnow swimming within easy range. As an experiment, researchers lowered a bottomless bell jar into a pike's aquarium and placed several minnows in it. The pike immediately lunged at them several times, only to bang its sensitive snout sharply against the glass. After many painful attempts, the pike finally gave up and ignored their presence completely. The bell jar was then removed from the tank, allowing the minnows to swim about freely. But even when they swam right past the pike's nose, it continued to ignore them. If allowed to, the fish will proceed to starve itself to death even though it is surrounded by a plentiful food supply because of a fixation based on a false belief.

How many fixations are holding you back? What "reality" about yourself are you assuming? Is there an imaginary chain tied around your leg or an invisible bell jar separating you from your ultimate goal in life? What abundance is there right in front of your nose, yet you continue to ignore it?

The human brain and nervous system can be compared to a light bulb screwed into a lamp. The lamp, by way of a cord, is attached to an infinite power source, the electrical power grid of North America. The lamp's intensity is directly proportional to the power rating of the bulb being used, either a 15, 60, 100, or 200 watt bulb. Each of these bulbs creates light. The bulb in question simply draws out of the grid the power it needs to perform at the appropriate level.

How much power are you drawing out of your personal power source? Have you screwed a 15 watt bulb into your success system or a 200 watt bulb? Remember, whatever you present yourself to be is what is drawn out of you in the end.

How Perceptive Are You?

As a result of faulty perception, it is possible to end up with a lot of garbage stored in your memory files. You then tend to recycle it in its original form.

Let's look at one example of selective perception. It has allowed certain information to enter your consciousness and be recorded, while allowing other information to be completely ignored.

Experts tell us that you look at your wristwatch about one hundred times each day. Assuming you have owned it for at least a year, that means you have looked at your watch about 36,500 times. That is a lot of looking at a display face that is usually less than one square inch in total area.

Here is a test that shows how selective perception works. Please DO NOT look at your watch as you ponder the answers to the following questions. Assuming your watch is not digital:

1. Does it have regular or Roman numerals, slashes, or dots to indicate each hour?
2. Is the display the same for all twelve numerals or are there different symbols to denote 3, 6, 9, and 12 o'clock?
3. What is the color of the background of the display face?

Take a minute to decide your answers. Now check your watch very carefully to see how many questions you answered correctly.

The vast majority of people fail to answer all three questions correctly. Isn't it amazing how you concentrate on narrow information "bytes," and in so doing, eliminate up to 90 percent of all the information that is available to you?

Let's consider the terms *conscious* and *subconscious* as they relate to the brain's two hemispheres. In about 95 percent of the population, the left hemisphere is the conscious part of the brain and the right is the subconscious. Until recently, the left also has been called the dominant hemisphere, but in fact it is dominant only for specific tasks.

The *left hemisphere* of the brain is usually the logical, analytical part that controls language skills such as reading and writing, and the remembering of names, dates, and various facts. It evaluates material in a rational, logical way, performs literal interpretations of words and concepts, and processes data sequentially. It performs analytical calculations, understands time, and controls all movements on the right side of the body.

The *right hemisphere* is usually the intuitive, artistic part where dreams and imagery originate and fantasies are born. It is dominant in thinking about problems holistically, that is, as an integrated whole. It deals in images and concepts, can process several pieces of information simultaneously, and perceives spatial relationships. It is responsible for artistic, musical, and imaginative creations and controls all movements on the left side of the body.

We live in a society in which conscious, left-brain thinking predominates, is most valued, and receives the most attention. The student who adds and subtracts correctly, remembers names, and works in a logical, organized manner gets the most recognition. The person who daydreams in class and fantasizes a great deal is considered less intelligent and productive, and hence is usually awarded lower grades. Not surprisingly, most children grow up believing that memory retention skills and conformity are more valuable than artistic or creative abilities.

When the two hemispheres are used properly, they work in complete harmony together and fully complement one another. Each is supportive of the other in that each contributes to the thinking process what it does best.

For example, a writer of fiction will draw upon the right hemisphere for imagery and creative insights regarding plot and characterization, but the left brain must find the right words and phrases to describe what the author wants to say.

In the same way, an engineer will use the right brain to conceive the spatial relationships and intricate design of a large bridge, but the left hemisphere must perform all the mathematical calculations regarding weights, dimensions, and stresses.

The hemispheres work together in almost every activity you undertake, although the amount of involvement of each depends upon the specific nature of the task. There are few meaningful pursuits you can think of where intuitive, creative inputs cannot add significantly to analytical, logical thinking.

The functional specialization of the two hemispheres appears to apply only to older human beings. Other primates and children under the age of five show little, if any, hemispheric specialization. Amazingly enough, as reported by Marilee Zdenek in *The Right-Brain Experience*, a young child who has lost a whole hemisphere through disease can grow up with normal intelligence, since each hemisphere alone seems to possess the potential for carrying out the full range of activities of both. This only goes to show the incredible inherent potential of the human brain. When called upon, 50 percent of it can perform what it takes 100 percent in others to do!

As we have seen, the conscious, directive part of the mind controls analytical, logical thinking. It draws specific conclusions from various inputs, resulting in decisions such as good-bad, right-wrong, yes-no, and so on. Conscious rational thought operates in real time and can concentrate effectively on only one thing at a time. It carries out the process of "experiencing." It selects information, compares it with past experiences, evaluates, and decides. It also selects goals and assigns problems to the subconscious for resolution.

You need the experience of success.

This introduces a very important role the conscious part of the mind can play. *By conscious effort, you can creatively imagine an event in your mind in every detail and it automatically becomes part of your memory profile.* Actual, everyday experiencing cannot always offer you what you need the most—the experience of success. You can more easily experience success in your imagination by using artificial experiencing. Scientific studies show that your brain cannot differentiate between an "actual" experience in real life and an "artificial" or simulated experience imagined vividly and in every detail. Either way, you are inputting new data into your memory bank. It's like running a dummy program and your computer accepts it as real data. Creative imagination is a primary reframing tool you need to use to move ahead in your life.

Consider the experiment reported in *Research Quarterly* that studied the effects of mental imaging on improving scores in sinking basketball free throws. A class of high school students with similar skills was divided into three test groups.

- Group 1 was told to practice shooting free throws in a gymnasium for twenty minutes each day for twenty days.

- Group 2 was told not to practice shooting free throws for twenty days.

- Group 3 members were told to practice shooting free throws in their imagination for twenty minutes each day for twenty days. They were to imagine shooting a perfect basket every time.

Based on tests on the first and last day, Group 1 improved its scores 24 percent, Group 2 showed *no improvement* at all, and Group 3 improved its results *23 percent!*

This very important discovery demonstrates that it is possible to use artificial experiencing as a purposeful and controlled method for changing basic beliefs about yourself that are now firmly entrenched in your subconscious mind. Later, you will see how this tool can radically improve your performance at any activity whether in public speaking, developing interpersonal skills, or playing tennis. To improve their concentration and performance, athletes, astronauts, and high achievers in all fields practice their routines in their mind before the actual event, whether the objective is to hit a home run or land safely on the moon. It can be likened to a mental dress rehearsal before the actual command performance, an imaginary dry run to increase confidence and coordination.

Studies show that there is a direct physiological relationship between artificial experiencing and actual performance. When a person vividly imagines performing a given activity in his or her mind, such as pole vaulting or running the hurdles, small but measurable amounts of neural activity can be measured taking place throughout the body. In other words, the same *neurological imprints* are created by vividly imagining a specific event as would be created had the event actually been real!

This ability to creatively imagine your future in the precise way you want it to evolve is *the second great wonder of the mind.* Many of your actual experiences during your upbringing were probably less than ideal. The odds are that you experienced more failure than success in your life, and now these events may be holding you back. But none of this need really matter. With this tool, *you can add new successes to your experience repertoire to fall back on* and help erase the effects of any negative programming from your past. Artificial experiencing puts you back in control, since when you are in charge of your thoughts, you are in control of your behavior. It helps to bridge the considerable gap between your current performance and your actual potential. Henry David Thoreau (1817–1862), the American naturalist, philosopher, and writer, described this phenomenon in this way: "If one advances confidently in the direction of his dreams, and endeavors to live the life which he has imagined, he will meet with a success unexpected in common hours."

Mental Images

As we have seen, the mental images you form are the key factor in how you think. For this reason, there is a great deal of renewed interest in this mental activity, and the latest research is helping us better understand how our brain carries it out.

In his book *Human Abilities*, Stephen Kosslyn describes several interesting experiments that show:

1.   The process of visualization, the forming of abstract mental pictures in your imagination, and the process of visual perception of an actual occurrence, are both exactly similar events in the brain. In other words, an image of an object formed mentally creates the same representations in the brain as actual physical perception of the same object. In addition, research shows that images produce the same analogous emotional effects as sensory input. For example, imagining a sad or happy experience evokes the same emotions the actual real-life experience would evoke. This becomes obvious when you realize how you reacted emotionally to such movies as *Love Story*, even when you knew the plot was based on pure fiction and the performers were merely acting out roles assigned to them.

2.   Objects represented by mental images act as if they have physical form and a distinct shape in space, and can be looked at, manipulated, and touched much as you do actual objects.

3.   The mental screen in your brain somehow is able to mimic the properties of three-dimensional space. It is as though brain cells join together to form an array much like an electronic computer, although cells that comprise adjacent parts of the mental image are located physically in different parts of the brain.

4.   Your mental screen is very much like the screen in your television set in that it has fixed physical dimensions and a grainy texture that make smaller details of a particular image harder to see mentally than larger ones.

5.   Imagery can effectively replace actual physical activity in learning a new motor skill, up to a point. Several experiments in various sports have shown that imagining a given exercise is always more productive than no mental practice at all, although it can never be as productive as actual physical practice at the sport. Imagining a specific activity simply cannot be as detailed an experience as actual practice of that activity.

Subconscious Thought Processes

Although there are literally thousands of activities that occur predominantly at the subconscious level, only three of the most important will be described here. All three occur automatically usually without your knowledge, although it is possible to affect these and some other types of subconscious thinking by deliberate conscious effort.

The first activity at the subconscious level is the *total management* of your immensely complex physical machinery. Breathing, blood circulation, and food digestion are prime examples of essential life-supporting activities that your subconscious carries out. You can affect each of these up to a point by conscious effort — decrease your heartbeat and lower your rate of breathing, for example.

Maintenance of all your bodily functions is no simple feat. In fact, it is so complex we don't understand most of what is going on. For example, in 1970, experts thought there were twenty hormones that regulated the human system. Now, only twenty years later, we know there are over two hundred. The brain regulates them all much like a conductor who makes music by controlling the sounds from a whole range of instruments.

Here are a few things we do know. *Every twenty-four hours,* without any real effort on your part, your subconscious

- causes you to breath 23,000 times, inhaling and exhaling 438 cubic feet of air;
- causes your heart to beat 100,000 times (about 2½ billion times in 70 years);
- causes your heart to pump 4,300 gallons of blood (enough to fill 13 million barrels in a lifetime); and
- causes your blood to make 1,450 complete circuits through 600,000 miles of capillaries.

Keep these statistics in mind as we continue to explore the power of your built-in success system and the extent of your full potential.

The second subconscious thought activity is the *storage and retrieval* of all information related to experiencing at the conscious level, whether the experience is real or imagined. All thoughts and feelings related to such events are treated the very same way. They are noted, accumulated, and stored to form the basis for your personal belief system. This, in turn, affects your day-to-day thinking and behavior. This is the activity that supports your built-in success system, your psycho-cybernetic or goal-striving mechanism that transforms the mental images you conceive into their physical counterpart. Each mental image you focus on leaves a photographic imprint or footprint in memory, and you proceed to retrace these steps each time you think in similar terms.

William Shakespeare spoke of memory as the "warder of the brain." Memory is all-important. Without the recording of information for later retrieval, there is no accumulated knowledge base or any historical reference points.

What do we know about the process of recording information in our mental archives? We know there is no single entity that can be called memory. Whereas names, events, and images are stored in some sections of our brain, recollections of how to do things are stored in other sections. In response to information largely from the sense organs, nerve cells in the brain grow branches called axons that connect with each other to pass electrical and chemical messages. The optic nerve in the eye is an extension of the brain, for example. These branches form a vast pattern of connections that are different for each person.

Researchers are still mapping out the anatomy of memory and trying to identify where the brain forms and stores it. The structures involved include the hippocampus, an S-shaped structure deep within both hemispheres of the brain; the cortex, the brain's wrinkled covering and seat of higher thought; and the cerebellum at the back of the skull which resembles a cauliflower. Formation of memories somehow brings about changes in the one hundred billion or so neurons in the brain—more cells than there are stars in the galaxy.

Although there are many theories about how the recording of information is actually accomplished, one suggests that a stimulus enters the cortex, then makes its way to the hippocampus area where it is checked for emotional content. Finally it enters the depths of the brain, where a chemical transformation along the information's path brings about a memory imprint. A memory imprint or trace is a chain of nerve cells linked by synapses, where nerve impulses jump from one cell to another. One theory holds that synapses themselves are the seeds of memory. Another presumes that brain tissue records sensory data much like a hologram, the three-dimensional photographs produced by laser light.

The third subconscious activity relates to *problem-solving or conflict resolution.* If you are consciously trying to solve a personal or business problem, or to create something new or original, your subconscious processes will go to work to help resolve the conflict. A search will be done in your memory files first to find a possible answer. If a suitable one is not readily available, the mind will transcend your own accumulated knowledge base and seek outside sources for ideas, concepts, or inspiration.

This area of metaphysics, known as parapsychology, can involve mental telepathy or the "sixth" sense. Although psychic phenomena are not fully understood even today, their presence and value are widely acknowledged both by practical users such as artists and writers, and by researchers who have studied clairvoyance and extrasensory perception. Emerson claimed that he read his essays with great interest and fascination because "they always contained concepts which were foreign to my thinking." Even Wolfgang Amadeus Mozart (1756-

1791), the renowned Austrian composer, claimed that much of his music came to him already fully composed, that he had only to write it down. He said, "When I am . . . completely myself, entirely alone . . . or during the night when I cannot sleep, it is on such occasions that my ideas flow best and most abundantly. Whence and how these come I know not nor can I force them. . . . Nor do I hear in my imagination the parts successively, but I hear them 'gleich alles zusammen' (at the same time all together)."

You probably have had similar experiences in your own life when, after failing to find the missing link to a particular problem facing you, the answer simply "popped" into your head out of nowhere. This often occurs at a time when you least expect it and are involved in a completely unrelated activity. Many find this happens at three or four o'clock in the morning; the answer, appearing fully formed, knocks at the door of your mind as if looking for a home. How it found your street address, nobody knows!

This ability to access information from a source beyond your conscious self is *the third great wonder of the mind.* Undoubtedly it will enable us to continue creating and discovering, to change our lives for the better. Scientists seeking cures for cancer and AIDS know that solutions to these dreaded diseases exist somewhere. It only remains for a person earnestly searching for them to discover their secret hiding place!

Some speculate that creative insights such as flashes of genius or startling new discoveries result solely from extrasensory abilities. In this view, new ideas are floating around in the atmosphere like particles of dust, and one need only "lock on" to their frequency to access them. This "cosmic ray" theory of creativity holds that new and novel ideas originate from somewhere in outer space. A more logical explanation may be that they are formed internally by the overlapping of two or more mental images already stored in memory to form a third, new picture that is not. This "combining-two-images" technique is often employed in the motion picture industry, where one image is superimposed on a background scene to give the impression of a single picture.

But how we are able to produce such original thoughts in our subconscious is not nearly as important as the fact that it can be done, such as whenever we attempt to think in a new direction or about something we haven't thought about before.

The key to stimulating creative thought is to learn how to allow your mind to let go, thus permitting creative ideas and concepts to bubble up to the conscious level. This is a relatively easy task and the technique can be developed with regular practice and used for specific purposes.

A main inhibiting factor is that our school system—indeed, our Western culture—has allowed conscious thought to dominate most of our thought activity. Conscious thought is language-oriented, logical, and businesslike. We allow it to occupy most of our waking hours, filling our mind-space to get us through each busy day.

There are proven methods for tapping the inner reservoir of the mind, and each requires entering into what is known as the *alpha brain-wave state*. The technique involves decreasing your conscious brain activity to a much lower level of arousal and awareness. Since subconscious thought enjoys a wider range of frequencies over which it maintains its normal functioning, it will continue to operate when conscious thought activity has been quieted and put to sleep. This lower arousal level of the alpha state allows the dreamlike creativity of the subconscious mind to flow freely up to the conscious level. Relaxation techniques involving imaging and meditation can be used to bring about this incredible effect.

Benjamin Franklin developed his own particular method to quiet his hemispheres. To reach a creative state of mind, he would lounge in his favorite chair and relax to the point of drowsiness. All the while, he would hold a metal ball or small stone in his hand above a plate on the floor to ensure he would not drop off to sleep. In this way, he discovered that there is a reality beyond one's ingrained reality structure, and that it lies in the subconscious mind. He learned how to tap into what is called universal wisdom, and applied it to the many literary and scientific pursuits that preoccupied him during the course of his long life.

Although your subconscious clearly has immense powers, it cannot pose a problem to itself. It has no imagination and relies totally on conscious experiencing for the information it stores. It is, however, the principal source of creative ideas and solutions to problems, and these cannot be forced out by conscious effort or willpower.

One point warrants further elaboration. The subconscious must be challenged by the conscious part of the brain before it can respond in a creative way. If you begin to consider some of your possibilities and potential for high achievement, for example, you will start to get some answers. Actively pondering your possibilities by conscious thought somehow triggers the subconscious into considering a variety of solutions. Purposely initiating a challenge to yourself is the most constructive way to get full mileage out of your internal success mechanism.

Why does this work? Your mind, like all things in nature, has a natural tendency to maintain the status quo. Stationary objects tend to stay stationary and moving objects tend to continue moving. Your subconscious, as well, will remain in neutral until challenged by an "outside" source, the conscious part of your brain. When finally challenged by a goal or aspiration, it will respond in such a way as to satisfy the demand and continue to work on the solution before returning to the neutral state once again.

In other words, your conscious and subconscious are always seeking out an internal equilibrium. Your conscious mind determines the level and the subconscious automatically follows its lead. The subconscious will endeavor to solve all problems directed its way until it is no longer challenged.

This ability to purposely activate the creative powers of the subconscious mind is available to anyone who chooses to use it. Of course, it takes a great deal of desire, wanting to get ahead, and an element of trust and faith. You cannot think you will fail and just hope that somehow you will succeed. Merely hoping shows a lack of confidence and commitment, and the strong desire and determination necessary to make the mental thought processes work together and in harmony with one another.

The Power of Suggestion

To better understand how you have been programmed, it is important to know the major role suggestion plays in your life. Suggestive elements are present in all aspects of everyday living. You are influenced by everything that you see, hear, and read, and everything that you experience. You are literally surrounded by a suggestive environment—friends, family, the home, the workplace, TV, radio, newspapers, and magazines—that significantly affects how you think and how you feel about yourself.

It is this power of suggestion, the impact of all these external persuasive factors, that has been most influential in determining the person you have become. Suggestion can be defined as:

1.   The inducing or the attempt to induce an idea, belief, decision, or action by one agent in another through stimulation, whether verbal or otherwise, but exclusive of argument;

2.   The stimulus, usually verbal or visual in nature, by which one agent seeks to arouse action in another by circumventing the critical, integrative functions.

You are constantly receiving suggestions from your external environment, and in most instances, you accept these self-instructions as valid. Unfortunately, no one has the time or ability to test everything he or she encounters or experiences in life by critical assessment and in-depth analysis. If you tried to do so, you would be reinventing every discovery ever made in history before moving forward with your own life. For this reason, you are forced to accept "exclusive of argument" many things about yourself and your world through blind trust and faith, and in the process you give credibility and power to the suggestive influences in your life.

Suggestions are "self-given" in two different ways. They may flow from the conscious to the subconscious self, which is part of the learning process, or from the subconscious to the conscious self, which represents habitual thinking as a result of prior learning. In either instance, self-suggestions have a profound effect on individual attitudes, and in turn a dramatic impact on individual behavior and performance.

Consider from the following poem the immense power *self-suggestions* have on you, and how they determine the way you continue to act today [emphasis added]:

YES I CAN!

If you *think* you are beaten, you are,
If you *think* you dare not, you don't.
If you'd like to win, but *think* you can't,
It's almost certain you won't.

If you *think* you'll lose, you're lost,
For out in the world we find,
Success begins with a fellow's will,
It's all in the state of mind.

If you *think* you are outclassed, you are,
You've got to *think high* to rise.

You've got to be sure of yourself before
You can ever win a prize.

Life's battles don't always go
To the stronger or faster man,
But sooner or later, the person who wins,
Is the one *who thinks he can!*

—Anonymous[3]

CHAPTER 5

The Human Success System

"The greatest discovery of my generation is that human beings can alter their lives by altering their attitudes of mind."
— William James

Most of us have some understanding of how a personal computer works. Although it is able to do many marvelous things, we know it cannot provide its own input. This remains the responsibility of an outside human operator. The raw data must be typed in to be processed according to the way the machine was designed to work.

Consider the word-processing function. You first type in the text of the letter to be printed according to a preset routine or word-processing program. After the basic information has been entered and automatically formatted, you press the PRINT key and immediately the printer begins to type out the text. An interesting phenomenon now begins to unfold: the quality of the text being printed as "output" is directly related to the quality of the data previously entered as "input."

In other words, as you type in errors, whether in spelling, punctuation, or layout, the machine prints out these same errors. "Errors in" result in "errors out," or "garbage in" produces "garbage out," a process commonly known as GIGO. If you change the quality of the input, you necessarily change the quality of the output.

In the case of the human computer, comprised of your brain and nervous system, it is much more sophisticated but works essentially the same way. Unlike the man-made variety, it produces its own input.

There are no external cables wired into your mind. Your sensors are internal, integral to your whole machine. The validity of their input, in the same way as the word processor, directly affects the quality of your output. Sensory perception and the thought processes that follow are done primarily at the conscious level, and the way you think and view the world determines what you "see." Thus it is a fact that thoughts, or thought-images, are always the primary input to your built-in success system, and results, by way of your performance, are always the primary output.

Let's look at the effect thought-images have on your performance more closely.

Your Built-in Success System

Until the mid-1940s, psychologists lacked any in-depth understanding of how the human brain and nervous system worked together when purposely trying to achieve a specific goal. Scientists setting out to build an electronic computer to support the war effort had to discover for the first time what basic laws and principles applied to goal-seeking mechanisms. Having discovered what these laws were, they wondered if the human brain worked the same way. In the opinion of early researchers designing goal-striving devices, the answer was a qualified yes, citing several important differences.

In his remarkable book *Psycho-Cybernetics*, the late Dr. Maxwell Maltz, a renowned plastic surgeon and author, compared the automatic guidance system in a mechanical computer to the human brain and nervous system. He described in some detail the workings of an on-board electronic computer in a guided missile whose goal is to destroy approaching enemy aircraft. To operate, the computer must have a way of knowing what the target is, and how to track and intercept it in order to destroy it.

A variety of electronic sensors provide all the information necessary to allow the missile's computer to perform the required calculations. It must compare the speed and direction of the target with its own in order to bring about final intercept. Positive feedback during flight indicates to the missile that it is on course and all is well, while negative feedback indicates it is off course and must make certain corrections. The computer responds by adjusting engine thrust or flaps to bring about the necessary changes in airspeed or direction. The missile thus accomplishes its goal by continually moving forward, sensing pertinent errors, and making small adjustments. It literally "feels" its way to the target by a series of corrections occasioned by negative feedback until it makes final contact.

While we are quick to marvel at the speed and efficiency of modern computers, we often fail to note that there is just as much wizardry in a football player trying to catch a long, forward pass. With the snap of the ball and the roar of the crowd still ringing in his ears, the player leaps into action. To be in position to catch the ball just as it approaches ground level, he must first judge the initial speed and direction of the ball, make allowances for any wind, and monitor the ball's changing arc and decrease in speed, all in relation to his own initial speed and direction. As he moves forward, he continually evaluates the ball's position and corrects his own progress, thus allowing himself to be in the precise spot at the right instant to make final contact.

The football player doesn't take a great deal of time to consciously "think" about this at all, but his mind is hard at work at the subconscious level. His built-in success mechanism accepts and processes all incoming information provided to it by his sight and sound sensors, compares it with memory in storage concerning past attempts at performing similar tasks, and issues instructions to his arms, legs, and other muscles in his body to act in the appropriate fashion. And, as he "envisions" he would, he catches the ball!

There are several significant differences in the way these two success systems operate in the accomplishment of their goal. One difference is the fact that the man-made machine is fed only real-time positive and negative feedback during flight to help it perform successfully. It has no stored memory to compare with regarding past experiences. The human machine, on the other hand, is fed both real-time and historical data based on past successes and failures relating to that particular ability. This historical information includes ideas, beliefs, opinions, and interpretations of past personal performance, complete with a strong emotional component. If the information fed into the player's success mechanism says that he is unworthy, inferior, and incapable (for example, negative self-image feedback), then this is the data that is processed and supplied to his nervous system. And, as he "envisions" he would, he drops the ball!

Another major difference is that the mechanical computer, unlike its human counterpart, cannot "want" or "not want" to intercept a plane or anticipate being successful or not. It is totally immune to either positive or negative emotions that, if present, would affect its performance.

Finally, the computer cannot "learn" to do something through repeated effort. On each occasion, it must be told precisely what to do. Nor can it be creative by deciding to perform a given task in a different way. It cannot make any decision by itself that has not been preprogrammed into its circuitry. In short, a mechanical computer does not have a "mind" of its own. It only has a success system that carries out specific instructions given to it.

Your built-in success system "succeeds" on every occasion whether the ball is caught or not.

Notice that the football player's built-in success system, unlike the missile's computer, "succeeds" on every occasion whether the ball is caught or not. Whatever dominant goal-image is focused on and held firmly in mind, positive or negative, then this is what is brought about. You can choose between desire— what you want, or fear—what you don't want. In either case, it faithfully processes the information made available to it and brings into reality precisely whatever you keep telling your mind you want. Since it always succeeds in the way described, it exercises no judgment and feels no remorse about the result.

Thus we see that the automatic guidance system within you works as a success mechanism regarding *all results,* depending on the mental picture you focus on and hold firmly in mind. Positive thinking will bring about successful outcomes when the goal-image in mind is positive and consistent with your self-image. But you cannot force a successful outcome upon the system by sheer willpower from without. You cannot consciously go about a task hoping to succeed, all the while imagining and fearing the things that will go wrong. Nor can the mind concentrate on the reverse of an idea. You cannot say, "I don't want to drop the ball," if you want to catch it, for the mind will focus only on the "drop the ball" aspect of the concept. The thought must be positive and expecting success, for example—"I see myself catching the ball, I have done this successfully many times before, and I know I can do it again"—if this is what you want to bring about.

Your Success System Never Fails

We see that the success system in you is designed to bring into reality *whatever image you accept and project onto your mental screen.* The role of the conscious mind in this process is always to *produce the picture.* The role of the subconscious is always to ensure that all of your actions, feelings, and behavior are *consistent with this picture,* your self-image. Whatever you keep telling your mind you want, whatever you continue to focus on and dwell upon, then this is what is brought about. Whatever you imagine in your mind is a preview of what you will soon bring about.

The subconscious is always the obedient servant, the obliging slave to the conscious perception process, and it is activated by mental pictures. But once it has received its instructions, *it becomes the most powerful influence in your life.* It accepts all of your instructions without question, records them in every detail, and refers back to them on appropriate occasions. The subconscious becomes "intelligent" unto itself in the exact way it has been programmed to *think* and proceeds to bring into physical form whatever it has been told to do. "BOSS WANTS THIS IMAGE AND HE SHALL HAVE IT," is its credo.

Thus you are destined to repeat as habit all learned behavioral patterns over and over again until you make a conscious decision to change the image. In other words, you have to provide your subconscious with a new goal-image if you want to bring about change; otherwise, it will automatically refer back to previous programming for its instructions. You always act the part, unconsciously, of the person you see yourself to be. You always dance to the tune recorded on your mental tape.

As a success system, your subconscious can do no wrong. It has no equal, works night and day—never complaining and never failing to deliver precisely *what you keep telling your mind you want.* If ever you are victimized, it is by your conscious mind, not the subconscious. It is the conscious perception process that you rely upon to accurately reflect reality and to select your goal-image. All failure can be traced back to the objective faculty of the mind, to your *conscious thought processes.*

The Self-Concept

This brings us to the major psychological breakthrough of the 20th century, the understanding of the role of the self-concept as it affects human personality.

The term *self-concept* refers to those beliefs you have acquired that relate directly to you and your relationship with the outside world. Your personal belief system includes all of the beliefs you possess about everything in your life. That particular subset of beliefs, the bundle of mini-beliefs you have about every aspect of you as a person, comprises your self-concept. Your self-concept determines the way you think, the way you behave, and the way you perform at every activity. Your self-concept is the result of the averaging of several hundred mini-self-concepts that answer this question: *"Who do you think you are?"*

—What kind of mother?
—What kind of father?
—What kind of employer?
—What kind of employee?
—What kind of storyteller?
—What kind of driver?
—What kind of gardener?
—What kind of cook?
—How attractive are you to the opposite sex?
—How well do you read?
—How well do you write?
—How well do you sing?
—How well do you dance?
—How well do you paint?
—How well do you dress?
—How good are you at languages?
—How good are you at mathematics?
—How good are you at drawing?
—How good are you at mechanical repairs?
—How good are you at remembering names?

In every case, the self-concept acts as a regulator or control mechanism that governs how well you perform. Remember, *you are who you think you are*. Recall that we all think in a three-dimensional format. The self-concept represents the awareness or idea component of this belief system, the self-image represents the picture or conceptual component, and self-esteem represents the emotional or feeling component. The self-image, then, is what your mind focuses on and your self-esteem is how you feel as a result of this specific image. Feelings refer to the emotional "stamp" you place on each knowledge element. For example, your self-concept has "PERSONAL" emblazoned all over it. Hence it is one of the more difficult beliefs to change.

The most important component of "who do you think you are" is the image component. It is also the only component over which you can exercise any control. The feeling component is automatic, it is a direct result of the picture you hold in your mind. But it is also the main factor you must contend with when you experience negative emotions such as fear, anger, guilt, jealousy, despair, or despondency.

The Self-Image

An entire school of thought has arisen as a result of the discovery of the self-concept. This, in turn, has led to what is called *self-image psychology*. Your self-image is simply the belief system you have adopted about yourself and the equivalent thought-images this produces.

Educator Prescott Lecky is credited as being one of the first to advocate self-image enhancement as a means to improve personal performance. In his book *Self Consistency: A Theory of Personality*, he argues that people fail to succeed because of a failure-oriented self-image, not because of a lack of ability. Lecky shows how negative, preconceived beliefs and expectations build up "mental roadblocks," convincing people in advance that it would be impossible for them, with their "limitations," to succeed.

For example, if a woman believes that speaking in front of a large audience would be impossible, her self-image will fight to the bitter end to ensure that she is "successful." The moment she enters the auditorium, she looks for all the outward signs to disrupt her concentration, lessen her confidence, and increase her nervousness — all to "allow" herself to fail. Then she proceeds to be successful — at failing!

The person becomes so preoccupied and worried about failing, and all the embarrassment and humiliation this will entail, that she actually proceeds to bring it about.

Lecky explains how the self-image initially rejects any new view of itself: "The center of the nucleus of the mind is the individual's idea or conception of himself. If a new idea seems consistent with the ideas already present in the system, and particularly with the individual's conception of himself, it is accepted and assimilated easily. If it seems to be inconsistent, however, it meets with resistance and is likely to be rejected."[1]

Lecky's theory of internal self-consistency is supported by educational researchers who have found that *a person's self-image is a more accurate predictor of performance than I.Q.* This amazing discovery has yet to be fully recognized and exploited by those attempting to improve the performance of others, whether parents in a home, teachers in a school, or managers in a business environment.

The importance of the self-image was also widely publicized by Maltz in *Psycho-Cybernetics*. He describes personality changes that took place in his patients after he had removed their physical scars and deformities through corrective plastic surgery. Most people who had lost their confidence and self-respect because of the way they viewed their physical abnormality became normal, well-adjusted human beings after corrective surgery. But some of his patients did not change, and continued to feel inferior and dejected as before. He wrote, "The change in their physical image meant nothing to them, so weak was their concept of themselves as people — so weak was their self-image."

Maltz's discovery demonstrates that the key to changing personality and performance is *not* in changing a person's physical face; it lies in changing the person's *"mental"* face, his inner mirror or the way he "sees" himself.

"The self-image is the key to human personality and human behavior," Maltz wrote. "But more than this. The self-image sets the boundaries of individual accomplishment. It defines what you can and cannot be. Expand the self-image and you expand the area of the possible. The development of an adequate, realistic self-image will seem to imbue the individual with new capabilities, new talents, and literally turns failure into success."[2]

Another facet of the self-image is the consideration of the "ideal-self." We all have a bundle of ideas, pictures, and feelings that represents our self-ideal, the person we would most like to be, with the qualities and abilities we would most like to have. It is usually a composite of all the people we knew during our upbringing, and ended up admiring the most.

Each of us is a product of the primary role models in our life. We were shaped by how our parents, other family members, teachers, and friends acted and responded to us. Many of the qualities and personality traits we adopted—our interests, goals, values, and beliefs—are far from ideal, yet they are the ones most characteristic of the important people in our lives.

Everyone aspires to being successful, in whatever sense this is meaningful to an individual. Success is synonymous with a high level of acceptance and approval by society in general, and contributes a great deal to self-liking and self-esteem. We all want to possess winning attributes that will bring more happiness and more prosperity into our lives.

Consider the following exercise to give yourself a new self-image and winning personality through positive and assertive imaging techniques. It uses what could be called "minimize-maximize" fantasizing, and demonstrates how you can effectively direct your mental thought processes in whatever direction you desire. You can "turn up" the volume of messages to your brain of positive, desirable things you want, and "turn down" the volume of negative, undesirable things you don't want. Your body then responds accordingly.

In this example, it is assumed that you are right-handed. If not, reverse the hands in the exercise.

NLP Reframing Exercise #2
"THE SELF-IMAGE MAKER"

Place both your hands about 15 inches in front of your face, with the palms facing you. Imagine the "old you," the way you are today, in a typical scene in your mind. Frame this undesirable picture, and center it in the palm of your less dominant (left) hand. Make sure it shows all of your warts, scars, and flaws, both physical and mental.

Now imagine the "new you," the person you want to be, in a typical scene in your mind. Frame this picture as well, and place it in the palm of your more dominant (right) hand. Make sure it shows all of the new positive attributes and characteristics you desire.

Focus on the "old you" for a moment. See the picture in black and white, fuzzy, and not very animated. Imagine the scene as being dull and undesirable, and slowly shrinking in size.

Switch your focus to the "new you." See this picture in bright color, and full of sound and animation. Imagine this scene as being totally delightful and desirable, and beginning to expand in size.

Now "swish" the two images as follows. As you are focusing on your left hand, quickly bring your right hand in front of it right up to your face, saying "swish" out loud in a firm, confident voice. You literally burst it through the old, undesirable image with the one you really want. Repeat the exercise, each time saying, "see this (left hand), do this . . . swish! (right hand). See this (left hand), do this . . . swish! (right hand)" until the old picture instantly triggers the new picture and all the positive feelings associated with it.

Repeat this exercise ten times in quick succession each day for one week. Now you will find that you conjure up in your mind this new picture every time you think about who you really are. And soon you'll notice in your life that others are beginning to see you the same way you are seeing yourself!

The world forms its opinion of you primarily from the opinion you have of yourself.

The fact is, you are mainly responsible for how you are accepted by others. Most people mistakingly are preoccupied about what others think of them, not realizing that the world forms its opinion of you primarily from the opinion you have of yourself. In effect, others see in you precisely what you see in yourself.

The "image-to-behavior" transformation process takes place entirely at the subconscious level. It involves something called your inner mirror. The process works like this. Your self-image is reflected onto your mental screen which then activates your nervous system to have you perform in a manner consistent with it. You cannot consciously see your self-image, even though you wear it like a coat. But everyone else does. In other words, your inner mirror is transparent in that others see your behavior and performance, which represents the physical manifestation of your self-image. From this, they form an opinion of who you think you are. Only 7 percent of what you communicate to others is in the form of words. Thirty-eight percent comes from your tone of voice, while the other 55 percent is represented by your body language, including your facial expression, general posture, and various body movements. Usually you are aware only of your words.

Although your self-image is not clearly evident to your conscious self, you can begin to understand something of the images you hold by listening carefully to your self-talk, monitoring the way others react to you, and comparing your current performance with previous performance. *You must accept full responsibility for the self-image you now possess.*

Self-Esteem

Self-esteem is the emotional component of the self-concept and represents the real core of human personality. It is generally agreed upon by all schools of modern psychology that self-esteem is the most critical element affecting all human performance. The best definition of self-esteem is "how much do you like yourself," or "how good do you feel about being you." Your self-image may be high or low, and it may be consistent or inconsistent with reality. But your self-esteem is always true to the image you hold in your mind, to the person you keep telling yourself you are. Thus how much you like yourself is totally dependent on who you think you are. It is either your inner catalyst or your inner brake. It either propels you forward or holds you back. It is the most important single statement you can make about yourself as a person.

Dorothy Corkille Briggs makes the following comments in her book *Your Child's Self-Esteem*:

What is self-esteem? *It is how a person feels about himself.* It is his overall judgment of himself—how he likes his person. A person's judgment of self influences the kinds of friends he chooses, how he gets along with others, the kind of person he marries, and how productive he will be. It affects his creativity, integrity, stability, and even whether he will be a leader or follower. His feelings of self-worth form the core of his personality and determine the use he makes of his aptitudes and abilities. His attitude toward himself has a direct bearing on how he lives all parts of his life. In fact, self-esteem is the mainspring that slates each of us for success or failure as a human being [emphasis added].[3]

People who genuinely like and accept themselves as valuable human beings find they can broaden their horizons, accept new challenges as a normal process of growth, and can perform at higher levels of effectiveness at everything they attempt.

Most people are afraid to like themselves, at least to like themselves too much. We are all familiar with the arrogant, conceited person who acts as if he or she is better than everyone else. Few of us wish to associate with pompous, presumptuous people. Actually, individuals who have what we call a *superiority complex*, they are aggressive and overbearing, and those who have what we call an *inferiority complex*, they are insecure and defensive, are on opposite ends of the same affliction—namely low self-esteem. Both have a "self-image" complex since they don't like themselves very much.

People with a positive self-image, who genuinely like and accept themselves, always manifest their high self-esteem in positive and constructive interactions with other people. They simply cannot hide their zest for life. Alternately, people with low self-esteem always attempt to compensate for their sense of inadequacy with actions of either superiority or inferiority. Everyone—from the pauper, to the prisoner, to the professional — can benefit from increased levels of self-esteem.

Another aspect of self-esteem and self-liking concerns interpersonal relationships. The way you relate to others is directly affected by how you feel about yourself. The result is that you are unable to like or love anyone else more than you like or love yourself. This is only logical, since you cannot hope to give away something to another that you don't already have yourself.

Also, you cannot allow anyone else to like or love you more than you like or love yourself. In other words, you are not able to accept an opinion about yourself from another that is higher than the one you already hold and believe to be true. This, too, is only logical since you generally value your own opinions above those of others.

Hence the measure of your self-esteem, the degree to which you like yourself, determines both the quality and extent of all your interpersonal relationships. Only to the degree that you truly like yourself are you able to enjoy good relationships with others and allow others to enjoy good relationships with you.

Low self-esteem has a profound negative effect on human personality and behavior. Most psychologists believe that low self-esteem, more than any other single factor, is the root cause of most psychological disorders, the main reason behind the epidemic in human failings, and the resulting misery in our society today. Witness the surging increase in drug and alcohol abuse, violent crime, teenage pregnancy, domestic violence, rape, indiscriminate promiscuity, and child molestation. People who do not accept themselves as valuable and worthwhile human beings, who hold low opinions of themselves, always manifest their frustrations and insecurities in their interactions with other people. Something very basic is lacking in the heart and mind of our modern society. It lies in individual, low self-esteem.

Consider this example of how low self-esteem can be the chain that binds you, or the cage that imprisons you.

Assume that you go through the following potentially disturbing experience. Analyze the natural cause-and-effect relationship that occurs in this way:

- *Event,* which is out of your direct control, leads to

- *Perception,* which is within your control, leads to

- *Self-talk,* which is within your control, leads to

- *Feelings,* which are out of your direct control, lead to

- *Behavior,* which is out of your direct control.

Event: You are passed over for promotion once again. Although you have more seniority and a better education, a younger person is selected as the new manager of product development.

Perception: Others are luckier than you. The appraisal system gives preference to younger people. The organization appreciates others more than you.

Self-talk: "I am not deserving; I am not a productive employee; I am not as good a person as the one selected for promotion."

Feelings: Rejection, insecurity, unhappiness, frustration, anger, and depression.

Behavior: Less interest, less enthusiasm, and less effort in your present job, all leading to lower performance.

RESULT: You are out to prove that your false interpretation is correct, as evidenced by your perceptions and self-talk! In the process, you are creating a problem in your mind that does not exist in reality. Note that if you simply changed your perception of the event and your own self-talk, you would totally change your feelings and behavior.

For example, if you only removed the single word "not" from your inner communications, your self-talk becomes: "I am deserving; I am a productive employee; I am as good a person as the one selected for promotion."

Every now and again in life, you need to step back and try to see the world as it exists in a different context. A good beginning is to appreciate that happiness exists everywhere. It can be found in the faces of your friends and loved ones, the laughter of children, in ocean waves, and the clouds in the sky. It is in the grass, the flowers, and the trees in the park. It is all around you. *But to have it, you must first "see" it in all these things!*

Frazier Hunt shares with us her appreciation of this very fact by recounting a moving experience she had with Helen Keller. Her short article appeared in *Redbook Magazine* titled "Our Unseeing Eyes:"

> One July afternoon at our ranch in the Canadian Rockies I rode toward Helen Keller's cabin. Along the wagon trail that ran through a lovely wood we had stretched a wire, to guide Helen when she walked there alone, and as I turned down the trail I saw her coming.
>
> I sat motionless while this women who was doomed to live forever in a black and silent prison made her way briskly down the path, her face radiant. She stepped out of the woods into a sunlit open space directly in front of me and stopped by a clump of wolf

willows. Gathering a handful, she breathed their strange fragrance; her sightless eyes looked up squarely into the sun, and her lips, so magically trained, pronounced the single word "Beautiful!" Then, still smiling, she walked past me.

I brushed the tears from my own inadequate eyes. For to me none of this exquisite highland had seemed beautiful: I had felt only bitter discouragement over the rejection of a piece of writing. I had eyes to see all the wonders of woods, sky, and mountains, ears to hear the rushing stream and the song of the wind in the treetops. It took the sightless eyes and sealed ears of this extraordinary woman to show me beauty, and bravery.

Perform the following simple test to further illustrate how you are able to control your thoughts and feelings. Close your eyes for a minute, take a few slow, deep breaths, and try to feel happy. Do this by recalling a happy experience from the past, or imagining what one would be like. Put a big, bright smile on your face. Pause, and sense the positive feelings this generates.

Now take another minute, and try to feel sad. Recall a sad experience from the past, or imagine what one would be like. Put a big, dark frown on your face. Pause, and sense the negative feelings this generates.

Note that nothing changes in the external environment as you create these new feelings and sensations. The only change that has taken place is in the way you have communicated with your inner self, in the way you have chosen to perceive your world.

Become more aware of your inner communications, what you see and say to yourself as a result of daily events, and learn to control it. *Adopt the key core belief that there is some benefit to be had from every adversity,* that you are wiser as a result of every experience.

As an experiment, monitor your self-talk for one full day. Consciously pay attention to all the thoughts you originate yourself and everything you communicate to yourself as a result of all the events that occur. Write them down on a pad of paper for assessment later at the end of the day. You will be amazed at the extent you have been conditioned to see so many things in a negative, unproductive way. As you become aware that you are doing this, change your perceptions and self-talk to reflect a more positive interpretation of what is actually happening.

If you do not control the way you perceive and react to all the things that happen in your life, you are allowing your feelings and behavior to run wild. You end up reading negative messages into developments that have no basis in reality. You become a victim of your circumstances and lose control over your life. The way you see yourself determines the way you feel about yourself. *All your behavior is shaped by who and what you think you are.*

It is this realization that is so important. Everything in life is indeed attitudinal. For it is your beliefs about yourself that formulate your self-image and it is your self-image that determines your level of self-esteem. Your level of self-esteem determines everything else.

There is no judgment you can pass that is more significant than the one you pass on yourself, no single factor more responsible for the path your life takes. Self-acceptance is the foundation for all personal growth and meaningful change. It provides the courage and determination to step out in front of the crowd and *be somebody* — to be everything you were meant to be.

CHAPTER 6

How the Mind Works

"The highest possible stage in moral culture is when we recognize that we ought to control our thoughts."
—Charles Darwin (1809–1882)
English naturalist

Just as there are basic laws and principles that control your physical world, there are basic laws and principles that control your mental world as well. Before you can hope to operate your human success system properly, you need to know the basic laws that determine your behavior and affect your very being.

In this regard, you have no choice. You cannot decide to bypass these laws in an attempt to negate their application. They are present in all mental workings and will always operate successfully to bring about the results you keep telling your mind you want.

We have seen how the human mind is very much like a sophisticated electronic computer. When you acquire any new piece of advanced equipment, you normally take some time to carefully read the owner's manual and basic operating instructions before turning it on to make it work. Operating instructions are important. They tell you how to get maximum performance out of the device, taking into account the specific tasks it was designed to perform. It should be the same with operating your own miraculous built-in machine.

You were born as the most advanced living organism in the world, yet you lack the precise knowledge to get the most out of your internal success system. Of course, your automatic goal-striving mechanism is always successful. But it is probably more successful at getting you what you *don't* want in life rather than what you *do* want. Understanding the mental laws will help you get what you do want more often.

Five Mental Laws

One overriding, fundamental law and four basic laws govern the operation of the human success system. You need to know these mental laws that control your behavior, for only by understanding the causes can you learn to control the effects and bring about the positive results you really want.

The first mental law is called the law of cause and effect. The law of cause and effect is a basic law of the universe. It says that for every action or event in your life, there is first a prior cause. It is the reason why everything happens in this world. As you learned in physics, for every action there is an equal and opposite reaction.

In the very same way, there is a prior cause for every effect in your life. In the human system, your thoughts are the cause and your circumstances are the effect. Your particular manner of thinking will always be the primary cause of your station in life, of the effects or results you are now experiencing. If you want your life to change in the future, you have to change how you are thinking in the present. You are continually changing and growing, always evolving in the direction of what you keep telling your mind you want.

The following mental laws are all corollaries of this first master law of cause and effect. Together, they show the natural linkage between controlling your thoughts from minute to minute and day to day, and the performance or output you eventually achieve. You experience the greatest amount of happiness and prosperity in your life to the extent you achieve the greatest number of successes in your endeavors.

The second mental law is the law of control. The law of control says that whatever you first decide to accept responsibility for, you are able to control. Like the pilot of an airplane or the driver of a bus, the person behind the steering wheel has the responsibility for the operation of the vehicle. And he knows he must accept full responsibility for whatever results his actions bring about. He appreciates and accepts the responsibility that lies in his hands, realizing that failure to correctly operate the mechanical machine he controls can bring death and destruction to everyone onboard. Failure to accept full responsibility for your thinking machine, the steering wheel of your life, will also bring you continued frustration and unhappiness. For you cannot feel good about yourself until you know you are deserving and bringing good things into your life by systematic, purposeful effort and responsible behavior.

There will always be unexpected events in your life over which you have little or no control. Serious accidents and death are everyday occurrences. But even in such instances, you have the ability and responsibility to manage and control how you react to such unpredictable events, and therefore to control their effect on your life. To manage your thoughts and, in turn, your actions and behavior, is to control your destiny.

Control of your life requires accepting 100 percent responsibility for all of your thoughts and actions. There is no way you can gain control over your thoughts and actions without accepting full responsibility for them. In this sense, control and responsibility are necessary companions down the road to positive thinking and positive living. The law of control is essential in maintaining a high level of energy, peace of mind, self-confidence, and positive emotions. Control begins with your thoughts, which in turn determine your performance, and the quality and amount of happiness you enjoy in your life.

The third mental law is the law of belief. The law of belief says that whatever you first come to accept and believe, becomes your reality. Many people don't understand that you choose what you believe. *Each one of your beliefs is a choice — a key core belief if you hope to move ahead with your life.* You are a direct result of all your belief systems. They form a screen of logic or a screen of prejudice that creates your world. You allow in only that information which is consistent with your innermost beliefs, whether these beliefs are consistent with reality or not.

Beliefs are the most powerful force for creating *positive change* in your life. For even though you may hold beliefs that are based on insufficient, inaccurate, or irrational information, they have a direct effect on the way you think and the way you perform. Beliefs send direct signals or commands to your brain that can help you tap the richest resources that lie deep within you. John Stuart Mills (1806-1873), the English philosopher and political economist once said, "One person with a belief is equal to a force of ninety-nine who have only interest."

The most damaging effect on you and your performance comes from false beliefs that you hold about yourself, for self-limiting beliefs only lead to self-defeating behavior. Self-limiting beliefs, whether based on fact or fiction, become true for you to the extent you honestly *believe* in them. You then end up performing at a level consistent with your beliefs and not at a level consistent with your potential. As the Bible says, "If thou canst believe, all things are possible to him that believeth."

You see, these mental laws are not of recent creation. They have been known for centuries. Unfortunately, only a few people have understood and applied them consistently in their daily lives. An excellent book on the law of belief is Claude Bristol's *The Magic of Believing*. First published in 1948 and still a best-seller today, it shows through meaningful anecdotes and real-life experiences how beliefs have an immense suggestive power over the believer. This power either moves you ahead or holds you back in everything you say and do.

Acquired beliefs necessarily affect individual expectations, especially expectations about personal performance and future outcomes. If you expect positive results, you tend to bring about positive outcomes; if you expect negative results, you tend to bring about negative outcomes. It is as if what you expect becomes a self-fulfilling prophecy, since you help bring it into reality. High achievers always talk to themselves and others as though they expect things to turn out well, that they will succeed in what they have set out to do.

Consider the following example to illustrate this point. Researchers studying peak performance have found that a person's perception of whether or not he or she is doing well is a prime factor for success. In one experiment, volunteers were asked to solve ten identical puzzles. But the scores they were given were fictitious. Half of the subjects were told that they did well, seven out of ten correct, and the other half that they did poorly, seven out of ten wrong. On being given another set of puzzles to work on, the half who had been told they did well on the first batch actually did better on the second, and the half who had been told they did poorly actually did worse.

It appears that association with past successes and the resulting positive expectations of future success were a prime motivating factor. *Note that individual expectations were not based on anything factual.* It was only the beliefs that were generated and accepted, not whether they were true or false, that made the difference.

The fourth mental law is the law of concentration. The law of concentration says that whatever you first concentrate on and dwell upon, grows in your experience. You can control what you concentrate on. You can develop a success consciousness by concentrating on successful outcomes; equally, you can develop a failure consciousness by concentrating on unsuccessful outcomes. You must first create mentally what you want to bring about physically, for when you adopt the mental view, you move more than halfway toward the goal.

We know the conscious mind can hold only one thought at a time, either positive or negative; it can never hold two thoughts simultaneously. If you find yourself with a negative, unproductive thought in mind, especially one that has progressed to near phobic proportions, you must find some effective way to erase it. One way is to punch it up on your mental screen, firmly push the ERASE button, and watch it disappear. Another way is to repeat the word *"stop"* to yourself, mentally or out loud, over and over again. Both these thought-stopping techniques must be followed immediately by a positive thought, by purposely focusing on the desired outcome.

The third and most effective way is the following exercise that uses the "minimize-maximize" fantasizing technique first described in Chapter 5.

NLP Reframing Exercise #3
"THE THOUGHT STOPPER"

With your eyes closed, make a medium-sized, black-and-white picture of the behavior you want to change. See it as a framed snapshot, and mentally place it out in front of you at a distance of about 12 inches. Next, make a small, bright, colorful picture of the behavior you want, and center it between the posts of a large slingshot that are lodged in the ground just a few feet away. In your mind, see this desirable scene being pulled farther and farther away from you, with the rubber sling being stretched further and further. At its absolute limit, let it go. See the new picture literally explode through the old picture in front of you and penetrate your brain. Repeat the word "swish" as it becomes part of your consciousness.

The key to doing this exercise successfully is speed and repetition. If it's done correctly, you'll actually feel your head snap back as the new scene hits you head-on. After each swish, open your eyes for a brief second to break the state. Repeat the exercise. See this, do this . . . swish! Pause, and absorb the impact. Open your eyes. See this, do this . . . swish! Pause, and absorb the impact. Open your eyes.

Stop for a moment and think of some limiting thought or behavior that may be holding you back. Swish it using this slingshot exercise to change it. Now all you should see directly in front of you is a bigger-than-life, bright, colorful picture of the precise behavior you want.

Techniques such as this demonstrate conscious thought control. You must find some technique to keep you on track and avoid negative, unwanted thoughts.

The fifth mental law is the law of attraction. The law of attraction says that whatever first grows in your consciousness, you attract into your life. You will always attract the people and circumstances that harmonize with your current dominant thoughts. It is as if you operate like a large communications center that transmits and receives thought energy. Your thoughts all have a certain intensity and frequency that is communicated to those you come into contact with. People who go about their day expecting good things to happen literally radiate self-confidence, enthusiasm, and a sense of purpose. They attract to them people and circumstances of a like kind and repel people and circumstances of a different kind.

You'll be surprised at how many good things and circumstances you'll instinctively attract to yourself if you are positive, feel good about yourself, and are up on life. But it works both ways. You'll also be surprised at how many negative things and circumstances you'll attract to yourself if you are pessimistic, feel bad about yourself, and are generally down on life.

What actually takes place is this. You will see more positive things in your life that you would normally not see and do more positive things you would normally not do if you are positive in your outlook. Likewise, you will see more negative things in your life that you would normally not see and do more negative things you would normally not do if you are negative in your outlook. What you see and what you do then create the world you live in.

---

*You will always bring into physical reality
what you first create mentally.*

Now let's combine the five mental laws to show their natural cause-and-effect relationship. First consider the law of belief.

Whatever you decide to believe, you adopt the value much as you consume food. It becomes internalized, assimilated into your consciousness, a part of the fabric of your mind. The belief then gives power to your outlook, the expectations you hold concerning a given outcome. You dwell upon what you believe will transpire and it grows bigger than life. The law of concentration tells you that. Finally, the law of attraction will bring to bear on the process the people and circumstances consistent with the expected outcome. You will always bring into physical reality what you first create mentally — the original adopted belief you began with and have control over.

Whatever you picture in your mind tends to actualize in physical form equivalent to the mental image being held. You can take charge of this cause-and-effect process by virtue of the law of control, for whenever you are in control of your thoughts, you are in control of your behavior. The thoughts you hold are the key determinant in your life, the dominant force in your existence.

The following examples illustrate what we have just discussed. They support the contention of Andrew Carnegie (1835-1919), the American industrialist and philanthropist who was born in Scotland, that "any idea held in mind that is either feared or revered will begin at once to clothe itself in the most convenient and appropriate physical form available."

The story is told about a man who as a youngster once thought about . . . robbing a bank. One day, the thought just crossed his mind, then he quickly dismissed it because he knew it was something he shouldn't be thinking about.

For several years, the experience continued to repeat itself, and each time he saw a bank, he allowed this negative, destructive thought to linger for a few seconds in his mind. As time went on, he began dwelling on the image for about a minute. Eventually, whenever a bank came into view, he spent several minutes thinking about what that experience would be like.

Some years later, his fantasy became his reality. Everyone who knew him was so shocked. How could a respected man of the community commit a crime of this kind?

The story is also told about a woman who as a child used to think about . . . flying through outer space as an astronaut. One day, the thought just crossed her mind, but she quickly dismissed it because she knew it was something that would probably never happen.

For several years, the experience continued to repeat itself and each time she allowed this positive, constructive thought to linger for a few seconds in her mind. As time went on, she began dwelling on the image for about a minute. Eventually, whenever she looked up at the sky, she spent several minutes thinking about what that experience would be like.

Some years later, her fantasy became her reality. Everyone who knew her was so impressed. How could a woman with humble beginnings accomplish such an incredible thing?

It was because these people had been harboring a particular thought for a very long time and progressively allowed themselves to nourish the image attached to it. Consider for a moment what thoughts and images you harbor in your fantasies. Do you think about fear, failure, and lack? Or do you see opportunity, challenge, and abundance all around you?

Consider the case of an acorn. Although an acorn appears outwardly as a solid object, like everything else in the world, it is a mass of molecules all vibrating at very high speeds. Nature has determined the rate of these vibrations, and has preset into its molecular makeup a precise plan that determines how it will expand and grow.

We know that all processes in nature are designed to be successful. As soon as the acorn is planted in the ground, its vibrations set up an attractive force that instinctively draws to it water, minerals, and other nutrients in harmonious vibration with its nature. There is, literally, a parade of complimentary particles drawn toward the seed, while other particles not in harmonious vibration are repelled.

Soon little shoots begin to sprout from the top and bottom of the seed to become branches, leaves, and roots. Particles from the earth and particles from the atmosphere combine together in a never-ending, progressive partnership leading, finally, to the creation of a tall, stately oak tree. The tree's ultimate composition is a product of the original plan or success system preprogrammed into the small seed.

But unlike the acorn, you are not destined to be anything specific. You are a co-creator of your existence. You can change your current programming to anything you choose. The way you "see" yourself in various real-life situations becomes your nucleus or orderly plan for eventual development and growth.

Mental Attitude

We now come to the subject of mental attitude. Your mental attitude is defined as your habitual manner of acting, feeling, and thinking that shows your disposition, opinions, and beliefs about life. The three key words are *habitual, thinking, and beliefs*. We know you are a function of what you think about most of the time. The most outwardly visible characteristic of what you think about is your attitude. Your personality, the person you present yourself to be, is simply the outward expression of your inner attitudes and feelings; your behavior can be likened to your attitudes in action. Your attitude, then, is a reflection to the world of all the beliefs you hold and of the quality of all the thinking you have engaged in.

Extensive research into how people become successful shows that one essential factor is present in every instance—a positive mental attitude. Along with other key factors of success that we will be describing later, it is an indispensible prerequisite for moving ahead in your life. W. Clement Stone, author of several self-help classics, refers to a positive mental attitude as "PMA," and asserts that "PMA is the catalyst which makes any combination of success principles work together to attain a worthwhile end."

Executive recruiters at Harvard University found in a study that 85 percent of everything a person accomplishes after university in the way of wealth, position, and status was the result of attitude; only 15 percent was the result of aptitude and abilities. Similar research has found that there is no correlation between lifetime earnings and academic achievement. Attitude accounts for a person's performance and progress at least 85 percent of the time.

Allan Cox, author of the widely acclaimed book *The Cox Report on the American Corporation*, surveyed top executives of Fortune 500 companies in 1982. Ninety-four percent of those surveyed attributed their success in life more to attitude than any other single factor.

If we have all this evidence that supports the need for a positive mental attitude, why do so many of us still lack one? Surely we are intelligent enough to know a good thing when we see it. Yet is this knowledge alone sufficient to allow us to change our attitude? Clearly, it is not.

We have seen that your attitude is a function of your beliefs — your fundamental beliefs about yourself, your abilities, and your world. We also know your beliefs determine your expectations about results and future outcomes. If you have a positive attitude, you tend to expect favorable outcomes; if you have a negative attitude, you tend to expect unfavorable outcomes. To paraphrase Denis Waitley in his book *The Psychology of Winning*, successful people make a habit of manufacturing their own positive expectations in advance of the event. They have developed an attitude of positive self-expectancy, even though they cannot be certain things will always turn out exactly the way they want. A positive attitude leads to positive, enthusiastic expectations that affect other people in a positive way and help bring about positive, productive results. Positive attitudes are a powerful suggestive force that helps create its own reality.

Samuel Johnson wrote this comment about mental attitude long ago: "He who has so little knowledge of human nature as to seek happiness by changing anything but his own *disposition* will waste his life in fruitless efforts and multiply the griefs which he proposes to remove" [emphasis added].

Judge for yourself the effect of attitude in the following job interview. As you read the verbal exchanges, compare attitudes versus facts as presented to the interviewer by the applicant, and decide which are more important.

Q.   **Interviewer:** Good day, sir. And how are you today?

A.   **Job Applicant:** *Just like yesterday, I guess. No better, no worse. I'm surviving.*

Q.   Could you give me some information about yourself, please? First, your name?

A.   *Shelley Clarke. But don't blame me for it. My parents dreamed that one up. Imagine! Shelley Clarke. What a way to go through life.*

Q. And your address, please?

A. *Twelve Backwater Road. It's over near the county dump. We get quite a breeze from it at night.*

Q. And how have your grades been, Shelley?

A. *Consistent D's. But it's the school I go to. Poor instruction and poor facilities. You can't expect someone to do well when nobody cares. If only I could have gone to that new school across town . . .*

Q. Can you tell me why you want to work for the ABC Company?

A. *Well, because you're hiring, I guess. Besides, I heard you have a good medical plan and pension benefits. I get sick quite often and always wanted to retire young.*

Q. I see. But what skills can you offer our company?

A. *Skills? I've never thought about that. I don't like paperwork and people get on my nerves. They're always after me to do things I don't want to do.*

Q. What prior experience and qualifications can you bring to this position, Shelley?

A. *Gee, no one's given me any experience. I've been waiting for that first big break. I'm not going to do just anything, you know.*

Q. Shelley, are you sure you want to work for the ABC Company?

A. *Well, my mom and dad said I should stop sponging off them and take advantage of someone else for a change.*

Q. Okay, Shelley, what is your ambition in life? Where would you like to be five or ten years from now?

A. *Well, I'd like to be far away from here, that's for sure. There's no future for me in this town. And my name. How can anyone with a name like Shelley Clarke expect to get a fair shake? I feel like I'm on a treadmill that's speeding up, and I'm going nowhere fast!*

From his comments, consider for a moment some of the mental images Shelly clings to. How **productive** are they? Are they a **realistic** portrayal of what actually exists? Or is he simply creating a negative reality of his own choosing? Could he not change it to a more positive view just as easily? Many others with simple names such as George

Bush, Paul Newman, and Steve Jobs are managing to do very well for themselves.

Clearly, attitudes are more important than facts in all of our lives. Attitudes are within your control, whereas most facts, like the name you are given and where you are born, are not. It is the way you react to your circumstances that is most important.

The Learning Process

Every adult is a product of the social learning he or she experiences as a child. There are four specific steps involved in the learning process. They include drive, cue, response, and reinforcement.

1.   *Drive* refers to the motive behind any act you engage in. A drive can be either inherent or learned. Inherent drives include basic needs such as food, water, air, sleep, security, approval, and love. Learned drives include such things as obedience, conformity, and social acceptance that in turn can lead to the development of various attitudinal traits such as patience, honesty, integrity, and resourcefulness. There are many more learned drives than inherent or innate drives.

2.   *Cue* is the perceived stimulus that triggers the thought, feelings, and physical action. It tells you when and where to begin responding to a drive.

3.   *Response* is the reaction to a stimulus that a person engages in, often solely by way of thoughts and feelings. Response has to do with the way you react to specific cues, the positive and negative habit patterns of thought you acquired during your upbringing. A habit pattern of thought is simply a learned response by way of a mental picture that has become firmly ingrained in your subconscious reality.

4.   *Reinforcement* refers to the reward or punishment you receive as a result of a given action. When you perform an act successfully, you receive positive reinforcement that encourages you to repeat the act on other occasions. When the act is not successful, you receive negative reinforcement that encourages you not to repeat the act.

Consider the NLP reframing exercise on confidence building at the beginning of the book to underscore the importance of the *stimulus-response* effect. When you perceive a stimulus that makes you anxious, for example, it is because this particular cue triggers this ingrained response as a habit. To counter this undesirable effect, it is necessary to override it with another stimulus-response effect that also has become firmly ingrained through repetition. The anchor or trigger you use can be one of your own making, or it can be the original cue that brings on the anxiety in the first place. For example, if the thought of public speaking makes you nervous, use the image of a microphone and podium to trigger the positive, desirable response you want.

All learning is a gradual, repetitious process and involves passing through four levels of competence. The first is referred to as the "unconscious incompetence" level, where you are totally unaware that you lack a particular skill or ability. The second level is "conscious incompetence," where you lack a particular skill or ability but now know it because someone has informed you of this fact. The next level is called "conscious competence," where you are aware that you know how to do a particular thing well. The final level of learning is "unconscious competence," where you do automatically what you do well and never think about it. At this point, your behavior is habitual and is carried out totally at the subconscious level.

Take the example of a mother teaching her son how to tie his shoelaces. In the beginning, the child doesn't even know he has shoelaces to tie (unconscious incompetence), but soon does once his mother explains it to him (conscious incompetence). After being taught this new skill, the child proceeds to tie his laces at the conscious competence level. After considerable practice, he proceeds to the unconscious competence level, where the learning experience is fully ingrained and automatic.

It's interesting to note that the word *learn* has both the words *ear* and *earn* in it. This tells us something about the process involved in learning!

Inherent Versus Learned Drives

Let's proceed to a description of the fundamental, inherent drives common to the human species. Although inherent drives are basic to the human character, they often differ in degree among people. In his classic work *Motivation and Personality*, Abraham Maslow (1908–1970), American psychologist, proposed the following hierarchy of human needs and wants as a basis for understanding human behavior and motivation:[1]

Figure 6

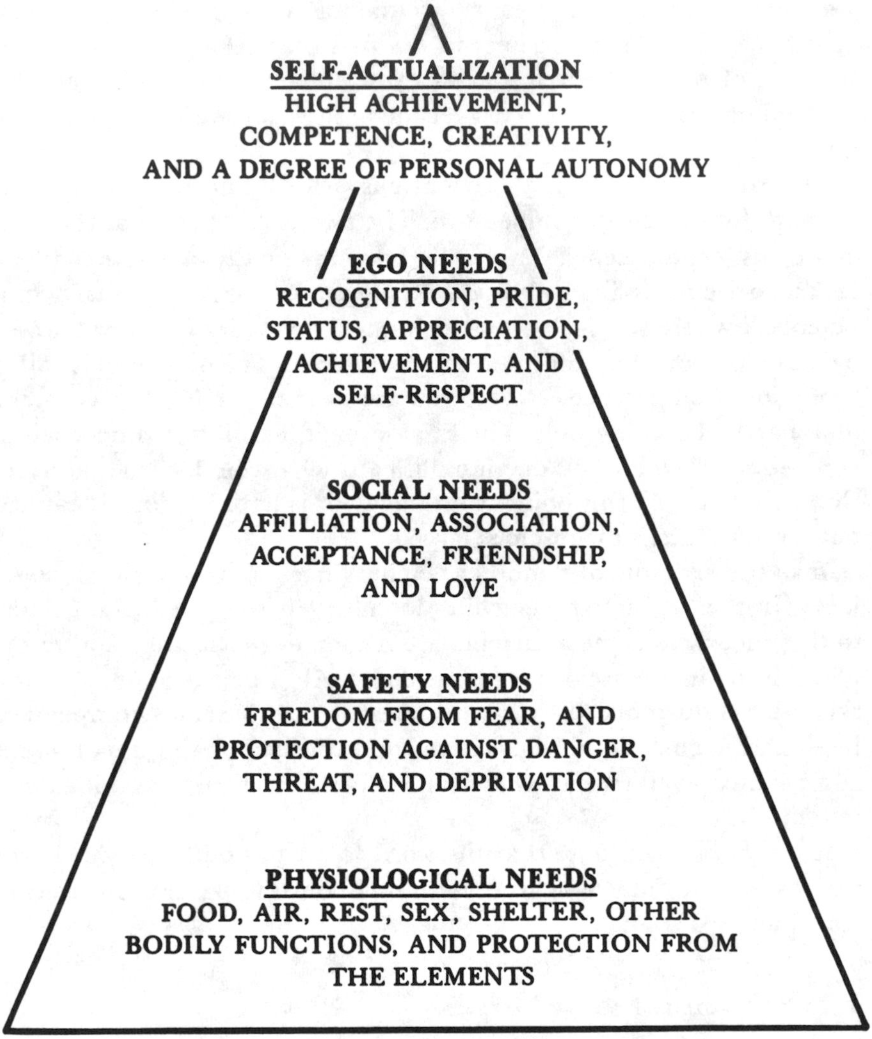

SELF-ACTUALIZATION
HIGH ACHIEVEMENT,
COMPETENCE, CREATIVITY,
AND A DEGREE OF PERSONAL AUTONOMY

EGO NEEDS
RECOGNITION, PRIDE,
STATUS, APPRECIATION,
ACHIEVEMENT, AND
SELF-RESPECT

SOCIAL NEEDS
AFFILIATION, ASSOCIATION,
ACCEPTANCE, FRIENDSHIP,
AND LOVE

SAFETY NEEDS
FREEDOM FROM FEAR, AND
PROTECTION AGAINST DANGER,
THREAT, AND DEPRIVATION

PHYSIOLOGICAL NEEDS
FOOD, AIR, REST, SEX, SHELTER, OTHER
BODILY FUNCTIONS, AND PROTECTION FROM
THE ELEMENTS

INHERENT DRIVES PROPOSED BY A. MASLOW

Fortunately, you don't have to learn to want to breathe, protect yourself, or seek out close, loving relationships as these and other drives are inherent in your being. But the way you actually go about striving for higher levels of satisfaction is more complicated. This is something that is programmed into you after birth. Primarily from modeling others in their environment, people learn to be either honest or dishonest, gracious or vain, or resourceful or lazy in pursuit of their goals. They learn either to seek out short-term gratification or to be patient in their quests, becoming either opportunistic or committed to long-term goals. Learned drives, then, are critical to character formation and personality development, for they determine to a large extent how people go about achieving their goals at all levels of the human needs and wants spectrum.

How is it that you are today the person you are? When you first entered the world, you were almost pure potential, with practically no self-concept at all. What you did inherit, of course, was the genetic background of your parents. This clearly has had a significant impact on you, but it is only one of the many influences determining your current makeup.

Most of the ideas, beliefs, values, attitudes, and feelings you now have as an adult did not exist at the time of your birth. You acquired these characteristics during the course of your upbringing through the process of learning. You began with your memory files as all blank pages waiting to be filled in. The manner in which they were filled in and the contents of the pages themselves have determined the direction your life has taken.

The essential elements that today form the basis for your adult personality were acquired during the first few years of your life. During this time, you should have experienced the love and touching of your parents and other family members, and learned how lovable, acceptable, and worthwhile you are. The quality of care and treatment you received have marked you for life. In this way, through the behavior and responses of others to your presence, you have developed a sense of self, an impression of your being.

You were born practically fearless. Most children have only two fears at birth, a fear of falling and a fear of loud noises. Even these may have been learned in the womb. Almost all other fears are acquired through the process of learning and repetition. If you wish to rid yourself of such fears, you have to do so through the same process.

There are two primary ways you learned your current habit patterns of thought. The first involved the process of imitating your parents and adopting their beliefs, mannerisms, and behavioral traits. You spent the most time with them, you attached great value to their presence, and you were led to consider them as worthy role models to emulate.

The second process involved reacting to your parents' behavior toward you, especially regarding the way and extent they expressed love and affection. You, like all children, needed all the love and attention you could get in the formative years. Everyone has an insatiable appetite for love, acceptance, and approval. This is even more important for a child whose only reference group is his or her parents.

The Two Principal Fears:
Failure and Rejection

The two principal fears most people have are the fear of failure and the fear of rejection. Both result from low self-esteem brought on by negative or traumatic experiences in childhood. These two fears, representing learned emotional responses, hold more people back from achieving their full potential than any other aspect of human personality.

A common mistake many parents make is to practice destructive criticism and arbitrary punishment with their children. This transmits to a child the message that his self-worth and behavior are one and the same thing. A child then begins to associate his sense of self and his estimate of his value as an individual with his parents' opinion of how well he is conforming to their standard. When destructive criticism or arbitrary punishment is practiced repeatedly as a normal behavioral response, the child suffers psychic discomfort or even trauma, which can handicap him for life. Inevitably this treatment robs a child of his individuality, saps his inner strength, and lowers his chances of reaching his full potential.

The fears you have acquired are always translated into verbal messages you repeat to yourself all the time. The fear of failure is characterized by self-expressions like "It's no use," or "I can't." It is brought about by being told over and over again as a child, "No," "Don't do that," "Stay away from there," or "Leave that alone." Children by nature are curious and inquisitive. They do not understand why parents respond this way. All they can understand is that whenever they try to do something, their parents respond negatively. They criticize, they threaten, and they punish. Children can only think it is because they are neither capable nor worthy of praise.

It is not possible for children to differentiate between valid and invalid criticism at a very young age, and they grow up with this negative habit pattern of thought well ingrained. Whenever a new challenge or opportunity arises later in life, they repeat to themselves, "I can't," "I'll fail," "It's too risky," or "I'll only be criticized and embarrassed." This fear of failure leads to what is called an ***inhibitive negative habit pattern***, and it is one of the greatest obstacles to success most adults face in life.

Destructive criticism and arbitrary punishment always lower a child's self-esteem and self-confidence. Both decrease a person's ability to perform in all aspects of life. Children who have been subjected to a steady routine of destructive criticism grow up to be hypersensitive adults, incapable of accepting any criticism from others at all, whether constructive or destructive.

In his book *Language in Thought and Action*, American linguist and former senator S.I. Hayakawa cites an experiment performed with laboratory rats that demonstrates how arbitrary punishment, one type of destructive criticism, immobilizes them permanently and prevents them from making new choices.

> Professor N.R.F. Maier of the University of Michigan performed a series of interesting experiments in which "neurosis" is induced in rats. The rats are first trained to jump off the edge of a platform at one of two doors. If the rat jumps to the right, the door holds fast, and it bumps its nose and falls into a net; if it jumps to the left, the door opens and the rat finds a dish of food. When the rats are well trained to this reaction, the situation is changed. The food is put behind the other door, so that in order to get their reward they now have to jump to the right instead of to the left. (Other changes, such as marking the two doors in different ways, may also be introduced by the experimenter.) If the rat fails to figure out the new system so that each time it jumps it never knows whether it is going to get food or bump its nose, it finally gives up and refuses to jump at all. At this stage, Mr. Maier says, "Many rats prefer to starve rather than make a choice."[2]

Another mistake many parents make is to practice conditional love with their children. This involves withholding love or threatening to do so as a means to control a child's behavior. Often parents don't realize that they can damage their children's psyches, sometimes permanently, by demanding obedience and conformity in exchange for expressions of love and affection. Children need love so much that they'll do almost anything to get it. If he receives only conditional love, a child quickly loses his innocence, natural spontaneity, and fearlessness. Although this manipulative technique is very effective, it can be very destructive. It often leaves deep psychological scars that remain for life, and creates severe psychological impediments that a child neither understands nor is able to overcome as an adult.

Fear of rejection is characterized by the self-expressions "I must" or "I have to." It is learned by a child who receives only conditional love and acceptance. It is caused by parents who demonstrate to their children that they are not loved in and of themselves, but only when they engage in behavior that is acceptable to the parents. When children are told repeatedly, "Do what I say or else," "I told you not to do that," or "Now you're going to get it," they do not understand why they are being treated this way. They can only think they are not worthy and valued in and of themselves, and that they are not safe and secure. They begin to believe their parents will not love them unless they do exactly what they say and approve of. They know they have to do what their parents want them to do, whatever pleases them.

This fear of rejection leads to what is called a *compulsive negative habit pattern*. Children subjected to a steady routine of conditional love and acceptance manifest in adult life a preoccupation with what others think about them and what they do, and they let it control their life.

These two negative habit patterns of thought, the inhibitive and the compulsive, can hold you back throughout your life. The worst situation of all is a case of both negative habit patterns working together against you: "I can't, but I know I have to" or "I have to, but I know I can't." You feel compelled to act yet you are afraid to try. You are faced with what you perceive as an impossible situation. These two fears can only undermine a positive sense of self. We know a lack of a positive self-concept is the primary cause of most of the misery and failure people experience in life. More adults are held back from realizing their full potential by a negative self-image and low *self-concept* than any other single factor.

"The debilitating mental and emotional difficulties that plague normal people are the most powerful and universal constraint on human performance," according to John W. Gardner, author of *Self-Renewal*.

Freedom from Fear

Negative habit patterns of thought reflect the many fears you learned early in life, practically all of which are unnatural to the human psyche. All negative thoughts necessarily lead to negative emotions, which detract from your mental health and contribute to poor performance. The key to happiness and success involves enjoying the greatest number of positive emotions as a result of all your efforts. As Helen Keller noted, all the joys and pleasures in life are neither seen nor heard; *they are felt.*

We have seen how negative habit patterns of thought can be eliminated from your life. The presence of negative emotions need not be a permanent state of affairs. You can learn to replace the old with the new, the negative emotions of fear and self-doubt with positive emotions of *"yes, I can!"* by carefully repeating the same learning process that brought on the negative emotions in the first place.

This ability to banish negative thoughts and emotions from your life is *the fourth great wonder of the mind.* It is a matter of accepting responsibility, taking control, and repeating the learning process over and over again so that you always choose the thoughts you want to have in order to generate the feelings you want to experience.

Through repetition, you can develop new, more positive patterns of thought which eventually become habitual. Your brain uses a vast number of these mental routines or programmed thought sequences to get you through each day. They resemble the routines and subroutines that an electronic computer uses to process data. Becoming more aware of your habit patterns of thought and their effects will help you identify areas where you are having difficulty. These patterns can range from simple perceptual misinterpretations of daily events to your overall pattern of living. Of particular significance is the way you relate to others. How do you handle interpersonal relationships such as socializing, compromising, and arguing? Are you in the habit of escalating or diminishing personal conflicts? The type and the quality of your interpersonal relationships are a key aspect of your life.

You must realize that all external events lack any emotional component in their makeup. All external events are inherently neutral until you respond mentally and assign an emotional context to them. About 90 percent of all fears are imaginary. They are a product of your mind and do not exist in reality. Unfortunately, you are trampled most often by forces you yourself create. As Rudyard Kipling (1865–1936), the British poet, short-story writer, and novelist, wrote, "Of all the liars in the world, sometimes the worst are your own fears."

All external events are inherently neutral until you respond mentally and assign an emotional context to them.

The key to eliminating unnecessary fear from your life is to create and hold firmly in mind a positive image in the present tense. Concentrating on the present keeps you from digging up what happened in the past and imagining that it will repeat itself in the future. It is impossible to experience fear if you hold your mind in the present moment and concentrate solely on what is currently taking place. You have to go back into the past or look into the future to experience fear.

In the vast majority of cases, there is no reason at all to be afraid. Your fear is real only to the extent that you allow your mind to create it, and in turn your body to sense it. You only devalue the present and condemn the future when you concentrate on past failures.

PART II:

The Application
of Expectation Theory

CHAPTER 7

Reprogramming Your Mind
for Success

*"It is not enough to have great qualities. We should
also have the management of them."*
—Duc François de La Rochefoucauld (1613–1680)
French moralist and writer of maxims

By now you should be convinced that the most critical factor in determining how well you perform in every aspect of your life is your self-esteem, and that the only way to raise your self-esteem is to change the way you see yourself.

What techniques are available to help you change your self-image and the way you think and feel about yourself? To answer this question, we first must have a better understanding of the magnitude of the problem at hand. Let's start with a description of your mental room.

Your Mental Room

Imagine your subconscious mind as a large, square room with only one door at the front. This front entrance is protected by a guard who represents your conscious mind. His primary job is to limit entry into the room according to certain specific criteria.

When you were born, this whole room was empty and the guard let in anyone who asked. As you grew older and experienced various new events and happenings, your room began to fill up with a variety of beliefs and opinions about yourself and your world. These beliefs and opinions joined together to form a kind of exclusive club, eventually determining your personality and becoming somewhat assertive about

137

it. In fact, this club became so assertive at some point that it began to tell the guard just who he could let in to join the group and who he could not. In other words, when the subconscious mind didn't feel comfortable with the qualifications of a particular applicant (a new belief or opinion), he was refused access. The club was exercising its right to allow in only new members who were compatible with long-term residents. If the current residents strongly believed that you were not a good athlete, for example, the group would not entertain the thought of letting in someone who thought you were.

The contents of your mental room represent the total programming your mind has been subjected to up to now. The most powerful occupant in your room is your self-image "clique," which together forms a consensus about who you are and what you are capable of achieving. Collectively, it controls the way you think about yourself, the way you feel, and most importantly, the way you perform in everything you say and do.

Recall how we compared your subconscious memory files to the data entered into a computer. If garbage is entered, then garbage is stored in memory. The most prominent feature of all garbage is its smell. If garbage has been stored in your mind, and there is a lot of it in all of us, then the unfortunate guard at the front door acquires the same characteristic—he begins to smell as well. He can't help but smell because he guards the only door the stench can exit from.

This gives you some measure of the serious problem many people face: a smoldering pile of garbage in their mind that is protected by an obedient, well-trained guard who has clear instructions to allow only more garbage in! Can you imagine the reception a positive thought or compliment gets at the front door of a room filled with decaying garbage? It becomes overwhelmed, suffocated by the more powerful stench of all its adversaries—the well-entrenched negative thoughts that are much more numerous and hence who are very much in control.

How Have You Been Programmed?

You entered the world as a blank slate, with little basis for thinking or acting in any particular way. As new experiences entered your subconscious mind, they began to define for you the world around you. For example, *a newborn baby forms a million new nerve connec-*

tions in the brain every second for the first two years of its life.
Every detail of all your experiences is stored in memory for future reference.

This programming began by other people in your life tapping on your computer keyboard—your sight, sound, smell, taste, and touch sensors. For example, by the time you were eighteen, you were told "No!" about 150,000 times. Eighty-five to 95 percent of all the programming you received from external sources was negative, while most of the remainder was neutral. The few hundred "yes's" you received hardly made any impact. In this purposeful way, you have been force-fed and conditioned to perceive and believe in a manner consistent with the experiences you have had and the people you have associated with. You ended up adopting the opinions and beliefs your primary reference groups acquired during their own upbringing. Now, as an adult, most of your programming is from the inside-out. Instead of listening to outside suggestions, you tend to rely on self-suggestions to decide on who you are and what you can do with the rest of your life. You cannot turn off that little voice inside you and just pretend not to hear its messages.

Previously, we examined the learning process by considering the simple act of crossing the street. Let's look at another example of how you formed a particular habit pattern of thought as a result of learning the multiplication table in grade school.

When you first learned the specific response to what is nine times nine, it occurred totally at the conscious level. You were made aware of the answer and you began to train your mind and nervous system to accept it. With continued repetition and practice, you began to act out the response more and more habitually, and the direction moved from the conscious toward the subconscious. When the response became fully ingrained, you didn't really think about the answer at all. You simply let the subconscious take over.

Thus a habit pattern of thought becomes either right or wrong, or positive or negative, depending on what is first entered into your subconscious mind. If you were told and believed that nine times nine was eighty-four, then this is what you'll repeat, even though it is not the correct answer. In the very same way, you have developed conditioned responses to a wide variety of external stimuli. They required a pattern of repetition over and over again, sometimes hundreds, often thousands of times before they became firmly ingrained. They can be changed only by the same process.

Recall that **WHEN YOU CHANGE YOUR THINKING,** you change your beliefs; when you change your beliefs, you change your expectations; when you change your expectations, you change your attitude; when you change your attitude, you change your behavior; when you change your behavior, you change your performance; and when you change your performance, **YOU CHANGE YOUR LIFE.**

Such are the causes and effects of human thought and human behavior. Everything begins with thought, representing the beliefs you adopt and plant in your subconscious mind.

Your Mental Light Switches

Imagine the 100 billion neurons in your brain as small light switches that are either on or off, indicating yes or no to your beliefs about each of your abilities. If you believe, for example, that you are an average parent, a poor communicator, an expert driver, or an inept athlete, then the appropriate light switch in your mind is lit up accordingly. It is either off or on, and low, medium, or high in intensity. The way you talk to yourself is the way you see yourself, and it controls the regulators to all these switches. Once the level is set, the regulators lock firmly into place and become very, very difficult to change.

What you come to believe about yourself determines what you say to yourself. This then becomes the controlling element in how you perform.

Do you recall ever saying to yourself any of the following?

"I would like to do it, but I don't have the education."
"I would like to do it, but I lack the experience."
"I would like to do it, but I don't know the right people."
"I would like to do it but I don't have the time, the ability, the energy, and so on."

From all of these statements, you'll notice that the only thing separating you from high achievement is one big "butt," and, of course, you'll realize it is your butt! You are forgetting that your butt is behind you and you should only be looking forward to what is ahead. Foresight rather than hindsight will get you where you want to go!

You probably have heard perfectly healthy people rationalize an occasional problem by saying, "I must be getting old. I have trouble remembering names, and I lack the concentration and energy I once had."

What do you think this kind of self-talk does to their mental light switches?

You're right. It lowers their intensity. In the previous example, the "memory," "concentration," and "energy" lights all dim appreciably. An idea, once planted in the mind, is like a seed that is sown. It quickly takes root and begins to grow. The feelings and behavior, slaves to the belief, automatically conform to the thought. Such people begin to feel older, and actually begin to experience a loss of memory, concentration, and energy in order to be consistent with the perceived notion. The rule here is *never* contemplate or verbalize anything that you do not want to bring into reality.

Had such people talked positively and believed they were maturing gracefully with renewed energy and mental powers, they would have found ways to bring these characteristics into reality as well. The body as a result of what is perceived and believed always manifests the thoughts innermost in the mind. Resigning yourself to defeat is the one sure way to get there. You are your own worst enemy when you continually tell yourself you cannot succeed. You must learn to become your own best friend by making your internal success mechanism work to your advantage.

You have to find some way to bypass the guard, your conscious mind, as it currently exists with all of its biases and prejudices, *principally about you!* Remember, it is standing proud and protective of all the negative and destructive beliefs it has already entered into your subconscious mind. It will not give in easily to a series of revisions, to a whole new set of ideas and aspirations that are counter to all of your prior experiences. It will intercept and reject anything it views as new or different, as contrary to whatever is already acceptable and compatible with your prior programming.

Recall Maltz's view that self-image psychology was the most successful technique yet discovered to bring about dramatic improvement and change in personality. He held that the subconscious always works like a goal-oriented mechanism to bring into physical reality the goals you have planted in memory. It processes a negative self-image, data reflecting beliefs you hold that say you are inferior, unworthy, and incapable, just as readily as a positive self-image. It functions impersonally, without malice or favoritism. It is a machine — *efficient, cold, and calculating* — but it can be controlled through new habit patterns of thought that result in new thought-images.

It is not enough to realize that you have a lot of talent, ability, and intelligence to work with. Positive thinking by itself is not the answer. Logic and reason alone will not bring about the changes you need in order to move ahead, since they are external to your subconscious self. If change could be effected from outside your subconscious memory bank, how different your life would be! You could eliminate unwanted habits such as drinking, smoking, and overeating simply by thinking about them at the conscious level and saying, "I'm going to stop." Anger, worry, guilt, and feelings of failure and rejection would no longer be part of your daily life. Supreme self-confidence and a feeling of total control would drive you steadily forward toward a life of increasing prosperity and personal fulfillment.

Unfortunately, it doesn't work this way. Sheer willpower and determination are not enough. It is not enough to keep telling yourself, "I am a likeable, capable, positive-minded person. I am self-confident, I can do anything I set my mind to," because, deep down, *your subconscious does not believe you.* You are filled with a multitude of self-doubts and fears. Your prior programming—all of the garbage stuffed into the mental warehouse of your mind—is your principal obstacle to success.

Is there any way to break free from this bondage of the past, to reprogram your mind to offset all of the negative, self-limiting ideas and notions you have ingested during your lifetime?

All of your potential exists at a lower level of consciousness.

The answer, thankfully, is an unqualified yes. There is a tried and proven method that works. It involves a three-dimensional technique that combines progressive relaxation, positive affirmations, and creative visualization. It allows you to tap into your full potential, all of which exists at a lower level of consciousness.

Autogenic Conditioning

The only way to reprogram your mind for success is to change what has been entered into your memory files using autogenic conditioning.

The term *autogenic* simply means self-generated. Autogenic conditioning involves repeating *a positive statement* to yourself while in a state of deep relaxation, and combining it with an associated *visualization* that is representative of exactly what you want to accomplish in your life. This leads us to an explanation of the progressive relaxation technique and the alpha state.

The human brain is constantly generating a series of pulses of electrical energy that reflect its level of activity. Most of the time these pulses are quite rapid, between thirteen and thirty cycles per second. These higher frequencies are called beta waves, and they are the ones you are now generating as you read this text. Beta waves are associated with being fully awake and mentally alert, and involve such activities as talking, listening, and concentrating.

Slower brain frequencies, those between eight and thirteen cycles per second, are called alpha waves. They predominate when the brain is relaxed and on the edge of sleep, a sort of dream-like state of mind. Alpha waves are almost always present during periods of high creativity.

A third type of wave, theta, pulses between four and eight cycles per second. The slowest waves of all are delta waves, which are associated with very deep sleep.

When you are wide awake, there is usually a mixture of waves operating in your brain in an ever-changing pattern. Beta waves primarily predominate, with occasional fluctuations of alpha waves mixed in. On the few occasions of alpha wave dominance, you are more likely to experience flashes of creativity and new ideas.

In the relaxed alpha state, you have improved access to your subconscious mind, the power base representing your true potential. The way is not blocked by the conscious mind which is always making judgments and editing out any thoughts deemed inconsistent with your current beliefs. All of the usual concerns, problems, and preoccupations of everyday life represented by the beta brain wave state are not present to complicate your thinking.

The alpha state is experienced naturally just before falling asleep and just after waking up. These are ideal times to condition your mind. Another option is to *induce* an alpha state by conscious effort at a suitable time during the day by simply practicing progressive relaxation. There are several ways to achieve this lower state of awareness. All aim at one thing: completely relaxing both the mind and the body until you are in a transformed state of consciousness.

Autogenic conditioning was developed by Dr. Johannes H. Schultz, a Berlin psychiatrist and neurologist, who practiced the technique earlier this century in Germany and throughout Europe. It amounts to an advanced method of mind control now commonly used by Olympic and professional athletes as part of their rigorous training programs. The East Germans in particular demonstrated the value of the technique with their phenomenal record of Olympic medals during the 1980s.

Autogenic conditioning involves a simple, seven-step process.

1. Find a quiet place.

2. Create a peaceful mood to relax both your mind and body.

3. Repeat to yourself the specific behavioral change you want to bring about in your life, detailing the new belief you wish to adopt.

4. "See" yourself exhibiting the specific behavior you want to emulate in your mind in as much detail as you can.

5. Accept this scene and the change it represents as already being part of your life.

6. Bathe in the positive feelings this new accomplishment generates.

7. Execute a specific anchor such as forming a fist and repeating the phrase "Yes, I can!" over and over to yourself in a firm, confident manner.

This sequence involves three essential elements. You must

- verbalize,
- visualize, and
- emotionalize

the new belief, representing the idea component, the image component, and the emotional component — the three-dimensional elements that comprise all new thought creation.

Why does this technique work? We all have ideas and images in our mind as a result of the thoughts and experiences we have had. After all, these are the things life is made of. When you think about something, you also *experience* it; in other words, you create an image in your mind that is entered into memory. As well, when you experience something, you also *think* about it; in other words, you respond to the stimulus, and store both it and your response by way of images in memory. This process of thinking and experiencing, and the forming of ideas and mental images, is then transformed into specific physical behavior in a way that is identical for all humans.

Although this image-to-behavior process is the same for all humans, we all end up with different images stored in memory. This is because people are exposed to different stimuli, have varying degrees of ability to perceive the outside world accurately, and make different interpretations even of identical experiences because of their previous programming.

These different behavioral targets that end up in memory represent your current models of excellence. The quality of these models in turn determines the quality of your performance. If the internal representations you now have aren't getting you the results you want, then clearly you need to look for more effective models. These you can acquire by discovering what has made other people successful in various fields of endeavor after years of trial and error, and using their models as your own. This is what autogenic conditioning allows. It is a modeling exercise that enters improved behavioral targets into your subconscious reality, making these your new models of excellence.

Whatever you can picture in your mind and firmly believe, you can achieve. And feeling the effect of accomplishing your goal helps activate the subconscious to go to work to find a way to bring it into reality. When you feel a certain way, you tend to act that way.

This feeling is the triggering mechanism that drives the new belief deep into your subconscious reality. Your relaxed mental state allows more easy access. Now **YOU** are the programmer, **YOU** are the master of your fate, **YOU** are the dominant force in your existence. You can repeat to yourself as often as you like what you really want out of life.

Recall that you always get what you keep telling your mind you want. But many of your self-instructions are now negative, stressful, and defeatist. If you were not programmed for success through your upbringing, then you simply must take on this challenging task yourself.

If you want to grow a field of nourishing wheat, you must first plant healthy wheat. So it is with the subconscious, the fertile garden of your mind. Just as you need to sow the seeds of the crop you want to harvest, you need to plant the thoughts that change the way you "see" yourself.

Failure to do so leaves the ground to negative weeds that will simply grow and multiply by default.

Just as your fabulous mind has been programmed by self-limiting beliefs, so it can be reprogrammed with more realistic beliefs. All skills, abilities, habits, personality traits, and performance characteristics can be changed by employing positive affirmations and creative visualization while in a state of deep relaxation. Autogenic conditioning helps you discover latent talents, skills, and abilities buried deep within you, and brings them to the surface and puts them on display.

One proven progressive relaxation technique involves the following guided imagery.

> Sit in a comfortable chair in a quiet room. Allow your eyelids to gently close. Imagine you are in an elevator traveling slowly down a series of levels to a place of total peace and tranquility. Begin to count from one to ten, and as you do, pay attention to the growing feeling of complete relaxation in your body. Count one. Feel relaxation beginning to spread all over your face. Your jaw, forehead, and scalp are totally relaxed. Count two. You are going down further and becoming more relaxed. Count three. Your neck, shoulders, and back feel soft and supple. Count four. Your arms, hands, and wrists are more relaxed. Your breathing is deep, slow, and easy. Count five. The elevator is moving down . . . you are experiencing deeper relaxation. You feel calm, comfortable, and at peace with the world. Count six. Your stomach, buttocks, and thighs are all relaxed. Tension is literally evaporating away from all your body parts and extremities. Count seven. Your legs and feet, even the tips of your toes, are relaxed. Count eight. You are drifting down, deeper and deeper, and getting closer to your special place. You feel calm all over. Count nine. Almost there. Feel the freedom. Count ten. You have arrived. You are in your special place. Enjoy the feeling of total peace and serenity.

Now you are very, very relaxed and receptive to new ideas. Clearly affirm the goal you want to accomplish or the performance you want to achieve. In this relaxed state, visualize yourself as already possessing the new qualities and attributes you want to have, as being the ideal person you want to be.

A typical conditioning session aims toward *a new belief and new expectations,* leading to a change in attitude and a change in behavior. Improved performance should always be the goal, leading to feelings of increased confidence and higher self-esteem.

Consider the following affirmations as a new beginning, the door to a new reality. In each instance, actually "see" yourself acting in the prescribed fashion and getting the desired results:

- Today, I have a positive mental attitude. I have eliminated criticism and impatience from my life, and replaced them with praise and tolerance.

- Today, I totally believe in myself. I believe I am capable and worthy of high achievement.

- Today, I have a big, challenging goal I am working toward. It is adding meaning and momentum to my life.

- Today, I accept full responsibility for all of my actions. Whatever results I achieve, I know they are the result of the thinking I am engaged in.

- Today, I manage my time effectively. I know every minute is precious and irreplaceable, and must be used to the best advantage.

- Today, I am pursuing a personal development program. I dedicate at least one hour each day toward improving myself.

- Today, I value my health, physically, mentally, and spiritually. I am taking very good care of myself.

- Today, I am a creative person in setting and attaining my goals. Possibilities abound in all of my thoughts and actions.

- Today, I have a service-minded approach toward my employment and fellow human beings. I always do more than what is expected of me, knowing I will receive more of what I want in return.

- Today, I am excellent at what I do. I believe it is through excellence that I will find my true self.

- Today, I am effective in all my interpersonal relationships. I believe people take priority over problems, and that they deserve my total respect and attention.

Notice three things about all of these affirmations: (1) they are in the first person, singular "I"; (2) they are in the present tense, since the subconscious can relate only to the now; and (3) they are positive. For example, you never say, "I no longer have a negative self-image" or "I don't feel nervous speaking in front of a large audience." You say, "I have a positive self-image" and "I speak with confidence and authority in front of a large audience."

You should also aim in your visualizations to focus on the external environment in order to become fully associated with the experience. Imagine being yourself *looking out through your eyes,* getting *the precise results* you desire, not someone else watching you from a distance. In this way, the correct neural imprints are registered, reflecting you as the initiator of the activity rather than you as a spectator watching yourself.

Finally, allow yourself to feel the positive emotions associated with the new belief throughout your body. Tingle with excitement, with the realization that you are more than you ever thought you were, that you are what you believe and say you are.

Your Book of Beliefs

Here is a suggested sequence of mental steps you can follow once you have entered the alpha state. The same steps can be used to bring about whatever new reality you want to create for yourself in your life.

NLP Reframing Exercise #4
"THE BELIEF CHANGER"

Imagine walking down a long, dark tunnel as vividly as you can and descending a series of steps until you come to a large, brightly lit, subterranean room which represents your subconscious mind. In the center of this chamber, on a large stone altar, lies an immense, gilt-edged manuscript titled *My Book of Beliefs.* The book is covered with a thick blanket of dust and cobwebs that you must wipe away with your hands.

You begin by turning to the index for the subject you most want to change. In this example, we'll consider your ability to speak in public. You note that the pages are like huge tablets and each seems to weigh several pounds. Mentally see yourself turning over each of these ponderous pages with considerable difficulty, with dust and dirt puffing up into your face on every attempt. Imag-

---

ine saying to yourself how old this book appears to be when in fact it is only as old as you are. Finally, you arrive at the desired page and, to no great surprise, you find the following words burnt into the paper as though they were etched in marble:

I NEVER SUCCEED AT PUBLIC SPEAKING.

Now you ponder this discovery for just a moment. Didn't you really know, deep down, that this would be the belief you would find? After all, surveys show that most people fear public speaking more than death itself. How many times have you tried to deny its existence, yet could not escape from this reality? Can you think back in time and recall specific events from your past that allowed this belief to develop and finally become entrenched in your subconscious? You are well aware you create your own reality, that it is a result of your past programming.

But you also know it can be changed. Your *Book of Beliefs* is only a book with words written on paper. So you decide to grab hold of the particular page with the unwanted belief, and proceed to rip it out with great gusto. You then walk over to one of the many flaming torches that ring the walls of the cave and set the page on fire. You hear it crackle, pop, and sizzle as it twists and curls up, finally falling to the floor completely engulfed in flames. Soon all that remains are scarlet embers and black ashes. You proceed to rub these paltry remains into the rough stone floor until only faint traces of fine powder bear testimony to its former existence. In effect, you have minimized the effect of this negative belief.

You walk back to your *Book of Beliefs* and turn to a crisp new page. You pick up a golden pen from its holder and proceed to write in solemn, capital letters:

I ALWAYS SUCCEED AT PUBLIC SPEAKING.

You slowly repeat the phrase out loud to yourself, over and over again: **I ALWAYS SUCCEED AT PUBLIC SPEAKING; I ALWAYS SUCCEED AT PUBLIC SPEAKING; I *ALWAYS* SUCCEED AT PUBLIC SPEAKING.**

Next, decide on a simple scene or scenario that best symbolizes what you most earnestly desire. See yourself living out this successful scene in your imagination, and hold it in crisp focus for a full thirty seconds.

Stare at each of these precious words. Deeply desire this outcome with as much emotion as you can possibly muster.

Now let the picture go and allow your mind to become completely blank. Accept the scene you have created as totally valid. Feel in your bones that you deserve it, that you are worthy of having it as part of your reality. And *expect* this successful scene to be part of your future whenever the occasion demands its presence.

You slowly close the book. *It is done!* You have begun to create a new belief. *Celebrate inside!* Rejoice in the realization that you are now in control, that a new reality will always follow a new belief once it has been fully accepted. In effect, you have maximized this positive belief.

The simple scene or scenario you decide upon that best symbolizes what you really want is critical in this process. You must return to this same image with great intensity several times each day for several days to finally drive it deep into your subconscious reality. It must become as familiar to you as your mother's face or the lake you used to swim in as a child. Let this picture become your talisman, the symbol that best represents your success in bringing into reality what you most desire in life.

For example, you could take the picture from a magazine or brochure of someone you particularly admired in the field of public speaking, cut out his or her face, and substitute your own. Then place copies of this picture in prominent places throughout your home, office, and in your automobile to remind you that this is now who you are. On each occasion that you look at this picture, "see" yourself getting the same positive results that this person gets when talking to an audience. Write the appropriate affirmation under the picture to reinforce this strong visual message:

> I speak with confidence and enthusiasm in front
> of people. The audience always reacts positively
> and supportively to what I have to say.

The Power of Affirmations

More than sixty years ago, Emile Coué (1857–1926), the French psychologist and pioneer in the field of autosuggestion, wrote these simple words: "Every day in every way, I'm getting better and better." He believed that great benefit would accrue to the person who merely repeated this simple phrase out loud one hundred times a day. Modern medicine has since confirmed his belief. Patients with chronic pain who have repeated these words over and over again with strong desire and conviction have been able to conquer their maladies.

Autogenic conditioning is based on the fact that improved performance will always result from improved models of excellence. No simple slogan is going to transform your personality overnight. You cannot hope to change everything all at once. But you can become more patient, more empathetic, and more confident if you concentrate on one behavioral trait at a time using a positive affirmation with an associated visualization. You can develop a new habit pattern of thought in five to seven days if you practice it regularly in your imagination. This is accomplished by thinking, talking, and acting in the manner consistent with the person you most want to be, with the attributes and characteristics you most want to have.

Assume you want to improve the quality of your interpersonal relationships in your home life. Repeat this affirmation:

> I enjoy happy, harmonious relationships with my spouse
> and children. We show respect and love for each other
> by our verbal exchanges and sympathetic behavior.

When you "see" yourself achieving a goal in your
imagination often enough, you begin to believe that
you can achieve it in real life.

By simultaneously repeating this affirmation out loud and visualizing yourself getting the desired results in your mind, you'll move that much closer to the goal. When you "see" yourself achieving a goal in your imagination often enough, you begin to believe that you can achieve it in real life.

Recall that you cannot always clearly differentiate between an artificial experience imagined vividly and in every detail, and a real-life experience. When you imagine yourself achieving a goal in your mind, your brain accepts the experience as real, so real in fact that you will feel the same emotions and experience the same sensations as those that would exist had you already achieved the goal in real life. In the process, you are building up a pattern of successful behavior in your subconscious mind, a sort of success consciousness.

Clearly there is hope for everyone. You need only program your subconscious mind with artificial, winning experiences as effectively as real-life experiences. You can use your own resources, knowledge, and imagination in this positive, purposeful way instead of waiting for your circumstances and environment to take care of you.

Research shows that you forget over 90 percent of everything you hear once in about twenty-four hours. But if you hear the same thing repeated fifty to a hundred times over a period of time, you tend to remember it. This type of learning experience takes advantage of what is called "spaced repetition," and it is the type represented by autogenic conditioning.

Each day, take fifteen to twenty minutes and repeat your affirmation of the week out loud while in a state of deep relaxation. You can use a series of three-by-five index cards for this purpose or an audiocassette that you have prerecorded. Choose a specific belief or characteristic you wish to change. Repeat it to yourself over and over again, and imagine yourself acting in the prescribed fashion and getting the desired results in as much detail as you can.

The effect with persistent, concentrated effort will astonish you. This simple technique, coupled with deep conviction and sincere desire, will bring about almost any change you want to make in your life.

The main benefit of autogenic conditioning is that it allows you to act with confidence in accordance with new, *imagined* behavior that is more desirable than old, **habitual** behavior. You change by playing the part. Once you have experienced what it is like to feel confident, competent, and successful in your imagination, you are more able to repeat the same behavior and experience the same emotions in real life. You simply act the part of the person you want to be, with the qualities and attributes you want to have. As William Shakespeare counseled, "Assume a virtue and it is yours."

This concept allowed author Dorothea Brande to reach new heights as a writer and public speaker. As she recounts in her wonderful book *Wake Up and Live*, she witnessed what she considered was an amazing display of ability by an average person under hypnosis. Later she read that such feats were possible by hypnotized subjects because past failures and mistakes were completely purged from their memory. She reasoned that similar results could be achieved as well by average people in the wakeful state if they simply ignored past failures and *acted as if* they could not fail. So she began to act on the assumption that she possessed the necessary qualities and abilities she desperately wanted and aggressively forged ahead, reaching within a year a level of success and accomplishment she never dreamed was possible.

This ability to act the part of the person you most want to be is *the fifth great wonder of the mind.* It recognizes the fact that all causation is mental, that everything that happens to you in your life today, tomorrow, and in the future will be determined by the contents of your mind. You are and will become the person you spend the most time being each day.

You must remember one critical point in this regard. You are able to bring into reality an act or event only to the degree that you are able to picture it clearly and in every detail in your imagination first. In other words, if you cannot believe it and see it in your mind, you will not be able to actualize it in your experience. You will stumble around and fail, not knowing exactly what you are trying to accomplish.

As the Reverend Robert Schuller notes, a pessimist says, "I'll believe it when I see it," whereas an optimist says, "I'll see it when I believe it." What you see is what you get.

Take any desired goal you may have—to give a rousing speech, to deliver a successful sales presentation, or to perform with confidence during an important job interview—and you'll discover that you can hope to do any one of them only to the degree that you can successfully "see" yourself getting the desired results in your imagination. The critical first effort is mental. You must believe and be able to see the possibilities in your mind before you can hope to realize them in your life.

Consider something you are trying to accomplish at the present time to prove this point. Do you firmly believe in your goal, and are you able to see yourself achieving it? If not, you will not be successful.

Breaking Through Fear

If some major fear or phobia is holding you back, you may find the following exercise useful. But please note: some fears and phobias are too complex to deal with in such simple terms. In such instances, you should seek professional medical advice.

NLP Reframing Exercise #5
"THE PHOBIA BUSTER"

Assume you are extremely nervous about something such as public speaking to the point that it is almost a phobia that consumes you. The particular fear or phobia you have is irrelevant to the technique that follows.

Access your most confident state by repeating NLP Reframing Exercise #1, "The Confidence Builder." Recall and fully associate with this *"think like a winner!"* feeling that puts you into your most powerful, confident state. Believe you can overcome any hardship or any ordeal, since you are wearing a suit of shining armor that is impregnable by outside forces. Anchor this feeling by forming a fist.

In this state, imagine yourself sitting in the middle of a large movie theater. Now imagine rising up out of your body, and floating through the air to the projection room at the back. From this position, look down and see yourself looking up at the screen. Your "other self" is seeing a large black-and-white still picture of yourself as you are just prior to your normal phobic response.

While focusing on your other self, see the original snapshot on the screen turn into a black-and-white movie that runs at very high speed from the beginning to the end of your phobic experience. As you watch this, imagine that music from a merry-go-round is playing in the background. Now see the same scenario run in reverse, again at very high speed. See everyone and hear everything go backward as though it were a home movie being

---

rewound. You feel nothing as all this takes place since you are twice removed from the experience. Note how comical it all looks. Freeze the film at the very beginning. Each of these showings lasts for only a second or two. Form a fist.

Next, float back down and enter your body sitting in the seat. With greater confidence than your former self ever had, stand, walk up to the screen, and jump inside the picture. Looking out of your own eyes, run the same film forward in your favorite colors at normal speed and go through the same experience, only this time *see, hear,* and *feel* everything going perfectly well. Replay the film in your imagination several times, each time experiencing only positive feelings. Acknowledge the fact that you are in absolute control. Form a fist. Take a moment and try to recall what it was you were phobic of. . . .

In this exercise, you have moved in your mind from a completely **disassociated** vision of the undesirable scene to a completely **associated** vision of the desirable scene. You have changed the old experience you don't want to the new experience you do want, and firmly anchored it into your subconscious reality. Now every time you think about your fear or phobia, this stimulus will trigger in you new feelings of confidence and greater control. You have provided your subconscious with a more acceptable and desirable alternative to its former response.

A variation of this visualization is to change the person you see on the screen, in the above instance, you, to a frog. Imagine the audience as being a bunch of frogs as well. See yourself croaking out in a strong, firm voice a particular message, and all the other frogs croaking back their approval. This particular lily pond is full of excitement! The object is to make the experience light and comical, as something you are comfortable with. After all, it isn't very hard to make a bunch of frogs croak! If you can see yourself doing this, how hard can it be to have a live audience give you a standing ovation at the end of your presentation?

This approach is not as absurd as you may think. Dale Carnegie (1888–1955) recounts in *How to Win Friends and Influence People* how he practiced as a youngster speaking to the animals on the farm where he lived to develop inner confidence and poise. Invariably, they were all totally enthralled with what he had to say! He went on, of course, to teach public speaking skills to thousands of people throughout the world.

Many experienced public speakers are known to run through their presentation successfully several times in their imagination before ever giving a speech. Looking out through their eyes, they see the audience responding and being receptive to their remarks in the *exact way they want.* When they are finally introduced and step up to the microphone, they are only going through their routine one more time. Their success system goes to work to have them affect their audience in the precise way they have previously envisioned it. To the degree that they were able to believe and see themselves doing well and affect their audience in the desired way, they will perform well. Their nervous system simply retraces the neural imprints etched onto their mental map. The quality of their performance—their behavioral response—is totally predictable. Their "trip" is as successful as the map or blueprint they have previously drawn up for themselves.

Using autogenic conditioning in this way, you can see that your future is virtually unlimited. Whatever image you can create and hold in your mind on a continuous basis, you can be, have, or do. You need only decide who it is you want to be and what it is you want to do. You become your ideal-self by imagining being ideal in your mind. Practice the part in your imagination first, then act the role in real life. Play a game of "Let's Pretend," a sort of progressive mental posturing. Learn to lean in the direction you want to go. The advice is this: If you continue to practice and act the part, you'll eventually bring it into reality, since you always get what you keep telling your mind you want.

Modern technology is now available to help us take advantage of this new learning process. Biofeedback equipment and courses in its use are readily available to help people relax through conscious effort. People can be taught by a professional in a few hours how to gain control over their nervous systems.

Another helpful tool is the audiocassette player. Many consider it to be the most significant development in self-help and self-learning since the invention of the printing press. You can now record your major goals on tape, appropriately accompanied by supporting affirmations that will move you forward faster than any other known method. You can listen to your goal program wherever you go, to the beach, on a bicycle, or in an airplane.

Finally, a breakthrough in advanced technology has made subliminal tapes available that completely bypass the conscious mental state. Subliminal mental programming was first used publicly in 1956 in the movie *Picnic*, starring Kim Novak and William Holden. Messages encouraging the consumption of popcorn and Coca-Cola were flashed onto the movie screen at millisecond intervals. Although they were not perceptible to the human eye, the subliminal messages had a dramatic effect on people's subconscious awareness. They resulted in a 56 percent increase in movie theater sales of these products. When the practice was later publicized in the press, the public naturally reacted with outrage, believing the technique was too intrusive. The FCC has since outlawed subliminal advertising.

Subliminal audiocassettes now on the market have a series of positive, assertive affirmations recorded on them at very high frequencies. Although the messages are not audible to the human ear, they are perceptible to the subconscious mind. Often several thousand affirmations are recorded together onto a one-hour tape that usually features ocean waves, singing birds, or classical music. The technique holds great potential, since it bypasses the normal sense organs and conscious awareness, and programs its messages directly into the subconscious reality.

This learning technique is another example of the tremendous power of suggestion in your life. In fact, you are already "hypnotized" to a large extent by the wide range of messages and ideas you have received from your environment—information you have uncritically accepted and now are convinced is a true and accurate reflection of reality. But very often, it is not.

You probably have witnessed on television or read about the many feats a professional hypnotist can render. A hypnotist can easily convince a person that she cannot stand up, lift a pencil, or remember her name simply by planting these suggestions directly into her subconscious mind. Obviously this person is capable of performing each of these tasks under normal circumstances. But conscious knowledge of these common skills is thwarted if the subconscious is convinced otherwise.

You must consider for a moment the many inherent talents and abilities you have that are now being denied existence by self-limiting beliefs. By ridding yourself of these beliefs, you are merely "dehypnotizing" yourself. There are no secret or magic powers at work. You are only allowing various skills and abilities to show themselves, see the light of day, and go to work on your behalf.

Using the techniques described here, you can reprogram your mind for success. You can change your most intimate beliefs about yourself and set your sights on any goal you choose. At your disposal right now, you have all that you need to be happy and successful. You have the necessary skills and abilities to do the many things you want to do but never dreamed were possible.

All this power is available to you when you take the time to break free from your self-limiting beliefs.

CHAPTER 8

Planning Your Future

"We possess by nature the factors out of which personality can be made, and to organize them into effective personal life is every man's primary responsibility."
— Harry Emerson Fosdick (1878-1969)
American author and minister

This epigram is a fitting way to begin a discussion of the various key factors of success essential to high achievement and peak performance. Each factor is an essential building block that supports a larger structure, a stepping stone to sure success. Your knowledge and ability to use these success principles will determine your relative level of performance at everything you attempt.

In Chapters 8 through 12, we'll discuss in detail twelve key factors of success, collectively represented by FOS in the performance equation. They constitute various models of excellence applicable to your personal and professional life. They represent specific beliefs held by successful people that cause them to see the world in a certain way and allow them to take effective action.

Positive Mental Attitude

The first key factor of success (FOS) is a positive mental attitude. *You must think attitude if you want to think like a winner!* Attitude is where all change and all success begins. It is the filter through which you view the entire world and thus determines the messages you get from everything you experience. Your attitude decides who and what you are, and whether you respond to events under control or out of control. You can alter and improve your attitude only by analyzing and changing your personal belief system. This necessarily takes effort. As George Santayana (1863-1952), Spanish-born American philosopher and poet, observed, "People are usually more firmly convinced that their opinions are precious than that they are true."

The belief system you now have very likely does not allow you to perform at your optimum. In many areas it is simply unreliable, since often it is based on information that is neither accurate, sufficient, nor rational. Let's see how this applies to a particular skill such as public speaking.

Recall as a child how you began to communicate with others for the very first time. Chances are, each time you learned to say a new word, you sensed approval and encouragement from your parents and others close to you. You probably received positive reinforcement that gave you positive feelings about each of your successes. Some of the messages sent your way may have included:

"That's wonderful, David. You did it!"

"He said 'Mommy,' he said 'Mommy!' Did you hear that? He's so cute!"

In this way, you received as a child immediate and positive feedback that reinforced all of your achievements on a regular basis. You may have received not only the encouraging words and praises but the smiles, touches, hugs, and kisses as well. If you were very fortunate, you were smothered in love and affection that became solidly embedded in your memory profile.

As time went on, you learned many new words and expressions to communicate your ideas and wishes to others. Expressing yourself more fully should have been an exciting new frontier for you, and been effective in serving your needs and satisfying your wants in a limited, protected environment.

Later you were exposed to a larger environment where you encountered other children and new situations. You were no longer the center of attention and didn't necessarily receive positive feedback on a regular basis. A typical conversation with a playmate may have gone like this:

"Catherine, gimme that toy," you asked your friend.

"No, it's mine," she replied. "Go away. I don't like you."

For the first time, you began to experience conflict with others your own age and found yourself competing with them for attention and praise.

As you grew older, things may have gotten a little rougher on occasion, and your parents may have chided you: "David, you are interrupting us again. Please be quiet. And if you can't be quiet, then please shut up!"

It is not possible to predict with any certainty what effect such messages may have had on you. It was not only what other people said to you that helped formulate your attitude about yourself and your ability to express yourself, but also how you interpreted these comments. If, on balance, you received more negative responses than positive and you accepted them as such, it is reasonable to assume that you became less enthusiastic about expressing yourself than otherwise would have been the case. You probably began to look upon the exercise as less than a fulfilling experience.

Later you may have recited poems and given impromptu talks in school, and thus received further feedback on your performance from your teachers and classmates. Perhaps you also participated on a debating team and lost most of the debates because you lacked familiarity with the debating process or the subjects at hand. This would have discouraged you even further and made you believe you were not cut out to be an orator.

As a result, it is unlikely you would have pursued public speaking when you became an adult either as a hobby or as part of a career. You would have fallen back on your memory profile formulated mainly from your many negative experiences or, more accurately, from your negative interpretation of these experiences. In short, you would have developed a negative attitude toward this activity. When called upon to express yourself in church, at a public hearing, or in the course of your business, most likely you would not do very well, even though your performance had little or no relevance to your potential at this task.

Whatever is perceived by the eye of the beholder
is planted in the eye of his mind.

In our example, your belief system about your ability to speak in public is inaccurate because you are merely making a judgment on this matter based on feedback and impressions that are open to many interpretations. Also, the number of samples in your data base is insufficient since you have attempted to perform this skill on relatively few occasions. Any conclusion, then, that you lack ability as a public speaker is irrational because it represents a subjective opinion, not an objective fact. Unfortunately, whatever is perceived by the eye of the beholder is planted in the eye of his mind. Once you adopt a firm belief, it becomes a fixed attitude, creating your reality and your world.

Any belief you wish to change must be thoroughly tested in a logical and rational manner. Reassessment of current beliefs is a thinking exercise, a revalidation of the accuracy of what you now accept to be true.

In each instance, your ability to be successful at a given task is in direct proportion to your ability to see yourself getting the specific results you want in your imagination first. Until you honestly believe you can do this and can vividly see yourself accomplishing this in your mind, you cannot hope to bring it about in real-life.

All this supports various cliches we have already discussed:

- Garbage in equals garbage out.
- Change the input and you change the output.
- What you see is what you get.

Your behavior is not directly dependent on what is going on around you, as our culture and mass media would have you think. Are you unhappy? Then buy an expensive suit of clothes, a more luxurious car, and move into a prestigious neighborhood. These actions may make you feel better in the short term, assuming you can afford them, but in and of themselves they cannot make you happy. There is a key additional factor at play that is central to your behavioral response and emotional well-being: your mental attitude.

Dr. Albert Ellis, the founder of Rational Emotive Therapy, holds that the key to your mental attitude is your beliefs, and that your beliefs in turn determine the way you behave.

External events and circumstances, both good and bad, are to be found everywhere in your world. Ellis refers to these circumstances as the *activating events* in your life, which he labels "A."

The natural tendency in our culture is to blame these activating events for causing us to feel and act the way we do. Ellis refers to these emotional and behavioral consequences as "C."

This leads to the equation

$$A = C$$

For example,

A (I didn't get promoted) = C (I feel rejected)

or

A (I didn't win the contest) = C (I feel incompetent)

However, "A" does not equal "C," and to believe it does will only bring frustration and misery into your life. The correct causal relationship is

$$A + B = C,$$

where "B" represents your personal belief system. Your belief system causes you to make certain judgments and interpretations that in turn generate your expectations and behavioral response. These thought patterns collectively form your attitude profile.

For example,

Activating Event A (I didn't get promoted)

plus

Belief System B (I am a capable person, my turn will come)

equals

Consequence C (I feel good about myself and my future prospects)

Dr. Ellis states, "People and things do not upset us, rather we upset ourselves by *believing that they can upset us.*"

More than any other single factor in your life, your particular manner of thinking—referred to as your attitude—determines how you feel and the way you behave. People who attribute their situation in life to events outside themselves look outside themselves for the solution. Since it cannot be found there, they end up becoming frustrated and often bitter. Others who recognize that all causation is mental begin to look inward for a solution. They begin to rethink their current beliefs and accept an element of responsibility for the beliefs they finally adopt.

John Wooden, former UCLA basketball coach, once said, "Things turn out best for the people who make the best of the way things turn out."

This oft-quoted statement summarizes in an interesting way a positive approach to life. You cannot hope to control every event that comes your way. But you can control the way you react to such events by adopting a positive mental attitude.

The following quote by Charles Swindoll is titled "Attitude":

> The longer I live, the more I realize the impact of attitude on life. Attitude, to me, is more important than facts. It is more important than the past, than education, than money, than circumstances, than failures, than successes, than what other people think or say or do. It is more important than appearance, giftedness, or skill. It will make or break a company . . . a church . . . a home. The remarkable thing is we have a choice every day regarding the attitude we will embrace for that day. We cannot change the past. We cannot change the fact that people will act in a certain way. We cannot change the inevitable. The only thing we can do is play on the one string we have, and that is our attitude. I am convinced that life is 10 percent what happens to me and 90 percent how I react to it. And so it is with you. We are in charge of our Attitudes.[1]

So what is your attitude toward your attitude? What is your attitude toward your beliefs, personal goals, sense of responsibility, time management, personal development, health, creativity, service, excellence, human relations, and leadership skills? These are the areas we will now explore in detail.

Total Belief in Yourself

The second key factor of success (FOS) is total belief in yourself. *You must think belief if you want to think like a winner!* Have confidence in yourself. Believe in your abilities, for you are who you think you are. You have the necessary skills and abilities to accomplish great things. You need only accept this fact to move ahead with your life.

"There are two ways to slide easily through life; to believe everything or to doubt everything; both ways save us from thinking," according to Alfred Korzybski (1879–1950), Polish-born U.S. scientist and philosopher.

You need to give careful thought to what you believe. False convictions are the worst enemy of truth, for they result in a lifetime of underachievement and complacency. You are what your mind has been programmed to think you are. Your power lies in the thoughts you hold. As William James remarked, "Belief is desecrated when given to unproved and unquestioned statements for the solace and private pleasure of the believer. It is wrong always, everywhere, and for everyone to believe anything upon insufficient evidence."

By the time you were two years old, about 50 percent of your belief system had been determined. When you were six, this increased to about 60 percent, and by age eight to about 80 percent. Finally, at about the age of fourteen, approximately 90 percent of who you think you are had been programmed into your mind. It dictates to this day the beliefs you hold about yourself and your potential for high achievement.

In other words, regardless of your age, who you think you are today was decided primarily by the time you were fourteen. Few of us can remember very much about the first fourteen years of our life. Also during this period, you were probably the most insecure and immature. You could not make well-informed judgments about many of the things that were happening to you. Yet this critical time in your upbringing can haunt you to your grave, unless you choose to reassess your true worth based on new information that challenges your preconceived ideas.

People have a habit of taking their assets for granted and concentrating only on their limitations. In this way, they are giving more credibility to what they believe they cannot do rather than to what they can do. Such behavior is inherently defeatist. It holds you back, eliminates any initiative, and essentially cripples any prospect for success.

When you constantly focus on the forces that seem to be against you, you give them power and strength they do not necessarily have. Instead, focus your attention on your assets, and you will be able to see through these imaginary and temporary obstacles to what is possible.

The following anonymous poem titled "Believe in Yourself" helps put things in proper perspective:[2]

> ***Believe in yourself!*** You're divinely designed
>   And perfectly made for the work of mankind.
> This truth you must cling to through danger and pain
>   The heights man has reached you can also attain.
> Believe to the very last hour, for it's true
>   That whatever you will you've been gifted to do.

Believe in yourself and step out unafraid
   By misgivings and doubt be not easily swayed.
You've the right to succeed, the precision of skill
   Which betokens the great, you can earn if you will!
The wisdom of ages is yours if you'll read
   But you've got to believe in yourself to succeed.

If you feel defeated and that you lack the ability to move ahead in your life, prepare a detailed inventory of all your assets and liabilities.

Take a piece of paper, draw a line down the center, and list all of your assets on the right-hand side and all of your liabilities on the left. Are you healthy? Do you have a supportive spouse or other family members? Do you earn a reasonable income or have prospects of doing so? Have you developed any valuable skills? Have you been successful in small ways at anything? Do you enjoy reading? Have you any spare time to study? Are there community or church groups that you can join to help you explore new outlets for your talents and abilities?

There are hundreds of questions like these you could ask yourself to quantify all of your assets. If you took the time, you would discover many assets you have been taking for granted—two eyes, two hands, two feet, and a brain to *think!* Many have achieved great things with less than some of these. If you explore both of these areas seriously, there is no way your list of liabilities can be longer than your list of assets.

You can assign greater relevance to your liabilities if you choose. However, this is a result of making judgments that can be changed based on new information or by reassessing old information. You can, and must, update your belief system if you want to provide new direction and purpose to your life.

This balance-sheet exercise makes use of the "minimize-maximize" technique to help you see your assets and liabilities in an entirely new light. The English poet and writer, Robert Southey (1774–1843), had his own way of perceiving his environment:

   I have told you of the man who always put on his spectacles when about to eat cherries, in order that the fruit might look larger and more tempting. In like manner, I always make the most of my enjoyments, and, though I do not cast my eyes away from troubles, I pack them into as small a compass as I can for myself, and never let them annoy others.

---

*Failure is a vital and necessary part
of the achievement process.*

There will always be setbacks and disappointments in the pursuit of any worthwhile goal. Most people do not understand a simple truth: it is almost impossible to succeed at anything significant the very first time. Failure is a vital and necessary part of the achievement process. No one learns to walk, ride a bicycle, or drive a car on the first attempt. The fear of failure is a primary reason most people do not set meaningful, challenging goals in the first place. They do not have the self-image to live with the possibility of failure. *But you are never defeated until you accept defeat as a reality, and decide to stop trying—a key core belief.*

History shows how failure is essential to all achievement, that great success is always accompanied by great failure. Babe Ruth held the strikeout record at the same time he held the home-run record. He knew and took advantage of the simple law of averages: the more you swing the bat, the more likely you are to hit the ball out of the park. It's the same in the game of life. The more often you try, the more likely you'll eventually succeed.

Thomas Edison had to discover over ten thousand ways a light bulb would not work before he discovered the one way it would. He had a very different attitude toward his work. He looked upon each unsuccessful attempt not as a failure but as a success, a success that took him one step closer to his ultimate goal. He kept his focus firmly on the goal he was striving for and was willing to do whatever was necessary in order to reach it. It worked for him. He was the most prolific inventor in modern history, with 1,097 devices patented in his name.

Abraham Lincoln (1809–1865) also struggled and faced adversity on more than one occasion. Here is a brief glimpse at his record that shows quitters don't win and winners don't quit. He failed in business in 1831. He was defeated in his bid for the legislature in 1832. He failed in business in 1834. In 1835 his sweetheart died, and the following year he had a nervous breakdown. He lost his bid for Speaker of the House in 1838. He lost Congressional campaigns in 1843 and

1846. He lost his bid for land officer in 1849. In 1855 he was defeated for the Senate, and in 1856 he lost the nomination for vice-president. He was defeated again for the Senate in 1858. Yet in 1860 Abraham Lincoln was elected president of the United States.

Lincoln had a reputation for never giving less than his best effort in any of his undertakings, regardless of the odds against him. As a young man he vowed, "I will always try to do my best no matter what, and some day my chance will come." He persevered, his chance came, and he went on to become one of the most respected presidents in U.S. history. His life personifies the expression, "To succeed, you must keep on keeping on!"

Thomas J. Watson, an early president of IBM, offered this famous advice on how to be successful: "Double your failure rate." He recognized that the only way to escape from what James Newman calls your comfort zone and improve on past performance was to fail more often.

In the 1952 Olympics, Bob Mathias won the gold medal in the decathlon, with Milton Campbell placing second. Four years later, Milt Campbell won the gold and Rafer Johnson placed second. Four years later, Rafer Johnson won the gold and C.K. Yang placed second. Four years later, C.K. Yang won the gold, and broke the world's record for the decathlon. In each case, a significant failure was followed by a major success.

The natural tendency of people with low self-esteem, those who cannot deal with the prospect of failure, is to stay within their comfort zone. Such people avoid all risk, they play it safe, and are content to be mediocre rather than successful. They are satisfied with the norm, never set goals, and never try anything new. Yet to become a peak performer, you have to break out of this shell of complacency. You have to contemplate your possibilities!

Consider the chart below to put in context the importance of beliefs in relation to accomplishment.

As each cup reaches its threshold level, it spills over to fill up the next cup. Your cup of life is filled only to the extent the other four cups all reach their threshold.

Note that unless belief is exercised, nothing happens; if potential is not activated, nothing happens; if action is not taken, nothing happens; if results are not achieved, nothing happens. *Your cup of life is*

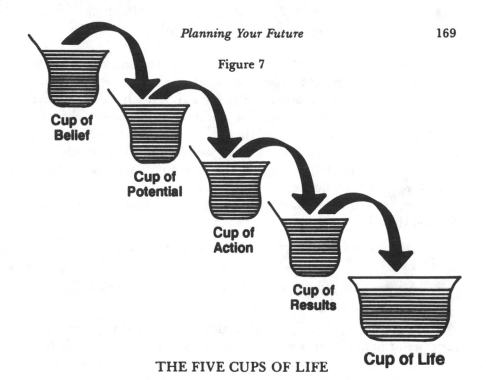

Figure 7

THE FIVE CUPS OF LIFE

filled only to the extent that specific things happen in a specific way.

You can have only two things in life—excuses or results. And of course, excuses don't count! They only represent your lack of faith in your ability to succeed.

One of the most important concepts in this book deals with your "area of excellence." This concept says that you have, on average, the same talents and abilities that everyone else has. In other words, you are slightly better at doing some things and slightly worse at doing others. But when averaged all together, your average equates to just about everyone else's average.

It also says that you already possess the ability to excel in at least one key area of your life—a key core belief if you intend to explore all of your possibilities. Each of us was put on earth for a specific purpose, and with the necessary skills consistent with this purpose. This means we all can excel at something, and it is our primary responsibility to find our area of excellence, and to channel all of our efforts in this direction.

You can achieve a level of excellence only in something you truly like to do. It then doesn't seem like work at all, although at first it may require more effort than other things you have attempted. Your area of excellence must be something that naturally interests you, that you are instinctively attracted to, and that you would perform whether you were paid to do it or not. It must make you feel unique, valuable, and important. It must help bring out the "real you," and allow you to express your own uniqueness and individuality.

One way to tell if you have found your area of excellence is to ask yourself these two questions:

1. Do you feel ecstatic about what you are doing on a regular basis?

2. Do you find you are surprised at your level of performance on a regular basis?

If you are not ecstatic about yourself and surprised regularly with your performance, then you have not found your area of excellence. This is a key secret of success—to find your area of excellence, the activity at which you excel, and then spend 80 to 90 percent of your time doing it.

For example, a pitcher whose specialty is a fastball doesn't throw a lot of sliders and curveballs during a game. Instead, he concentrates on what he does best and, in the process, becomes ecstatic about himself and surprised, even astonished, at his success.

Most people have no idea what their "fastball" is in life and certainly are not in a game where they are throwing it 80 to 90 percent of the time. They have difficulty trying to decide what they would really like to do and what interests them the most. They are caught in a rut trying to earn a living day after day, usually doing something they don't particularly like. They get up in the morning to go to work to earn enough money to come back home . . . to get up in the morning to go to work to earn enough money to come back home. They repeat this vicious cycle over and over again. Clearly, such people are too busy earning a living rather than living a life.

Here are five questions that will help you zero in on who you are and in what direction you may want to go:

1. *What are the principal values you want to live by?*

Do you value loving relationships of friends and close family? Do you want to accomplish useful things in your life, help others, and make a contribution to society? Do you want acknowledgment of your self-worth, to know that you are appreciated? These are some of the key questions you can ask yourself to elicit your innermost values and beliefs about what, for you, are the most important things in life. Many people never face up to the values they cherish and in so doing, never apply them consistently in their daily affairs.

2. *What activity gives you the most satisfaction, and the greatest sense of accomplishment and feeling of importance?*
Your answer here will help direct you to your area of excellence. It may be something you haven't tried yet but would like to do. If this is the case, try it! Get a taste of what it is like, then go from there.

3. *How would you change your life if you knew you had only one year to live?*
In this scenario, assume you are healthy during this twelve-month period. You don't have any medical bills to pay and you are on full salary, but don't have to go to work. In other words, your time is your own, and you have no health or money problems whatsoever. How would you spend your time?

4. Now consider Robert Schuller's favorite question: *What one great thing would you do if you knew you could not fail?*
Oh boy, *you cannot fail!* Your success is certain and everyone will be so impressed. So what is it you want to do?

5. *What do you most want to be remembered for when you are gone?*
This is like writing your own epitaph: *"HERE I LIE WITH A SIGH, WISHING I HAD DONE SOMETHING SIGNIFICANT!"*

You are dead a lot longer than you are alive, so it is important to use the short time you have to best advantage. Make a decision today to develop your area of excellence. We all have to start somewhere. And it's far more important to know where you want to go than where you are or where you have been.

Consider the following chart, based on a life expectancy of 70 years, to help you decide how to spend the rest of your life.

Figure 8

IF YOU ARE		YOU'VE SPENT		AND HAVE
20 years old	=	7,300 days	=	18,250 days left
25 years old	=	9,125 days	=	16,425 days left
30 years old	=	10,950 days	=	14,600 days left
Half Way	=	12,775 days	=	12,775 days left
40 years old	=	14,600 days	=	10,950 days left
45 years old	=	16,425 days	=	9,125 days left
50 years old	=	18,250 days	=	7,300 days left
55 years old	=	20,075 days	=	5,475 days left
60 years old	=	21,900 days	=	3,650 days left
65 years old	=	23,725 days	=	1,775 days left
70 years old	=	25,550 days	=	Are you spending them wisely?

The key question is: *What do you want to do with the rest of your life?* "Do not act as if you had a thousand years to live," Marcus Aurelius (121–180 A.D.), emperor of Rome, warned himself in his maxims.

There are many people who have accomplished a great deal. They may have succeeded academically, professionally, and as parents. They may be rich in the material things they have accumulated. But are these the correct yardsticks to measure your relative success in life? Or are there other considerations that may be more important? Consider this:

* *It is not what you have accomplished that benefits you that is important, but what you have accomplished that benefits others.*

* *It is not what you have accomplished in relation to others that is important, but what you have accomplished in relation to your full potential.*

* *It is not what you do in your life that is important, but what you cause others to do.*

What do you really believe in? How important are worthy goals and ideals to you? Today, like each day, can be a new beginning.

Big, Challenging Goals

The third key factor of success (FOS) is big, challenging goals. *You must think goals if you want to think like a winner!* Consider this advice from Lucius Annaeus Seneca (4 B.C.-65 A.D.), Roman statesman, writer, and Stoic philosopher: "Our plans miscarry because they have no aim. When a man does not know what harbor he is making for, no wind is the right wind."

Why is this subject of goals and being successful in life so important? Here are the statistics. According to actuarial tables, if you take one hundred people at random at age twenty-five and compare their progress at age sixty-five, one will be wealthy, four will be financially independent, fifteen will have modest savings put aside, and the other eighty will be totally broke, without any savings, and completely dependent on small pensions or Social Security for the rest of their lives. In other words, of one hundred people now working, only five percent are going to end up financially independent. *Only five percent!* This means that you have *one chance in twenty* of making it to retirement age with your financial affairs in order despite fully forty years of gainful employment in a free economy characterized by limitless opportunity and almost continuous growth. But of course you have the choice to do something to change these odds in your favor . . . *start setting some meaningful goals!*

We live in the richest, most affluent society in all of recorded history. We enjoy living standards today that were never dreamed possible at the beginning of the 20th century. Yet many people are not happy with what they have. They are not happy with their work, their marriages, their incomes, or themselves. People eat too much, drink too much, and smoke too much. They steal, take drugs, and are killing themselves almost as fast as they are killing each other.

People with such problems lack direction in their lives. As Zig Ziglar so aptly puts it, they are "wandering generalities" rather than "meaningful specifics." They don't know what they really want out of life. They take what is sent their way and if this proves insufficient, they try to take even more. But nowhere along the way do they accept any responsibility for their actions or the results of their behavior. The person who doesn't know where he is going has no hope of ever getting there.

We have explained how all peak performing men and women possess certain unique qualities. They have developed a positive sense of self—

high self-liking, high self-worth, and high self-acceptance. They accept full responsibility for their lives and the consequences of all their actions. They are also compulsive goal-setters. They are obsessed with big, challenging goals to which they have made a total commitment.

A strong sense of purpose in life is essential to all change and meaningful improvement. With a clear, central purpose comes direction, meaning, and positive expectations. With each step of progress comes a sense of fulfillment. With fulfillment comes a sense of pride, satisfaction, and other good feelings associated with high self-esteem and high self-worth. You feel that you are going somewhere, that you are making progress, and that this progress is a direct result of your own efforts. "Happiness," wrote Emerson, "is the progressive realization of a worthy goal."

Every study of high achievers—whether Olympic or professional athletes, famous industrialists, or self-made millionaires—has found that they all began with a commitment to a meaningful goal. A clear, well-defined central purpose in life allows you to focus your energy and discipline your behavior so that you are able to hurdle any obstacle that stands in your way. Hills fall as easy victims when your goal is to climb a mountain.

"You will become as small as your controlling desires, as great as your dominant aspiration," according to James Allen, author of *As a Man Thinketh*.

H. L. "Bunker" Hunt, the Texas oil billionaire, rose from being a bankrupt cotton farmer at age thirty-two during the Depression to earning more than one billion dollars a year by age fifty-six. When asked in an interview about the secret of his success, Hunt replied that he believed there were only two things necessary to succeed. The first was that you have to decide exactly what it is you want. This is the starting point and, in his estimation, this is where most people fail. They never decide what it is they really want. He observed that most people wander through life wanting a great many things but not wanting any one thing more than all the rest. They end up settling for far less than what could be theirs. Once you decide what you want, he continued, the second thing you must do is determine the price you have to pay to get it, then resolve to pay that price. But many who get past the first step never get to the second. They never realize there is a price you have to pay for success.

There is enormous wisdom contained in his remarks. Only a big, challenging goal can provide meaning and purpose to your life. It gives you something to aim at, to work toward, and to look forward to. Without a goal, you'll wander around like a chicken with no head, with no direction attached to your efforts. Since you cannot measure any progress, you cannot feel any sense of accomplishment.

"People who have no goals are doomed forever to work for people who do," says Brian Tracy in his best-selling tape program, *The Psychology of Success.* He estimates that more than half the college graduates in America today are working for people who never finished high school. Without pain there is no gain; without a goal there can be no glory.

Maltz compared the human mind to the homing system in a torpedo or an automatic pilot in a plane. Once a torpedo selects its target, a self-correcting system constantly monitors feedback and makes the necessary corrections until final contact is made. Failing to lock onto a target, a torpedo will go around in circles like a ship with no rudder and eventually run out of fuel. Similarly, people without a goal wander around aimlessly in life wondering why they aren't getting somewhere. It is impossible to arrive at a place if you don't know where you want to go. You must make a clear, conscious decision about what you want to accomplish in your life. If you fail to plan, you are planning to fail. Your subconscious can only be activated by a goal, a clear, focused picture of what you want. When you decide on a goal, you activate within you a cybernetic, goal-seeking function at the subconscious level, and it moves you toward your goal and your goal toward you.

Among all living organisms on earth, only humans are born without a built-in software program for success. Humans are free to imagine themselves as successes or failures, as winners or losers, or as positive or negative. Of course, you get precisely what you see and dwell upon. You can develop a success consciousness by deciding precisely what it is you want, and beginning to take specific steps toward it.

It has been said that once you have decided on a clear, focused goal for your life, you will have it because it will have you. A firmly entrenched goal literally forces you to stay on course until you reach your target. Commitment to a goal firmly embeds it in the subconscious and, once there, you cannot ignore its presence. In fact, everything you do must recognize the existence of the goal until you finally bring it about. Your subconscious will firmly guide and direct you down this path. It will keep saying to you "do this" and "don't do that" as you go about your daily routine. It will attract to you those people and circumstances consistent with your goal and repel those that are not.

Imagine that in five years from now, you want to be president of the company you now work for. Assume this is your major goal in life, the culmination of twenty-five years in a variety of senior positions, and that you are willing to do whatever is necessary to reach this goal.

Your goal now begins to "talk" to you. It stirs you up and makes you more alert. All of a sudden, you begin to see new opportunities all around you to offer your services and demonstrate your skills. You tackle normal work with renewed energy and a broader perspective. When you make a major decision, you give more thought to its impact on the company as a whole rather than on just one department. What in fact you are doing is beginning to see yourself as the president, beginning to think like the president, so that eventually you're more likely to become the president.

When you look in the mirror each morning, you'll see a president; when you buy new clothes, you'll buy clothes appropriate for a president; and when you relate to colleagues, you'll treat them like a president would treat them. Should you drift a little off course, your automatic guidance system will make the necessary corrections and get you back on track. In this way, your goal literally has taken possession of you. It has become an integral part of your consciousness. You cannot be anything but totally absorbed by the implications for everything that you do and say as they apply to your major life goal.

How important is goal-setting? Consider this evidence that demonstrates its relationship to achievement. In 1953, a study dealing with goals was conducted at Yale University. It found that 3 percent of the graduating class that year had carried out a comprehensive goal-setting program, 10 percent had carried out a modest and incomplete program, and 87 percent had carried out no program at all. Twenty years later, in 1973, the study was concluded with the following results. It was discovered that the 3 percent who had set comprehensive goals had accomplished *more during that period than all of the other 97 percent combined!* The researchers measured both financial and career status to indicate levels of achievement. These results are a monumental testimony to the value of setting clear, focused goals if you want to be successful in life.

Goals may be physical, mental, or spiritual in nature. They apply to all aspects of living, including your personal, parental, and professional life. You may want to lose weight, stop smoking, or start attending church regularly. You may want to spend more time with your spouse and children in leisure-time activities, begin a computer course, or start writing a book. There is no end to goal-setting, and invariably one goal leads to another, each one being progressively more ambitious than the one before. The most rapid progress is made if a single, major life goal is adopted, with several mini- or sub-goals selected to complement the major one. This way you are deciding on the kind of house you want to build for yourself, and then deciding on the building blocks you'll need to put it all together.

Here is a comprehensive list of ten key goal-setting principles that must be followed to achieve any goal of significance:

1. Identify a major goal that is challenging and important to you, one that is capable of being measured or quantified in some way. Examples are to earn a specific sum of money, sell a certain amount of life insurance, or lose a given number of pounds.

2. Specify the exact date by which you want to reach your goal.

3. Identify and explore various options that alone or together will enable you to reach your goal.

4. Define a detailed plan of action you have decided to follow, with specific reference to what actions you have to take to (a) acquire the knowledge you need, (b) develop the skills you must have, and (c) meet the people you need to know to assist you and give you the necessary advice.

5. Compile a list of the major obstacles you'll have to overcome in your efforts to reach your goal.

6. Compile a list of the major benefits you'll receive when you complete your goal on time.

7. Once you have completed steps one through six, write them all down to form a *master plan.*

8. Read your *master plan* out loud twice each day, once on rising in the morning and again on retiring at night. Better yet, record it on an audiocassette and play it back to yourself.

9. Believe, see, and feel yourself as already having achieved your goal.

10. Begin to implement your plan at once, ready or not.

Implement a measured amount of the plan each day, seven days a week. When aggregated over the total time period you have chosen, your daily efforts should total your ultimate goal. For example, you will have to earn a specific sum of money, sell a certain amount of life insurance, or lose a given amount of weight each day in order to reach your major goal in any of these areas by a certain date.

As the German poet and dramatist, Johann von Goethe (1749–1832), advised, "What you can do, or dream you can do, begin it; boldness has genius, power, and magic in it."

Goal-setting is a thinking exercise that activates
the natural success system within you.

Goal-setting is not an easy exercise. It requires considerable desire and dedication to sit down and work your way through each step. It also takes a sincere belief in the value of your goal and in your ability to reach it. Goal-setting is a thinking exercise that activates the natural success system within you. It engages your inner power and resourcefulness much like a car's transmission engages the engine when it is shifted out of neutral. A big, challenging goal causes the creative juices in you to flow. You'll find renewed energy, dedication, and enthusiasm as you head down the path you have chosen. When you think big goals, you automatically expect big results. Remember, the size of your goal is determined by the size of your belief.

As Daniel Burnham, Chicago's 19th century master planner, put it, "Make no little plans: they have no magic to stir your blood to action. Make big plans, aim high in work and hope."

One of the most difficult aspects of goal-setting and planning to understand is that progress toward any worthwhile goal can be made only one step at a time. A college degree is earned one credit at a time. A basketball game is won one basket at a time. New products are sold one unit at a time. Every major accomplishment is a series of little accomplishments spaced over a specific period of time.

A step-by-step approach involving a measurable achievement each day is the only effective method to get results. Each little success gives you a shot of confidence and a sense of accomplishment that will help sustain you in sticking to your program. It also makes the final goal seem more achievable, since all you have to do is put forth the same amount of effort each day. For example, if you were asked to write a book of two hundred and fifty pages without having written anything significant before, this task probably would seem insurmountable. However, if you were asked to write two pages of text each day for one hundred and twenty-five days, you would have to agree that this request is both reasonable and realistic.

The expression, "By the inch it's a cinch, by the yard it's hard," has a good deal of merit. Whenever you meet a particularly impressive individual who seems poised, confident, well-mannered, articulate, and has achieved a high station in life, always remember that such a person was not born that way. He or she developed these attributes and achieved their status over a considerable period of time as a result of persistent, dedicated effort. And so can you.

One of the most dramatic examples ever documented of goal-setting and its effect on achievement is the story of John Goddard as told in *Life* magazine in 1972. When he was fifteen years old, young Goddard overheard his grandmother say, "If only I had done more when I was young." Goddard resolved he would not grow old saying the same thing, regretting all the "if onlys" in his life.

So he sat down and determined what he wanted to accomplish. He wrote out in detail 127 specific goals. He listed ten rivers he wanted to explore and seventeen mountains he wanted to climb. He wanted to visit every country in the world, learn to fly an airplane, retrace the travels of Marco Polo, ride a horse in the Pasadena Rose Bowl Parade, and have a career in medicine. Goddard also wanted to read the Bible and all the works of Plato, Aristotle, Dickens, Shakespeare, Churchill, and a dozen other authors of classic works. He wanted to dive in a submarine, play the flute and violin, become an Eagle Scout, go on a church mission, marry and have children, and read the entire Encyclopedia Britannica. He committed his whole list to memory and could repeat it on request.

In 1972, at the age of forty-seven, John Goddard had realized 103 of his 127 goals. He built his whole life around setting and reaching his goals, and toured the world lecturing on his adventures and accomplishments.

Few of us have 127 goals committed to memory and being actively pursued. But what goals have you decided on and can you recite them on request? Do you wake up early each morning with your major life goal on the tip of your tongue? If not, this should be your first major goal!

CHAPTER 9

Working Hard on Yourself

"So long as a person imagines that he cannot do this or that, so long as he determines not to do it; and consequently so long is it impossible to him that he should do it."
— Benedict Spinoza (1632-1677)
Dutch philosopher

Responsible Behavior

The fourth key factor of success (FOS) is responsible behavior. *You must think responsibility if you want to think like a winner!* "The price of greatness," wrote Winston Churchill (1874-1965), "is responsibility."

Denis Waitley teaches that life is a "do-it-yourself" project, that your rewards in life are in direct proportion to your contributions. This philosophy again reflects the law of cause and effect. We know that for every effect in your life, there is a prior cause — basically you! You are today where all your thinking has brought you. You will be tomorrow a product of the thinking you are currently engaged in. You are the dynamic force behind your existence.

"Destiny is not a matter of chance, it is a matter of choice; it is not a thing to be waited for, it is a thing to be achieved," commented William Jennings Bryan (1860-1925), American statesman, orator, and reformer.

People accept responsibility for those things that are going well in their life, and forgo responsibility for those things that are going poorly. If things at work are not ideal, it must be your boss who is at fault. If things at home are not perfect, it must be your spouse who is to blame. If you got a "D" in history, it must be because your teacher doesn't like you. But this kind of thinking can lead nowhere. You can never hope to improve on what's right or correct what's wrong if your focus is always on those who you think are against you. Albert Schweitzer (1875-1965), Alsatian theologian, musician, and medical missionary in Africa, gave this advice: "Man must cease attributing his problems to his environment, and learn again to exercise his will, his personal responsibility."

You should study the "causes" in your life much more closely than the "effects," since they alone hold the prospect for improvement and meaningful change. Always consider what precedes and what follows. Winners always accept both the credit and the blame for whatever happens to them.

There is a direct relationship between the amount of control you enjoy and the amount of responsibility you accept. Winners accept full responsibility for what they think, what they say, and what they do. Hence they are able to control these aspects of their lives. Losers always blame someone or something else for the results they achieve. Since they are unable to control all the people and things around them, they are out of control and beyond help. They blow with the wind and are manipulated by every chance and circumstance that comes their way.

Let's list just some of the things that you can control. You can control your thinking, if you take the time to become aware of it and assume responsibility for it. You can control the beliefs you cling to and the way you see yourself. You can control what you imagine and the way you want the future to unfold. You can control the goals you set that are important to you and the way you go about achieving them. You can control the way you allocate your time and the way you spend your day. You can control the things you eat and the exercise you engage in. You can control who you associate with and the topics of your conversation. You can control the environment you learn and live in, and the people, places, and things that influence your thinking and behavior. You can control your response to situations and circumstances, the joy or sadness, the ecstacy or agony, of all your efforts. To a very real extent, you are master of your fate.

The most prominent feature of all fully mature, high-achieving human beings is their willingness to accept full responsibility for all aspects of their lives. Most people fail to grasp this key concept, that accepting 100 percent responsibility for everything is the only way to learn, grow, and move ahead in your life.

To not accept responsibility is to blame and criticize others, to make excuses, and bring down everything around you. But you cannot bring down everything around you without bringing yourself down to this same level in the process. You simply cannot hope to achieve at high levels if you are bitter, overly critical, and suffering from a host of negative emotions brought on by irresponsible behavior.

In many ways, our modern society even encourages irresponsible behavior. We witnessed during the boom years of the 1960s and 1970s a tendency for people to ask the government to solve many of the problems they would rather not solve for themselves. Everyone demanded jobs, housing, health care, and old age security as a right to which people were entitled. As noted by John Nesbitt in *Megatrends*, the result is that big government today controls more and more, and people are receiving less and less. This is inevitable since it is impossible to have something for nothing. Big government is very inefficient and very expensive. Many of the services it provides could be carried out at lower cost by the private sector. Yet most politicians continue to fall all over each other at election time to offer more and more benefits for which the voters must eventually pay more and more money. But since the price is greater than the voters can afford, this only results in higher annual budget deficits that are passed on to future generations. It is hard to contemplate anything so irresponsible.

Although people have passed along control of many areas of their lives to the government at one level or another, they cannot so easily pass on the responsibility. The government may or may not be able to provide you with a job, at least one that uses your unique talents and abilities, one you like, and that pays you what you think you are worth.

The alternative to taking whatever may be made available is to accept responsibility yourself to become qualified for a job of your own choice, even for one that you create. During the 1970s, over 60 percent of all new jobs created in the U.S. were by small businesses, most of which were in existence for four years or less. In 1950, new businesses were being created at the rate of 93,000 per year; by 1990, this increased ten-fold. Small businesses are indicative of people taking responsibility for their well-being into their own hands. They represent frustration with big government and big business. People want more control over their careers and their lives, and more freedom to express and fulfill themselves. Losers wait for the state to look after them. Winners seize control and make it happen. Only in a democracy can you enjoy such freedom. You are able to choose the path you want to follow, and you know in advance that each choice has a specific consequence. The responsibility for the choice as well as the consequence lies with each individual.

There is a side to human nature that can bring out irresponsibility in all of us, and it pays to know and recognize it when it appears. The first area of our psyche that is involved is our natural tendency to want to improve our situation in life. This could mean more leisure, more money, more power, more prestige, or more control over events and circumstances. It stems from our prehistoric drive for self-preservation and has expanded into other areas as they become available in our modern society. This inherent characteristic is basically constructive. It leads to desire, action, and change.

The second is our tendency to seek the fastest and easiest route to satisfy all of our desires. This, too, is only natural, since no one wants to do any more than is necessary to achieve a particular goal. This characteristic is basically constructive as well. It leads to efficiency, increased productivity, and innovation.

When these two human traits come together in their worst extremes, however, the problem of irresponsibility manifests itself as a continuous desire to have something for nothing.

Most people function at a level of simply wanting more for less. They want improvement and are willing to pay a certain price for it, one that is the lowest possible in terms of either effort or money. They would like to lose fifteen pounds by exercising once a week instead of three or four times, for example; and they would like to buy a new luxury car with all the options for $10,000 rather than $25,000. Only an irrational, irresponsible person would hope to have either of these two goals for nothing.

It's no wonder that a politician who preaches lower taxes and increased benefits attracts the attention of the average voter. Or that lotteries do a booming business by advertising, "We'll make you a millionaire for a dollar!"

*You must always pay a price
for everything that comes your way.*

If you'll take some time to think about it, you'll find that the law of cause and effect precludes ever having anything for nothing. You must always pay a price for everything that comes your way. The key is to determine what it is you want and what price you have to pay to get it. Then resolve to pay that price, or even more than that price, for this will bring you even more of what you want. You can expect to reap only what you sow.

Can you really hope to win the Boston Marathon by taking the subway?

Can you really hope to live a life of luxury by passing out counterfeit $100 bills?

Can you really hope to become the president of the company by shooting all the vice-presidents?

All of the above have been tried by irresponsible people at one time or another. Attempts at instant gratification may appeal to your ego in the short term, but in the long term they can lead only to disaster. They violate the basic law of cause and effect. The advice is this: avoid the quick and easy, and resolve to earn what you want.

The hallmark of losers is to blame others for all of the things that go wrong in their lives. They believe that the world owes them all the good things they want and they owe the world nothing. As a result, they exert little effort to bring about change and they feel out of control. Losers necessarily feel fenced in, that their options are limited. They believe their fate is sealed and that they cannot hope to achieve anything of any real consequence in life because it is beyond their ability to bring it about. When they fail, they often become aggressive and angry, and strike out against others. They suffer the consequences of their efforts, over and over again.

The hallmark of all winners is accepting total responsibility for everything they say and do. As a result, they are confident and feel in control. They understand that with control comes freedom of choice and a realization that anything is possible if only they are willing to pay the price to earn it. This necessarily expands their horizons and stirs positive emotions of belief and accomplishment. "I can do it! Anything is possible! The sky's the limit!" Winners reap the rewards of their efforts, over and over again.

Time Management

The fifth key factor of success (FOS) is time management. *You must think time if you want to think like a winner!* Take heed of these wise words of Benjamin Franklin: "Dost thou love life? Then do not squander time, for that is the stuff life is made of."

Few people appreciate the true value of time, for time wasted is time lost forever. Time is the only commodity allocated equally to all, whether rich or poor, male or female, wise or not so wise.

Control, a key concept in this book, applies to the management of time as well. The objective is not to become rigid, inflexible, and controlled by time but to be relaxed, flexible, and in control of time. The object is always effectiveness rather than efficiency, which means doing what should be done at the right time rather than doing well whatever you happen to be doing. With greater control comes greater freedom to do more, and to do more more effectively. No one has the choice in all situations to do precisely what you want to do at the exact time you want to do it. But you do have this choice most of the time, and it is these situations you want to maximize.

There is really no such thing as lack of time. Everyone has sufficient time to do what has to be done, at least the most important things that really matter. You probably know people who appear even less busy than you yet are able to accomplish much more. It is not a matter of having more time. It is a matter of using the time that is available to better advantage.

Time management involves setting priorities
and disciplining yourself.

Time management is really self-management. It is a thinking exercise that involves setting priorities and disciplining yourself in the use of time in order to derive maximum benefit. Not having the time to carry out a specific task usually means you have not given sufficiently high priority to it. The secret to finding the time to do the things that need to be done is to develop a real sense of urgency and commitment to the task, to really *want* rather than just *wish* to do it. Two key prerequisites of effective time management are:

1. A clear, focused goal that is measurable.
2. A detailed plan of action for its implementation on a daily basis.

To be effective, you need to know what you have to do to get where you want to go. You have to clearly identify the major goal that is important to you and formulate a master plan describing how you intend to go about achieving it. Every goal requires a decision; every decision dictates a process; every process involves a plan; and every plan needs time for implementation. Time must be controlled, since it is slipping away minute by minute, hour by hour. Either you catch it and use it as it comes your way, or it passes you by.

Let's look at a typical day in your life and see where you might spend your time more effectively.

Go to bed and get up at a reasonable hour each day. It is the quality of your sleep, not the quantity, that is important. Experts claim you should follow a regular sleep routine, retiring and rising about the same time each day, to get quality sleep. Sleep in a cool room, preferably with a window open. Aim at a temperature of seventy degrees or less.

Do your nightly exercises such as stretching, sit-ups, and push-ups before retiring. Then take a warm bath or shower. You'll be more relaxed and sleep better. Select and lay out the clothes you intend to wear the next day. Read out loud or play your tape of major goals before getting into bed.

As you lie in bed, visualize yourself as already being in possession of your goal. Repeat your affirmation of the week over and over to yourself, saying, *"I can do it!"* Bathe in the positive feelings this generates. Let the euphoria of this experience lull you off to sleep.

Have something specific planned to do first thing the next morning or something pleasant to look forward to. It could be that cold glass of freshly squeezed orange juice or your usual thirty-minute brisk walk in the cool morning air. Do not rush as you take time for yourself to wash, dress, and have breakfast. The first thirty minutes set the tone for the rest of the day. Greet the new day with a cheerful "Good morning!" After all, *each new morning is indeed a good morning*, for one day you won't have a morning to wake up to!

If you work outside the home and commute to work, always listen to tapes in your car or on the bus, not to the radio. You need something to inspire you in the morning, not to depress you with all the previous day's disasters. With only thirty minutes travel time each way to work, you can add five hours per week or twenty hours per month to your personal development program. The subject could be attitude, success, effective management techniques, or financial planning. Other choices include classical music or books-on-tape, which now include most of the classics. Make maximum use of your commuting time, whatever tape program you listen to. This time is too precious to donate to your local D.J.

If you listen to positive, uplifting tapes on your way to work, you'll arrive full of energy and enthusiasm — at least most days! As you enter your office, you'll find your daily list of "to do" things you prepared the day before placed neatly on top of your desk. It lists all of the major outstanding action items using an A-B-C order of priority that are to be dealt with that day. "A" items are those that must be done right away; "B" items are important, but don't require any action for a few or several days; and "C" items require no action at all, but may be of general interest.

To formulate your "A" list, you should follow the "Pareto" principle, named after Italian economist and sociologist, Vilfredo Pareto (1848–1923). This principle holds that 80 percent of the value is contained in 20 percent of the items. In other words, you may get done only the first two items on a list of ten, or 20 percent, but you will reap 80 percent of the list's total value.

With a prioritized list, you needn't rummage through all your files and outstanding correspondence to determine what needs to be done first. You get started immediately on the "A" items. Sticking to your list gets you off to a running start, and helps you avoid more convenient or fun things that only eat up time. You avoid the lower value items that make up 80 percent of the list, and concentrate instead on the few high value items that need your immediate attention.

As you proceed in this focused, purposeful way, you know you are organized, you feel you are in control, and you expect to make excellent progress. It is this single-minded approach of doing one thing at a time without distraction, sticking to a single item until it is finished, that will get you through your day accomplishing more than you ever thought possible.

Hunger pains? Think for a moment before you rush off to the nearest restaurant for lunch with co-workers or business contacts. A business lunch can sometimes accomplish a great deal, but there may be a less time-consuming way to get the same results. And most nutritionists do not favor three full meals a day. A heavy lunch can slow you down, not to mention the extra weight it adds to the total you are already trying to take off.

Alternatively, you could bring a lunch from home that suits your own particular dietary needs, and combine it with a brisk walk around the block where you work.

You continue to tackle your "A" items in the afternoon. If you haven't already done so, consider other options to get through your list faster. Can you delegate anything? Can your secretary, a staff member, a co-worker, or your supervisor play a useful role?

Another alternative may be to lump more than one action item together into a single item and deal with it in a more creative fashion. For example, should you write a memo, a report, a telex, or a fax? A single fax to five interested contacts could replace five long-distance telephone calls or five letters. What is more effective and less time-consuming? Consider all of the options. You needn't do everything yourself on all occasions in exactly the same way.

Periodically, consider the bigger picture, the totality of your job rather than just the individual activities or functions you are responsible for. You may be burying yourself in micro rather than macro issues, thus losing perspective and impact. The old motto of the French cavalry, *"When in doubt, charge!"* does not always work.

Fortune magazine reports that most of the people who run the world's fifty largest industrial companies share a penchant for delegating duties. They relax with their golf clubs or tennis rackets, have stayed married to their first spouse, and take normal holidays. Generally, they have similar views on how to manage their companies effectively. They believe that delegating, planning, and communicating are the most important responsibilities to operate and control any large organization.

As you wind down your business day, you'll need to reestablish your priorities for tomorrow in light of what has happened today. What new demands on your time have presented themselves? What new information has surfaced that requires changing the priorities on your current list? Rethink your workload for tomorrow, write it down, and place it in the middle of your desk. Wave good-bye to it until then.

After listening to tapes again on the way home, you can begin to plan your evening. This block of time is probably the most valuable period over which you can exercise maximum control. You should consider taking some quiet time for yourself, either by stopping off at a park along the way home or by taking a short walk on arrival. Set aside some time for reading the newspaper, helping with dinner, and assisting the children with their homework. But always keep in the back of your mind your primary life goal that is staring you right in the face. *You must set aside at least one hour each evening to work on a personal project that is consistent with your primary life goal.* Otherwise, you will lose interest and your commitment will falter. Block out a time slot, 8 p.m. to 9 p.m. or 9 p.m. to 10 p.m., as time to be dedicated toward your needs, whatever you decide this entails. Many people fritter this time away watching TV, reading the newspaper, or snoozing in the recliner after gulping down three martinis before dinner. Keep your self-interest first. Keep focused on your project.

As an architect, you may be trying to design the ultimate prefab dwelling for developing countries; as a nutritionist, determining how to feed a poor family of four on $25 a week; or as a civil engineer, fabricating a low-cost irrigation system for drought-stricken areas in Africa. There are currently more needs in this world than there are people willing and able to address them. Do you have unique skills to apply to any of the world's needs? Just having the desire to help others is one key requirement. We help ourselves most by helping others. Give it some thought.

However you decide to spend your free time in the evenings and on weekends, here are some ideas on goals for each of the key areas of your life:

1.   *Personal.* Spend some quiet time alone each day, for a moment of insight is more valuable than a lifetime of experience. Joseph D. Kennedy, John F. Kennedy's father, was asked how he started to become successful. "When I stopped pushing for it, and went up and sat on the Cape and gave myself time to think," was his reply. Do something for yourself each day that helps you grow and develop your latent

skills. Become **PROactive** in your life — *do something!* — rather than **REactive**. Be selfish with your time and in the process, become somebody!

2.   *Spouse.* Your relationship with your spouse is a separate area of responsibility and should not be lumped into "family" as is so often done. Plan to have a meaningful dialogue with your spouse every day. If you are out of town for a few days on business, always call home and chat. Try to spend one evening a week alone together, maybe a dinner/movie night on the town. Maintain a dating relationship throughout your marriage, with little courtesies and surprises every once in a while. Seek out common areas of interest and see if you can agree on a major life goal together. If you can, you'll benefit from mutual support and each other's contributions to achieve it.

3.   *Family.* Set aside time every day to spend with each of your children, regardless of their age. Do activities together as much as you can, even if you think you are too old. It'll help keep you young! Form a family council that decides family issues. Let your children decide how the family will spend some Saturdays and Sundays, even what to do on annual vacation. Have them actively participate in household chores, teaching them the basics of running a home. After all, they'll have to run one some day.

4.   *Career.* Learn to become excellent at what you do. Take pride in your work and encourage it in others. Regarding each activity, adopt the attitude that if it's worth doing, it's worth doing right. Always go that extra measure, doing a little more than is expected of you. Be creative. There is nothing like a new idea or a new way of doing something to make your job more interesting, more fun, and more fulfilling.

5.   *Health.* Analyze your diet to see if what you are consuming is healthy. Eat foods in their natural state as much as possible. Progressively begin to eliminate white sugar, white flour, red meat, and processed foods of all kinds from your diet. Substitute fish, fowl, whole grains, and raw fruits and vegetables. Do thirty to forty-five minutes of active exercise three to four times a week. Brisk walking and swimming are among the best forms of exercise for old and young alike, and they add to both physical and mental health.

Jack LaLanne, the seventy-five-year-old physical fitness and nutrition pioneer and operator of one hundred and one health spas, says it's better to wear out than rust out. He claims that the human body was designed and built to last one hundred and forty years, if properly taken care of. He points out that a few have succeeded as proof. This man, who at age forty-two set the world record of 1,033 push-ups in twenty-three minutes, is a living monument to physical and mental health and fitness.

"I eat sensibly, exercise vigorously, take no drugs or alcohol, think positively, and look and feel as young as ever," he told an interviewer. "The food you eat, the exercise you do, and the thoughts you think all manifest themselves in the way you walk, talk, look, and feel."[1]

LaLanne says he hasn't been sick since 1936, and owes it to the fact that he gets up each morning at 4 a.m. to lift weights and swim for two hours.

Regarding eating habits, LaLanne says that if man makes it, don't eat it. "I eat no processed foods, no sugar or white flour products, and no red meat. My diet consists mainly of fish, chicken, turkey, organic fresh fruits and vegetables, and natural whole grains. I eat three meals a day, but never between meals. For breakfast, I whip up a high protein drink with egg whites, bananas, apples, pears, wheat germ, bran, bone meal, and brewer's yeast."

LaLanne also strongly believes in a positive mental attitude. "Anything in life is possible if you want it badly enough. I keep making new challenges and goals for myself, that's what keeps me going. With proper diet, exercise, and attitude, you can live life to the fullest."

The advice—from a man who celebrated his 70th birthday by swimming a mile in Long Beach harbor with both his hands and feet tied, towing seventy boats behind him filled with guests—is plain and simple: take better care of yourself!

6.   *Finances*. Maintain a detailed record of all your financial affairs. Seek professional guidance when deciding on any major investment, then rely on your own judgment. Consider the tax and other advantages of starting your own small business at home. Try to borrow money only for assets that have the potential to appreciate. Learn to live on a budget. Robert Schuller recommends setting 10 percent aside for savings, giving 10 percent to the religious institution of your choice, and living on the remainder.

7.   *Community*. Consider volunteering your services or joining a club that supports local activities such as the Rotary, Kiwanis, or Lions

Club. You will have the opportunity to serve your community in any number of ways and learn from the new people you'll meet.

8.   *Spirituality.* A great source of personal strength for many comes from their spiritual beliefs, whatever religion they practice. Give some thought to this area, for it may hold the key to putting the rest of your life together.

All of the great religions teach ethics, values, and ideals to live by. If you study them, most have a common purpose: to live in harmony with yourself and your fellow humans. Choose your ideals and values with great care and thought. There is a wide choice available to you. Jesus Christ, Mohammed, Confucius, Buddha, and many others have suggested sets of values and rules. Consider them. And if you decide you don't like their rules, then decide whose others you would rather choose. Carl Schurz (1829–1906), German-born American statesman, once wrote, "Ideals are like stars: you will not succeed in touching them with your hands, but like the seafaring man on the desert of waters, you choose them as your guides, and following them you reach your destiny."

The purpose of self-image psychology is not to make you something you can never hope to be, but to help you become the person you are capable of being. If you happen to put your faith in the Bible, here are some statements in it that are truly inspiring:

First, it says that God created men and women "a little lower than the angels" and "in his own image." And, "If you have faith, nothing shall be impossible unto you."

In other words, you have been built to the highest of specifications, and have many unique talents and abilities within you that you cannot even begin to contemplate—until you accept on *faith* that you have them and begin to explore them through purposeful and consistent effort. Faith is simply unquestionable belief. By accepting the fact that you already possess the talents and abilities you need to be successful, you are only putting to use what was meant to be used. By taking the time and effort to express yourself fully and in your own unique way, you are simply showing gratitude for your gifts and returning some of the value invested in you.

It also says, "Verily, verily, I say unto you, he that believeth in me, the works that I do shall he do also; and greater works than these shall he do."

No one who believes in Jesus would deny that He did many kind and miraculous things during His lifetime. Yet this statement tells us that you and I are capable of even greater things than these. *Without doubt, this must be considered the greatest motivational concept in the world!* Few have ever considered they could aspire to such heights as the works of Jesus Christ. You must have a sense of what is possible, what needs to be done, and an unwavering desire to do it if you want to be successful.

All of these statements if understood, appreciated, and fully accepted cannot have anything but a powerful and persuasive effect on the thinking of the person who believes in them. They certainly open up the possibilities!

"Bad will be the day for every man when he becomes absolutely contented with the life he is living, with the thoughts that he is thinking, with the deeds that he is doing, when there is not forever beating at the doors of his soul some great desire to do something larger, which he knows that he was meant and made to do because he is still, in spite of all, the child of God." — Phillips Brooks (1835-1893), American clergyman and writer.

9.   *Fellow human beings.* Is there something you can contribute to enhance the welfare of others? To give abundantly is to receive abundantly. You have a fortune to share if only you would. You have empathy, goodwill, praise, encouragement, and love to give to your fellow human beings. By giving freely of these things and being nonjudgmental, you receive these same things in return. In your own way, you can *add value* to those you deal with, to your friends, colleagues, and loved ones. When you build others up and increase their self-esteem, you enable them in turn to add value to you and others in their environment. Each time you act to improve the lot of others, you set an example and send forth a tiny ripple of hope for a better world.

An individual is the basic element of a family.
A family is the basic element of a community.
A community is a basic element of a state.
A state is a basic element of a nation.
And nations together represent the family of Man.

Personal Development

The sixth key factor of success (FOS) is personal development. *You must think personal development if you want to think like a winner!* One of life's greatest challenges and hopes is to create and look forward to the next stage of personal development. If you dedicate yourself to a program of personal growth and development, nothing can stop you from moving ahead in your life. Whatever you end up accomplishing is a direct result of your efforts to improve yourself. You can never be a failure without your consent. Since no one can possibly care more about you than you care about yourself, the responsibility rests with you to set this process in motion, to take the initiative, and to make it happen.

Learning is a lifelong process. "The education of man is never completed until he dies," remarked Robert E. Lee (1807–1870), commander-in-chief of the Confederate army during the American Civil War. Education involves both learning of the new and unlearning of the old, and it can start anytime. If you haven't yet started your own personal development program, now is the time to begin.

Personal development requires two things: an admission that you don't know all you need to know in order to get ahead, and a commitment to begin learning these things. Of course, it requires a certain amount of dedication and hard work, a willingness to sacrifice some short-term pleasures for long-term gain. Winners always do what they have to do, when they have to do it, because they know this is the price of success.

Author Norman Cousins offers the view that "It is nonsense to say there is not enough time to be fully informed. Time given to thought is the greatest time-saver of all."

Personal development involves working on yourself, on the key mental skills that you must contribute to the performance equation. The more you improve yourself, the more you'll like, respect, and believe in yourself. You'll begin to see yourself in a different light, and your mind will open up to new challenges and opportunities. Opportunities and challenges always gravitate toward the person who believes in them.

Every study has found that peak performance begins with the preparation and practice phase, not in the execution phase, of a particular activity. Athletes spend many more hours on the practice field than they do in the actual contest. It is this repeated practice and training that makes the difference between an average performer and a peak performer. Peak performers are self-made. They are not born with the superior motor skills that make champions.

Men and women who have excelled in a particular field are often no more gifted than many others. But they stand out because they have taken the time to prepare themselves, to develop whatever potential they do possess to a level considerably above the average. The unique feature of a free society is that people can develop their individual talents and abilities, and strive in any direction they choose, as long as they are willing to put in the time and effort to earn what they are seeking.

People reflect without, what they are thinking within. The quality of your outer life will always be a reflection of the quality of your inner thinking. Each step you take, each slight improvement you make, will add to your outer circumstances. You will accumulate worldly benefits as you begin to develop your mental skills. You will accumulate material, financial, and emotional rewards in direct proportion to the mental preparation you undertake. You have to work hard on yourself. As Zig Ziglar says, "When you are hard on yourself, life will be easy on you but when you are easy on yourself, life will be hard on you."

For most people, life progresses in stages. In your early twenties, you are full of vim and vigor, and high hope for the future. In your thirties, you experience some of the difficulties and challenges life has to offer, and some of its setbacks. In your forties, you wonder why you haven't "made it" yet, and whether you ever will. This is an ideal time to re-assess your present circumstances and plan your future.

Dale Carnegie, Norman Vincent Peale, and Napoleon Hill were all over forty-five years old before their first major works were published. The average millionaire in the U.S. is over fifty-five. Michelangelo (1475–1564), the famous Italian painter, sculptor, and architect, was seventy-two when he was asked by Pope Paul III to design and build St. Peter's dome, considered the greatest architectural accomplishment of the Italian Renaissance. And as Abraham Lincoln predicted, his turn finally came when he was fifty-two years old. "Forty is the old age of youth; fifty is the youth of old age," according to Victor Hugo (1802–1885), French poet, novelist, and dramatist.

You can trigger desire and enthusiasm for beginning a program of personal development by setting a goal that is significantly higher than your current state of affairs. Would you like to double your current annual income? Can you even begin to conceive of earning *ten times* what you are now earning? The reality is that you can if you begin the process of learning what you need to know in order to be successful.

The majority of people waste virtually every evening and weekend on trivia.

Let's begin with a few "don'ts." Don't spend your free time doing things that contribute nothing to your further development such as watching TV, idle socializing, reading every page of the newspaper, or just plain goofing off. The majority of people waste virtually every evening and weekend on trivia. It is not that you have to eliminate any or all of these pastimes from your life, but you must reduce them significantly to fit more productive activities into your schedule.

Research shows that the average American adult female watches four hours and fifty-three minutes of TV each day; the average adult male watches three hours and fifty-nine minutes. Can you believe that? An average of almost four and a half hours of watching game shows, sitcoms, and old movies that ensures you will stay exactly where you are in life—that is, if you are lucky. Most people are actually sliding slowly backward but aren't aware of it because the descent is so gradual.

Today, there is a greater quantity and variety of material on the market to help you get ahead in life than ever before. Information on almost any subject has been produced by some of the most successful people who have ever lived. For a few dollars and some hard work, you can learn in a few hours what it took them decades to discover. By absorbing this information, you can leap into the forefront of any field and begin to make your own mark. You can acquire specialized knowledge in this way that does not exist in any other form. Books, magazines, tapes, and seminars are all available through your employer, community groups, and your local library or bookstore. The self-help movement is blossoming along with the entrepreneurial surge in

America, and seminars are one of the fastest growing industries in the country. As John Naisbitt points out in *Megatrends*, society today is moving away from the short-term consideration of what we have learned in school toward a lifetime of reeducation and retraining.

You need to plan each day and set aside at least one hour to work on yourself. It may be that you'll have to get up an hour or two earlier in the morning or set aside some time in the evening to fit it in. Whatever way you do it, make it a daily event, one that you look forward to and plan toward.

Any expert on time management will tell you that you will always "find" the time—you actually *make* the time available—to do what you place the highest priority on, on what you value the most. So the time is available if you seize it and use it to your advantage. For example, if you study for one hour a day, after five years you will have studied for 1,825 hours, the equivalent of about one normal working year involving forty-five 40-hour weeks. That's quite an accomplishment, taking only one hour, one day at a time.

Your personal development program is your stepping stone to success. Make it the last thing you give up each day, not the first. Usually the lawn can wait or you can skip that TV special or baseball game, but *never* let a day go by that you do not invest at least one hour in yourself. You deserve at least this much attention. Aim to work as hard on yourself as you do on your job, and you'll have things in just about the right proportion.

A comprehensive reading program is the first important step toward meaningful self-improvement. Books are a portable, permanent source of invaluable information. Almost any book you could want is available at your local library, or in any bookstore in softcover or mass paperback editions at very reasonable prices. For the cost of a movie, you can enter the minds of some of the greatest thinkers the world has ever known. You can study history, philosophy, or the lives and teachings of the masters such as Socrates, Plato, and Shakespeare. You can proceed at your own pace, reading over lunch or a cup of coffee. Reading offers a new reality. It can open up a whole new world of possibilities all for the asking—but only you can expose yourself to this opportunity. Only you can read, assimilate, contemplate, and take from the data what is useful to get ahead.

"Every man who knows how to read has it in his power to magnify himself, to multiply the ways in which he exists, to make his life full, significant, and interesting," English writer Aldous Huxley (1894–1963) observed.

Statistics show, however, that the average American reads less than one book per year and 58 percent never finish a nonfiction book after high school. The Bible is the all-time best-selling book, but it seems that less than 1 percent of the general population has read it from cover to cover. It is estimated that less than 20 percent of the population purchases about 80 percent of all the books sold in bookstores. Fiction outsells nonfiction at least ten to one.

Yet self-help psychology and management books continue to be extremely popular and are among the best-sellers today. Among the perennially best-selling self-help books are *Think and Grow Rich* (Napoleon Hill), *The Power of Positive Thinking* (Norman Vincent Peale), *How to Win Friends and Influence People* (Dale Carnegie), *Psycho-Cybernetics* (Maxwell Maltz), and *Unlimited Power* (Anthony Robbins). All are "must" reading for anyone serious about personal development.

If you spend one hour a day reading, you will read about one book a week or fifty-two books a year. The knowledge you'll gain from fifty-two books will set you apart from your peers and give you the winning edge in whatever field you are in. Like good food is to the body, reading is nutrition for the mind. It will force you to consider new ideas and concepts, reassess old beliefs, and broaden your horizons.

The only real limitations on what you can accomplish in your life are those you impose on yourself—a key core belief. By learning how others have succeeded, you too can learn to think smarter, think bigger, and think more about the "business" of success. Like any pursuit, some ways of going about it are better than others. If you learn from others and take the very best advice from experts, you can accomplish in a few years what it has taken others a lifetime to accomplish. Make time your ally, not your albatross.

Remember that according to Mark Twain (1835–1910), American novelist and humorist, "The man who does not read good books has no advantage over the man who cannot read them."

Listening to educational and motivational cassettes is the second important step toward self-improvement. Take control over your transition time, which is the time you take to commute to and from work, traveling time on business trips, and time walking or jogging. The average commute in North America is about one hour per day, totalling about two hundred and fifty hours per year. Imagine the opportunity of having Brian Tracy, Denis Waitley, or Zig Ziglar, all authors of best-selling audiocassette programs, talk to you in the privacy of your own car. These giants have helped thousands turn their lives around to become more confident and more accomplished in their professions, more successful in their relationships, and more fulfilled as people.

With accomplishment come feelings of greater value, higher self-worth, and peace of mind. You cannot afford to miss out on this experience, but you will if you continue to throw away these two hundred and fifty hours of prime learning time each year. You can become one of the most highly motivated, well-informed professionals in your field simply by reading a book one hour per day and listening to audiocassettes while traveling in your car.

The third important step toward self-improvement is "reading" other people. There are opportunities every day to learn from others, to seek out knowledgeable, successful people and ask them questions about the things they are particularly good at. Assume that everyone you meet knows something you don't, then ask for his or her advice. People who have mastered a particular subject are only too happy to share their knowledge with you, and even learn a little something from you in the process. As the American author William Channing (1780–1842) noted, "Every man is a volume, if you know how to read him."

Whatever your chosen profession, find an expert in your particular field, explain what you are trying to accomplish, and ask how you should go about doing it. Experts are not only those above you in an organization. Many are your peers and your subordinates. Everyone has some unique knowledge and expertise, and it can be yours if you simply ask for it. "Every man is my superior in some way. In that, I can learn from him," remarked Emerson.

The fact that successful people really want to help others is a difficult concept for many to accept, especially those who are just starting out. You must understand that asking others for advice is about the most sincere compliment you can give them. When you seek advice or guidance from others, you are recognizing them for their unique knowledge and expertise. Others are flattered that you think they have something of value to contribute. By placing a high value on what they know, you are placing a high value on who they are. Reading other people is a key step in avoiding needless mistakes and reaching your full potential much, much faster. Any self-improvement program is better than no program at all. And remember, self-fulfillment is impossible without self-improvement.

Personal growth must go hand-in-hand with professional development if you want to remain competitive in the marketplace. Not surprisingly, many people are finding themselves underqualified as new technologies and better-educated employees enter the professional ranks. As well, a large number of firms regularly cut back on their white-collar staff as a result of austerity, increased competition, or a fluctuating economy. Thus there are fewer promotional opportunities for those who do not keep current, especially those in middle management.

Increasingly, employees are having to accept the fact that "up" is no longer the prime option available to them to increase career and lifetime satisfaction. Along with personnel administrators, many are coming to the conclusion that self-improvement and career planning are more the responsibility of each individual than they are of the company. A personal development program that is self-designed and self-administered is appearing more and more to be the only option for people who have reached a plateau in their career, and whose prospects for future advancement are minimal.

Ralph J. Cordiner, former chairman of the board of General Electric, offered this advice in the early 1930s at a leadership conference: "We need from every man who aspires to leadership — for himself and his company—a determination to undertake a personal program of self-development. Nobody is going to order a man to develop. Whether a man lags behind or moves ahead in his specialty is a matter of his own personal application. This is something which takes time, work, and sacrifice. Nobody can do it for you."

His statement is just as valid for the men and women of today. *It demonstrates that there can be no great success without great commitment—a key core belief if you truly want to achieve your goal.*

Health

The seventh key factor of success (FOS) is health. *You must think health if you want to think like a winner!* Your physical, mental, and spiritual health cannot be ignored except at your peril. Poor health in any of these areas can cause you sickness, pain, depression, and despair, not to mention a shorter lifespan.

You must work hard at maintaining a high level of health and accept responsibility for all of your actions that are health-related. There is no cure for a lifetime of bad health habits.

"To know how to grow old is the master work of wisdom, and one of the most difficult chapters in the great art of living," was the comment of Henri Frederic Amiel (1821–1881), the Swiss writer. And English poet Robert Browning (1812–1889) added, "It is the last of life for which the first was made." Old age should be the icing on the cake, the dividend years of a full, productive life.

For decades, people relied on the government and a huge medical establishment to keep healthy. There was little concern for diet, exercise, and mental stimulation to keep fit and to stir the emotions. Beginning in the 1970s, a trend began to develop away from these institutions toward more individual responsibility for health and fitness. This change was inevitable at a time when the automobile was clearly king of the road and fast food was fashionable dining. People had been exercising less than ever before and natural food had virtually disappeared from the shelves of the supermarket.

Since this trend, which has become known as the holistic health movement, people have come to accept the whole body concept—body, mind, and soul—as central to good health. And people have put themselves at the center of the decision process: how much and what kind of exercise is appropriate, what diet and nutritional programs are advisable, and what attitudinal, lifestyle, and environmental changes are warranted to reduce stress. Enlightened practitioners rely less on drugs, surgery, and annual checkups to judge their level of health and more on self-designed, self-administered programs.

Dr. Tom Ferguson, author of *Medical Self-Care*, says, "I think we are on the edge of a very major change in our health care system. People are learning to make decisions about their own symptoms and to take care of themselves."[2] The objective of a preventive health care program is evolutionary improvement through holistic lifestyle changes versus the treatment of symptoms with temporary and artificial remedies.

The explosion in diet and health care books and exercise programs is indicative of the major shifts in people's attitudes in these areas:

- Almost half the U.S. population now exercises in some way.

- Diet and nutrition books head the non-fiction best-seller lists.

- Fat intake from red meat and dairy products is down significantly.
- Smokers are increasingly under seige in public places and office buildings.
- In-premise fitness centers in companies are almost as common as dining facilities.

Exercise is only one key element of a successful health regimen.

Jim Fixx's 1976 classic, *The Complete Book of Running*, sparked a fitness revolution. Suddenly there were more swimmers, cyclists, walkers, weightlifters, and joggers than ever before. According to the *Gallup Poll*, running reached a peak in 1984 when thirty million Americans claimed to be runners. That same year, Jim Fixx died of a heart attack while jogging on a country road in Vermont, tragically indicating that exercise is only one key element of a successful health regimen.

According to a 1985 study by the President's Council on Physical Fitness and Sports, walking is the most common form of exercise among adults over eighteen. The study also found that:

- Walking burns the same number of calories as running or jogging the same distance.
- Walking increases circulation and improves cardiovascular efficiency, while lowering blood pressure and reducing stress.
- Walking decreases appetite.
- Muscles are flexed 1,500 to 3,000 times during every mile walked, more than almost any other exercise.

Financial considerations have been a major factor encouraging greater individual responsibility for health care. Doctor and hospital costs have soared to once-unimaginable heights, leaving individuals, insurance companies, and government assistance programs unable to cope. In 1989, health-care spending topped $600 billion, representing 12 percent of the U.S. gross national product, compared to only 9.1 percent in 1981.

Corporate America sees significant cost savings as a result of having a healthier workforce. Employees who are healthier physically and mentally are more productive, more cooperative, take less sick leave, and don't run up high medical bills. Companies that have developed wellness programs employ full-time staffs to run their fitness programs. One corporate participant claims to have saved $5.52 in medical costs for every dollar spent on the program.

The U.S. Departments of Agriculture and Health and Human Services offer the following advice for families committed to healthier diets:

- Eat a variety of foods.
- Eat foods high in fiber and complex carbohydrates.
- Avoid foods high in fat, especially saturated fat, and cholesterol.
- Limit sodium intake.
- Cut down on sugar.
- Drink alcohol in moderation.

The new self-care phenomenon makes much more sense and is far cheaper in the long run. The emphasis has shifted from sickness and recovery to prevention and wellness, and has created a whole new growth industry. Health professionals are now treating the emotional as well as the physical causes of illness, and are actively counseling sick people to take more responsibility for their own wellness. They are recommending more attention to regular exercise, proper diet, and stress management through a positive mental attitude, and less dependence on drugs, alcohol, and withdrawal from society.

The holistic health movement has brought renewed attention to the major causal factor behind all health and wellness: the human mind. The most extreme view is that every disease that exists is 100 percent psychosomatic—created by the mind—and that any disease can be cured through the powers of the mind. Most experts would agree that a great number of diseases certainly have a major psychosomatic component and that many can be treated by changes in attitude if caught in time. Norman Cousins brought this to our attention when he showed in his book *Anatomy of an Illness* how he healed himself from what was considered an incurable disease with positive thinking, vitamin C, and laughter.

Numerous other cases have been documented where visualization and deep religious faith have caused remission of life-threatening diseases such as cancer. Visualization involves exercises such as imagining white blood cells as predatory fish swimming around in the bloodstream gobbling up grayfish cancer cells. Dr. Bernard Siegal, author of *Love, Medicine and Miracles,* describes how a person's attitude is the most important factor in healing and staying healthy.

> Love, laughter, and peace of mind are physiological. They create chemical changes in the body that are conducive to physical health. As a surgeon, my personal experience has been to see the positive effects of one's state of mind on healing. I can see it very dramatically in front of my eyes because I do the same operation on several people and their recovery rates are enormously different based on their attitude, lifestyle, and life experience. If you're depressed and your life is filled with despair, and you don't deal with those feelings, then you're telling your body you don't want to recover. By hiding feelings, you suppress your immune system, which then makes you more susceptible to illness.[3]

"The mind and body are one," says Dr. Joan Borysenko, author of *Minding the Body, Mending the Mind.* "Every thought we have translates into changes in our physiology. There's a different biochemistry for hope, for depression, and for love, and we're just beginning to understand those connections."[4]

Almost two thousand five hundred years ago, Plato (427–347 B.C.), the Greek philosopher, wrote, "The great error in the treatment of the human body is that physicians are ignorant of the whole. For the part can never be well unless the whole is well." Philippus Paracelsus, the 15th-century German physician who is often called the father of modern medicine, wrote: "The spirit is the master, imagination the tool, and the body the plastic material."

These views are supported by modern findings that the workings of the mind—attitudes, beliefs, and emotions—are primary factors affecting the body. Dennis Jaffe speaks for all holistic health proponents in his book, *Healing from Within*:

> In reality most diseases stem from not one but a long chain of contributing factors, which intensify and multiply over a period of months or years. Our behavior, feelings, stress levels, relation-

ships, conflicts, and beliefs contribute to our overall susceptibility to disease. Our power to prevent and heal illness is far greater than most of us realize.[5]

Tests on TV viewers show the validity of mind-body interaction. When four people are hooked up to electrodes, each one watching a different TV program—for example a mystery, a romance, a documentary, and a horror story—researchers can tell which person is watching which program simply by monitoring biofeedback data such as saliva and perspiration. When all the channels are switched, the new data allow a person isolated from the test area to determine which person is now watching which new program. For example, person A is now watching the documentary, person B is now watching the horror story, and so on. Without fail, what the body experiences is a true indicator of what the mind is perceiving. Emotional responses to mental activity have a direct effect on bodily functions such as heartbeat, breathing, digestion, and eye dilation.

Certain attitudes people adopt also produce specific behavioral responses. To illustrate these different effects, Meyer Friedman and Ray Rosenman described what they called Type A behavior in a 1959 study and later in their book *Type A Behavior and Your Heart*. People exhibiting Type A behavior are characterized by a feeling of lack of control over themselves and their environment. Such people are unable or unwilling to accept responsibility for what happens to them in their life. They cannot find contentment and satisfaction inwardly, and they are always seeking acceptance and approval from others to compensate for their own lack of self-esteem. Type A people are always in a hurry, they overcomplicate situations, cannot easily relax, and act insecure. Their sense of urgency and hostility often gives rise to irritation, impatience, and anger, and makes them high-risk candidates for coronary heart disease and heart attacks. In contrast, Type B people are more relaxed, more content, and easygoing.

Many life changes are unavoidable. We must all adjust and learn to go with the flow to some extent. But the manner in which you react to change in fact is more critical than the change itself. Inner-directed people, those who are willing to accept responsibility for their lives, tend to make adjustments better and with less physical wear-and-tear than those who believe outside events are in control of their lives.

The Holmes-Rahe scale of stress ratings that follows was first published in 1967 by Doctors T.H. Holmes and R.H. Rahe of the University of Washington Medical School. It assigned mean values or point scores to forty-three events on a Social Readjustment Rating Scale reflecting common life changes, both good and bad.

To use the scale, identify the events that have taken place in your own life during the past twelve months. Then add up the corresponding numerical values shown to determine your score. If you score 150 points or less, you are safe. Between 150 and 300 points, your chances of becoming ill or disabled during the next two years are about 50-50. If you score over 300 points, a critical plateau has been reached in your life and there is a high probability you will become seriously ill. This scale has proven to have remarkable predictability regarding the onset of disease.[6]

Figure 9

LIFE EVENT	MEAN VALUE
Death of spouse	100
Divorce	73
Marital separation	65
Jail term	63
Death of close family member	63
Personal injury or illness	53
Marriage	50
Fired at work	47
Marital reconciliation	45
Retirement	45
Change in health of family member	44
Pregnancy	40
Sex difficulties	39
Gain of new family member	39
Business adjustment	39
Change in financial status	38
Death of close friend	37
Change to different line of work	36
Change in number of arguments with spouse	35
Mortgage over $10,000	31
Foreclosure of mortgage or loan	30
Change in responsibilities at work	29
Son or daughter leaving home	29

Trouble with in-laws	29
Outstanding personal achievement	28
Spouse begin or stop work	26
Begin or end school	26
Change in living conditions	25
Revision of personal habits	24
Trouble with boss	23
Change in work hours or conditions	20
Change in residence	20
Change in schools	20
Change in recreation	19
Change in church activities	19
Change in social activities	18
Mortgage or loan less than $10,000	17
Change in sleeping habits	16
Change in number of family get-togethers	15
Change in eating habits	15
Vacation	13
Christmas	12
Minor violations of the law	11

THE HOLMES-RAHE SCALE

In the population Holmes and Rahe studied, 80 percent of the people who exceeded 300 points became seriously depressed, had heart attacks, or suffered some other serious illness. Bernard Siegel found similar results. Ninety-five percent of his patients with serious illnesses experienced some significant life change just prior to their affliction.

Heredity obviously is a major factor in many diseases but so is mental attitude. The average point scores shown do not have to apply to everyone. A person can learn to cope more effectively with significant life changes using techniques such as meditation, biofeedback, deep breathing, proper nutrition, and physical exercise.

To determine your relative level of health, you can undergo regular and routine medical examinations and physical fitness tests. If you are among the average, more than likely you have been eating too much and exercising too little.

But it is not so easy to measure your level of mental health. One approach is to look at yourself carefully and assess your ability to see and believe the best about everyone, yourself included, and everything on a regular basis. Do you habitually think, act, and feel cheerful and happy? Do you place the best possible interpretation upon the actions of others? Do you allow preconceived opinions to color your perception of daily events? Do you look beyond your common faults and instead focus your energies on developing new, desirable skills and personality traits? Do "worst-case" scenarios haunt your daily thoughts? Depending on your answers to these questions, you may have some serious thinking to do.

Emerson once said, "The measure of mental health is the disposition to find good everywhere." This is a very useful definition, for it shows that happiness isn't something that comes to you by chance, it comes to you by choice. Happiness must be cultivated by purposeful effort and made into a mental habit. There will always be pleasant and unpleasant aspects in your daily life to justify either an optimistic or a pessimistic outlook. But if you wait for all the unpleasant thoughts you can think of to go away before allowing yourself to be happy, then you're bound to wait an awfully long time. Happiness comes to the person who puts the best possible interpretation upon every event — to the person who chooses to be optimistic most of the time. As the English philosopher, L. P. Jacks (1860-1955), notes, "The pessimist sees the difficulty in every opportunity; the optimist, the opportunity in every difficulty."

Your physical and mental health are key factors of success. The way you think in your mental domain determines the way you act and feel in your physical domain, and the two combine to produce either constructive or destructive end-results. As Shakespeare observed, " 'Tis the mind that makes the body rich." Start to take much better care of yourself—your attitude, diet, and exercise—and assume greater control over your environment. If you believe you can, you will.

CHAPTER 10

Adding Value to Yourself

"There is no meaning to life except the meaning man gives his life by the unfolding of his powers."
—Erich Fromm (1900–1980)
German-born American
psychoanalyst and social philosopher

Creativity

The eighth key factor of success (FOS) is creativity. ***You must think creativity if you want to think like a winner!*** As American historian James Harvey Robinson (1863–1936) noted, "Creative intelligence in its various forms and activities is what makes man." Just look around you. All the objects you see are the result of the work of some creative human being. In reality, you are looking not at "things," but at thoughts manifested in their physical form. It was a thought that created the chair you sit on, the pen you write with, and the light you read by.

Fly over any major city and you will marvel at the many creations of human thought—the skyscrapers, sports stadiums, freeways, bridges, and parks. All were an idea in the beginning. It is people with ideas, dreams, and vision that create what you have. The world is governed totally by thought. Everything you perceive without is the result of what has been thought about within. You are what you think. You enjoy what human thought has created.

Creativity is an ability given to us at birth. Albert Einstein (1879–1955), famous for developing the theory of relativity, believed that every child is born a genius. When children are tested between the ages of two and four, typically 95 percent are found to be creative. When

211

tested later at age seven, only about 5 percent are still found to be highly creative. What happens? In his insightful book *Self-Renewal*, John W. Gardner suggests that pressure from society to conform is to blame.

We have seen that many children, who naturally seek out love and affection and try to avoid criticism, are brought up to fear failure and rejection. They are forced through subtle and not so subtle means to conform to adult wishes and standards, and to behave in a way that is not creative. They are told what to do, and when and how to do it. Often they are not encouraged to ask questions, to explore new avenues, or to satisfy their natural curiosity. They are rewarded for conformity with the norm and compliance with the rules, a sort of dehumanizing capitulation. In the process, they lose their spontaneity and identity as independent thinkers.

Later in life, many adults manifest this early programming by rigid thinking and fixed attitudes. People who have been cut off from their creativity tend to be insecure, inflexible, and unimaginative. They see everything in extremes: it is either right or wrong, black or white, relevant or irrelevant. They are unable to engage in any original thinking or approach a problem in a creative way. They think habitually and cling to the status quo.

Thankfully, creativity cannot be lost. It only goes into hiding and lies dormant from lack of use. It can be tapped and made to come alive again on demand. You need only accept the fact that you still possess what you were given at birth — the inherent wisdom, intelligence, and creativity that make up your particular brand of genius. Genius is the ability to make the common appear novel, the complicated more simple, and the seemingly unconnected connected. To combine known forms into a previously unknown form is the great triumph of genius.

Your ability to develop and use your inborn creativity in a purposeful way is a key factor of success. But it is very underrated and poorly understood. It requires persistent, focused concentration and effort on specific challenges you select, and a quiet confidence in a successful outcome. Each time you generate a creative insight or solution to a challenge, you automatically experience the positive feelings associated with accomplishment. Using your creativity in an organized, systematic way gives you a greater sense of control in your life, boosts your self-esteem, and moves you ahead in the direction you want to go.

An excellent definition of creativity is that it is the making of the new or the rearranging of the old in a new way. It represents the actualization of human potential, of the creative energy of your subconscious mind. Your subconscious is a vast storehouse. It contains the wisdom of the past, the understanding of the present, and the vision of the future. By tapping into its vast reserves, you can create new thoughts about anything you choose to think about. You may wish to develop artistic, scholastic, or professional talents, and reach specific goals that are meaningful and important to you.

When everyone thinks alike, no one is thinking at all.

If you wish to explore your full potential and identify new opportunities for high achievement, you must challenge your creative powers. Otherwise, you'll spend your time being like everyone else, with the result that you become a copy and not an original. When everyone thinks alike, no one is thinking at all. In this way, nothing very useful is ever accomplished.

Researchers studying the behavior of creative people have found a direct link between creativity and positive thinking. Positive people are those who habitually consider a wide range of possibilities, the various options that are available to achieve a particular goal. A positive attitude inherently implies confidence in other possibilities. The positive thinker can find value in any idea and the reasons why it *will work*. Alternatively, a negative thinker focuses primarily on reasons why an idea *will not work*. Creative ideas help you stretch to new limits and explore the possibilities. As Abraham Maslow said, "If you settle for less than you can be, you will be unhappy the rest of your life."

There are two distinctly different thought processes involved in creative problem-solving. The difference lies in the manner the brain processes information related to the problem.

The first thought process is known as *divergent thinking* and it consists of expanding all aspects of the problem itself. It involves stating the problem in different ways, assessing it from several points of view, questioning basic facts and assumptions about it, gathering additional information, and listing as many options as possible to solve it. Divergent thinking aims to expand the problem into all of its constituent parts in order to better understand its true nature, and to list all possible solutions for its resolution. It can be compared to blowing air into a balloon to determine its true size and shape.

The other manner of thinking is known as *convergent thinking* and it proceeds in exactly the opposite direction. It involves reducing the problem into smaller, more manageable parts. It zeros in on key factors for in-depth analysis, discards unworthy options, and selects others for implementation. Convergent thinking is reductive. It reduces a problem to a specific plan of action and a method to evaluate results.

A key skill in all problem-solving is to know when to diverge and when to converge, since most people habitually practice one type of thinking or the other.

A typical diverger is good at generating a great number of new ideas and considering many possible solutions, but is not able to make a decision. Such people are often labeled *indecisive*, since they never get around to taking action, preferring instead to keep studying the problem one more time.

On the other hand, a typical converger is prone to premature action, not having adequately studied the totality of the problem. A converger tends to make snap decisions based on insufficient information and inadequate exploration of all possible options. Such people are often labeled *impulsive*, because they never properly understand why they are doing something. They are in too big a hurry just to do it.

Some of the most typically rigid thinkers, people who cannot innovate well or accept others who can, are well known to most of us. Often they acquired their narrow thinking from the professional training they received and the analytical nature of their work. Among professional groupings, lawyers, accountants, military officers, government employees, and business executives tend to be the most unimaginative. They all have their approved forms, correct procedures, necessary approvals, and mandatory guidelines. Since everything is defined, dictated, and decided, there is little room for either initiative or creativity. Seldom do options exist. Either you qualify or you don't; either the rules permit it or they don't; either you obey the order or you suffer the consequences. It should be no surprise that these professions change very little over time and that innovation is not one of their hallmarks.

Creativity is a thinking exercise. It is a developed mental skill aimed at generating new ideas that may be more useful than the old ones. A new idea is usually only a combination of old ideas recast in a different light. You can produce new ideas more easily by adopting the habit of "free association," the linking of two or more ideas together to form a new one. Sony created an entirely new product with the introduction of the Walkman radio. It combined two known ideas to satisfy a consumer need that remained unsatisfied: to be able to listen to a radio while walking or jogging — both blossoming leisure-time activities.

Another example revolutionized transportation. At the end of the last century, a German engineer named Wilhelm Maybach observed a perfume atomizer at the end of the last century, and was intrigued by how it mixed liquid with air. He tried it with gasoline and came up with the carburetor. Gottlieb Daimler used the device to create an entirely new mode of transportation: the automobile.

Look around you and see what you can create that is of potential benefit to other people. Is there some way you can help humanity rise higher, suffer less, and enjoy more of life? The answer lies within you, deep in your subconscious mind. You begin to reach your full potential when you help others reach theirs first.

The only real wealth in the world is a new idea and someone willing to act on it. Wealth does not lie in luxury items such as cars, homes, and personal possessions. These items are merely the symbols of wealth. The causal factor behind all prosperity is a useful new idea with a practical application that has yet to be exploited. The individual, organization, or country that can generate the greatest number of useful new ideas is the one that will flourish and prosper.

As Victor Hugo once remarked, "An invasion of armies can be resisted, but not an idea whose time has come."

Here are some suggested techniques for new-idea generation that have proven effective:

1. *Incubator method.* This technique involves clearly identifying the question or problem you want answered, writing it down just before retiring, then sleeping on it. You confidently assign the problem to your subconscious mind, then forget about it but expect to have the answer during the night or first thing in the morning. Place a pad of paper and pen on your bedside table, and when the answer strikes you out of nowhere like a bolt of lightning, get up and write it down.

Otherwise, you'll fall back to sleep and never remember it. Many successful writers report that they use this method more than any other to come up with creative ideas and insights for their work.

2. *Brainstorming method.* This technique for new-idea generation is generally credited to Alex Osborn, author of *Applied Imagination.* The process involves two separate meetings of between four to seven people typically lasting thirty to forty-five minutes. The main objective of the first meeting is to get agreement on what the real problem is, then to generate as many problem-solving options as possible without any evaluation or judgment being rendered. Once the meeting coordinator receives group consensus on a clear definition of the problem, that person solicits ideas from the group to resolve it.

Care must be taken not to favor any particular approach or direction in the discussions, only to encourage the free flow of ideas and suggestions. At the end of the meeting, the coordinator arranges to have all the ideas presented typed up on a single page. This list forms the basis for a second meeting whose main purpose is to evaluate the merits of each proposed solution, select one or a combination of several, and agree upon a plan of implementation and follow-up. Action items should be assigned to specific individuals, with a time limit agreed upon for their implementation.

3. *Mind-mapping method.* This technique exploits free association to the maximum by forming a pictorial display or decision tree of new ideas. The subject or topic at hand is placed in the center of a page and spokes are drawn out radially from this point as each new idea or solution is identified. If a particular option brings to mind a related association, a sub-branch is drawn off that line. You'll end up with numerous spokes and a sprinkling of sub-branches, all directed at helping you solve your particular problem.

The mind-mapping technique was developed by Tony Buzan of the Learning Methods Group in England. The exercise is designed to take full advantage of a person's various mental capacities, and is called the "whole brain" approach. It combines the visual, intuitive qualities of the right hemisphere of the brain with the logical, analytical left hemisphere as described in Betty Edward's bestseller *Drawing on the Right Side of the Brain.* Most people habitually operate in either one mode or the other when problem-solving, seldom together. The meth-

mode or the other when problem-solving, seldom together. The methodology effectively brings together both the qualitative and quantitative capabilities of the brain.

Perception versus reality lies at the core of this concept. People often have a vested interest in sticking with a particular approach or the status quo without consciously being aware of it. They overlook new opportunities or options to bring about change or improvement, alternatives that others not so close to the problem can readily see. People tend to deal mainly with effects, the results of plans or policies, rather than with the causes. Causes represent reality, while effects represent perception. People who make decisions based on perception alone are operating with a distorted picture of reality. They are not likely to be very creative.

Consider the example of passenger trains, which certainly are not as numerous today as they once were. The operators of passenger trains perceived themselves to be in the "passenger train" business, when in fact they were in the "transportation" business. They failed to remain competitive with other modes of transportation and allowed their industry to languish.

The following mind map depicts the wide variety of ways books can be sold to customers. It depicts the various channels of distribution from the point of view of a person wanting to explore the many options available to sell books. Once all of the options are identified, it is easier to make judgments concerning the viability of each based on time, profit, and other considerations.

What we do is determined by who we are; who we are is determined by what we think; what we think is determined by what we learn; what we learn is determined by what we are exposed to and what we do with that exposure.

So purposely expose yourself to as many divergent people and situations as possible. What you expose yourself to is a key causal factor behind what you do with your life.

An important part of being a creative person, then, involves exposing yourself to a steady stream of new ideas from outside sources. You must read thought-provoking books, meet interesting people, attend lectures and speeches, engage in meaningful conversations, and question the status quo. Be inquisitive, curious, and always searching. These are the hallmarks of a creative person.

Figure 10

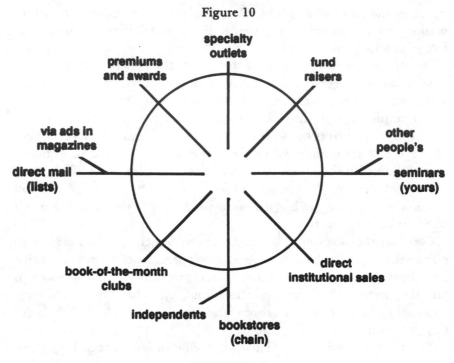

MIND MAP

Service

The ninth key factor of success (FOS) is service. *You must think service if you want to think like a winner!* The principle of service can best be summarized by the statement, "Give and you shall receive in kind." It is a reflection of the law of cause and effect — for every action, there is an equal and opposite reaction. When you get right down to the root meaning of success, you will find that it simply means to provide service. And the more service you provide, the more success you will have. "To do more for the world than the world does for you, that is success," according to Henry Ford.

Napoleon Hill fervently urged those who wanted success more than failure, wealth more than poverty, and happiness more than heartbreak to render more and better service than they were currently being paid to deliver. Emerson spoke about service in his famous essay titled *Compensation*: "But all the good of nature is the soul's, and may be had if paid for in nature's lawful coin, that is, by labor which the heart and head allow."

Your outward contribution in the way of services rendered to others is the key determinant of how successful you will be in your pursuits. The rewards you receive will always be in direct proportion to the value of your service. And if you want to increase the value of your rewards, it follows that you must increase the value of your service. There will always be naive and opportunistic people who strive to receive the most for the least possible effort — or worse still, try to get something for nothing. Such people are simply on the wrong end of the Bible's law of sowing and reaping: "Whatever a man sows, that will he also reap." If it were easy to have all of the rewards we seek without working for them, we wouldn't value them very much and hence wouldn't want them.

Service is the rent you must pay
for the space you occupy here on planet Earth.

Service is your contribution to the general scheme of things, to the interactions between people that determine the quality of human relationships and human output. It is the rent you must pay for the space you occupy here on planet Earth. A family reflects to the community the amount of love and affection shared by its members. A company reflects to its customers the amount of attention and care it directs toward satisfying their needs. Service is satisfying human needs and wants in the most efficient way.

Consider the effects of service in the home. We know children are largely a product of their upbringing, of the quality of their parents' treatment of them. Children who do not meet with their parents' approval, who are victims of destructive criticism and arbitrary punishment, grow up with low self-concepts, a poor self-image, and minimum self-confidence — only to live unproductive, uninspiring lives. On the other hand, children raised in an atmosphere of love and affection grow up to be healthy, self-confident adults with positive self-concepts and high levels of self-worth and self-liking. They are able to make something of their lives and contribute significantly to society.

With regard to a marriage relationship, every marriage reflects the contributions of its two members. If there is minimum mutual support, if each is asking more of the other than he or she is willing to contribute, the result can only be a tearing apart rather than a bringing together. If you want more out of your marriage, begin by adding more to the relationship. In each instance, add more of precisely what you want. If you want more affection from your spouse, first demonstrate more affection toward that person. If you want more understanding, first demonstrate more understanding. And if you sow the seeds of dislike and distrust, expect to reap the same rewards. Good begets good and evil begets evil.

Our capitalistic society is based on a service economy in which goods and services are freely exchanged according to individual needs and wants. It is through the services you render that you live, and only by rendering service can you hope to survive and prosper. The system does place great demands on participants—some would say it is even cruel. But it does provide the greatest rewards for the greatest number of people. Winston Churchill once remarked, "The inherent vice of capitalism is the unequal sharing of blessings, whereas the inherent virtue of socialism is the equal sharing of miseries."

Consider how capitalism evolved into what it is today. In its most elementary stage, a person consumed exactly what he or she produced. The food you gathered, the clothes you wore, and the weapons you fashioned all had to come from your own effort. As society matured, families began to produce items for trade with each other. You exchanged what others wanted for what you wanted. Clearly, the more you produced what others wanted, the more you could acquire what you wanted. You prospered as a direct result of your labor and ability to satisfy the needs and wants of other people. This is the basis of our modern, free enterprise system.

As the following poem shows, to aim high in life in search of prosperity requires no more effort than to aim low and accept poverty.

> I bargained with Life for a penny,
> And Life would pay no more,
> However I begged at evening
> When I counted my scanty store.

For Life is a just employer,
He gives you what you ask,
But once you have set the wages,
Why, you must bear the task.

I worked for a menial's hire,
Only to learn, dismayed,
That any wage I had asked of Life,
Life would have willingly paid.[1]

Jessie Rittenhouse

The simplest way to express the law of compensation is this: the more you put into something, the more you get out of it. It is a law of nature, not a law of man. Live by the law and you'll reap its rewards; live counter to the law and you'll pay the penalty. Winners in life always focus their efforts on how to put the most in, while losers always focus on how to get the most out.

Consider modern business practices where companies succeed or fail by this same immutable law.

A business can be a single person performing all of the tasks necessary to satisfy a customer's particular needs. This person could be a gardener, an accountant, or a consultant, none of whom needs a hierarchial structure to operate. In such a situation, the supplier and the customer meet "eye to eye" in the marketplace. However, when the scope of the business opportunity expands and demands specialization of effort, an organization becomes necessary. An organization's reason for being is very simple. An organization exists only because it can achieve goals that an individual alone cannot accomplish. Every organization results in some form of hierarchial structure where various levels of management and workers strive to coexist and cooperate in order to produce a product at a profit.

Business also must live by the law of cause and effect. The cause is to satisfy customers' needs and the effect is to market goods or services at a price above cost. Thus it is evident that the first focus must be the consumer and his needs, and the second is efficient production such that a fair, competitive price can be charged that results in a profit being generated. The customer must always be the primary center of attention. If a customer base of sufficient size is properly serviced at a price above cost, profits will automatically follow. But you cannot hope to generate a profit if you ignore serving the customer at a price that he or she can afford and is willing to pay in light of the competition.

Today in the auto industry in North America, we are seeing the effects of some manufacturers not being able to satisfy customers' needs at a competitive price. Japan in particular has done a far better job of making the customer its primary focus, the main reason behind the design of its product and the quality of its workmanship. U.S. industry has gone to great effort to try to counter this Japanese success. They have invested heavily in automated equipment in an effort to lower costs. They have improved their designs and built more quality into their product. But the results have not been spectacular. Worker productivity still lags behind levels in Japan. And American managers continue to be obsessed with quarterly and annual profit figures rather than customer satisfaction and increased market share.

In an effort to explain away massive recurring trade deficits with the Japanese, we in America are quick to criticize lack of access to the Japanese market, unrealistic exchange rates, generous Japanese government subsidies to its industry, and lower labor rates in Japan. And many of these complaints do have merit. But we always seem to overlook one prime consideration: *realization that the customer is supreme.* Our efforts increasingly must be to focus on each employee as the basic unit of production, on the organization as the mechanism to bring together diverse specializations in a cost-effective manner, and on satisfying consumer needs in a very competitive environment. Only in this way will American industry be able to compete with foreign firms in domestic and foreign markets.

In their book *In Search of Excellence*, Thomas Peters and Robert Waterman discovered that excellent companies have two distinct characteristics: they constantly sought increased productivity improvements through effective human resource management, and they had an obsession with putting the customer first. All the internal policies and plans of excellent companies have these two areas as their primary focus. Their aim is not to have separate departments of finance, production, purchasing, and marketing as excellent isolated areas of specialization. Rather, it is to have all these functional units work together to produce the best product that meets the needs of the market being served.

Everyone is self-employed, whether you work for others or for yourself. It rests with each individual to ensure that you make the greatest possible contribution to whatever organization you are part of in order to ensure its profitability and survival.

Here are eight attributes that extensive research indicates are characteristic of excellent companies that maximize employee input and put the customer first. Consider how you might go about doing some things differently in your own position that will add to the competitive advantage of the organization you now work for.

1. *A high level of communications* both vertically and horizontally throughout the organization, making contact with employees at all levels. To be effective, an organization must strive through some means to focus all the efforts, talents, and creative energy of its employees toward valued goals and objectives consistent with the organization's well-being. Excellent companies go out of their way to encourage frequent, informal discussions and meetings as often as possible, whether over lunch or after hours socially, in both written and verbal ways.

2. *A less formal structure* to increase communications and facilitate individual involvement in decision-making. A formal hierarchial structure cannot possibly accommodate all the lines of communication necessary for maximum employee input, since the number of lines needed increases exponentially as the number of employees increases in an organization. Excellent companies frequently convene ad-hoc groups or task forces representing smaller units in the organization to tackle multi-functional problems such as quality control. Many firms have eliminated whole layers of management, sometimes reducing the number in an organization from as many as twelve or fourteen to as few as three.

3. *High delegation of authority.* Excellent companies delegate authority to the appropriate working level to allow input where unique knowledge and experience exists. This helps stimulate individual initiative and creativity, and allows senior management to focus on other important issues. Delegation of authority also allows evolutionary rather than revolutionary changes in the organization to take place that are consistent with changes in the marketplace. Employees who deal directly with customers are in a much better position to note trends and changes in preferences than middle or senior management.

4. *A high level of accountability.* This involves individuals being made fully responsible for the contributions they make to the

organization and goes hand in hand with delegation of authority. It fosters a high level of trust and encourages acceptance of more responsibility. Accountability applies to both formal and informal groups where individuals accept personal responsibility for the quality of all their inputs and decisions.

5.   *Recognition of effort.* Employees want to be recognized for their individual efforts, especially accomplishments that can be attributed to themselves, or their particular unit or group. People want to feel they are part of a team that is succeeding. Excellent companies build positive reinforcement into their operations and day-to-day activities. They pay attention to employee needs and have found ways to show appreciation for work well done. They help employees feel important, that their contributions are valuable and meaningful to the organization.

6.   *Clearly defined strategic objectives* throughout the organization that are market-driven and emphasize the right things:

- not a preoccupation with profit at the expense of product
- not a preoccupation with shareholders at the expense of customers
- not a preoccupation with quantitative factors (units produced, units shipped, units sold) at the expense of qualitative factors (product, people, and process)

7.   *High creativity and innovation.* Excellent companies constantly aim for increased productivity through their people. They foster loyalty, high morale, commitment, and individual identification with the firm's success. The key in each case is the supervisor-employee relationship. The ideal supervisor shows each employee how to be more productive on the job. A supervisor must be a facilitator, the catalyst who is able to maximize individual effort and direct it toward the firm's primary objectives.

Seeking employee input is an obvious activity that enhances the quantity and quality of production. As much as 50 percent improvement in productivity can come from employee suggestions and involvement in the design and production process.

In 1980, for example, Toyota had 48,757 employees who submitted 859,039 suggestions, an average of 17.62 per person per year. Fully 807,497 or 94 percent of these were deemed to be practical ideas and were implemented that same year, resulting in $30 million in savings.

8. *A corporate mentality or culture* that promotes:
- flexibility in people, process, and problem-solving
- focusing company resources on key business issues
- facilitating customer needs by perceiving customer problems as business opportunities

All eight of these attributes are directed at satisfying the ultimate consumer, the person who pays all the bills. In a free-market society, the consumer does have a choice. People will patronize a business only to the extent they believe the firm has their best interests in mind, and that they are being served in a manner consistent with their needs and in proportion to their importance.

In the end, we are all in business for ourselves. Each individual represents a personal services organization, and must compete in the marketplace to survive and prosper. What can you begin to do differently that will add value to the services you have to offer? Give this question some serious thought.

Excellence

The tenth key factor of success (FOS) is excellence. *You must think excellence if you want to think like a winner!* Make the commitment to become excellent at what you do, for in excellence you will find your true self. As John Gardner points out in his book *Excellence*, "When we raise our sights, strive for excellence, dedicate ourselves to the highest goals of our society, we are enrolling in an ancient and meaningful cause—the age-long struggle of humans to realize the best that is in them."[2]

Only when you attain excellence in your chosen field can you hope to become truly successful in life. Anything less and you cannot hope to reach your full potential. Every study of high-achieving men and women shows that they persevered and labored at becoming only one thing—outstanding in their chosen profession. The market always pays in relation to performance. It always pays top rewards for top performance whether in sports, the arts, business, or the game of life.

A very fine line exists between high achievers and the rest of the pack. On the professional golf tour, only one or two shots separate the top money winner from all the others. In professional baseball, the league batting champion hits only ten or twelve times more often in an entire season than the runner-up. In the Olympics, the difference between the gold medal winner and the fourth-place finisher in the 100-meter dash is often less than two-tenths of a second. So the *winning edge* is only a chip shot here, a clutch hit there, or a fraction of a second on a stopwatch. A small difference makes all the difference in the world, regardless of the game you are playing.

Excellence translates into a labor of love.

Peak performers do not become outstanding by chance. Instead, they make the commitment to learn the skills and acquire the knowledge necessary to excel. They are dedicated people who enjoy what they do. They don't really "work" at their profession as most people do. Work can be defined as having to do something when you would rather be doing something else. Whatever you call it, excellence translates into a labor of love, a total commitment to perform at your maximum.

How small, seemingly marginal differences in performance result in enormous differences in rewards is well demonstrated in the classic Wimbledon final on Saturday, July 5, 1980, between Bjorn Borg and John McEnroe. The set scores were 1-6, 7-5, 6-3, 6-7, and 8-6. Borg won his fifth consecutive Wimbledon final on this occasion, winning twenty-eight games to McEnroe's twenty-seven, about a 4 percent difference in performance. But Borg picked up $50,000 first-prize money versus $25,000 for McEnroe, a 100 percent difference in rewards.

Numerous benefits accrue to peak performers. They are rewarded more both materially and emotionally. They are able to enjoy a higher standard of living and be more independent. They are also more likely to be happy, content, and positive in their approach toward themselves, their profession, and others. They are less likely to be sick, depressed, or unemployed. Each time they perform well, they receive a boost in self-confidence and self-esteem. They are easily reenergized and able to move on to new challenges. They readily accept advice and criticism from others, creatively approach problem-solving, and work well in cooperation with others. Such individuals are not outstanding in any one particular area so much as they are simply slightly more competent in several key areas. This is the key to excellence and discovering how to *be the best that you can be.*

The same rules apply to companies as they do to individuals. Companies develop one or more areas of excellence, a competitive advantage that sets them apart from their competition. They excel at particular activities that meet the demands of the marketplace, and the marketplace reacts accordingly.

Let's return to the automobile industry as our example. Japan vowed to become the world's number one auto producer by the end of the 1970s, and it was successful. To reach this goal, it had to penetrate the lucrative North American market, overcome a reputation for marginal quality, especially for inexpensive consumer goods, and compete head-on with the entrenched "Big Three" automakers that already had well-established sales and service outlets. Japan's strategy was to sell a car of outstanding quality in design and performance at a competitive price. This way, consumers were enticed to focus more on value and quality than on service and repairs. The Japanese success story illustrates that true service is not to be found in how well or how quickly you fix something that's broken, but rather in how good your product is in the first place.

The market will always pay a premium for quality. Quality is really a combination of performance and price which adds up to value, and value is still sought after by the discerning consumer. Every firm must have some competitive advantage to help distinguish itself from its competition. Any company whose product or service does not stand out from the competition in some way is not likely to succeed. It will be doomed to mediocrity and a slow but steady decline.

The Four Seasons Hotel chain is one example of an organization that has reacted differently to the trend in North America that has service becoming a thing of the past. You may have heard the story of the salesclerk who always tells her customers that saying "thank you" wasn't part of her job anymore because it was already printed on the sales slip!

To succeed in the international marketplace, the company formulated and sticks to this corporate goal: to operate the finest hotel in every market they enter.

Isadore Sharp, the company's chairman, president, and CEO takes pride in telling the story about a guest who left a briefcase behind at the firm's Toronto hotel. The gentleman called from Washington to explain that the contents were very important to him and that he needed them for an upcoming meeting. When hotel management tried to find the bellman to determine what had happened to the case, they discovered that he was already on his way to Washington to deliver the case to the guest personally on his own time and at his own expense. The bellman felt personally responsible because he had inadvertently forgotten to place the briefcase in the trunk of the taxi along with the guest's other luggage.

Business Week recently accused Four Seasons of an almost obsessive emphasis on customer service. The company's chairman heartily pleads "Guilty!" In a speech in Los Angeles on June 3, 1987, he explained, "We can take five years to design and build the most glamorous hotel. We can spend many millions of dollars on that hotel. The very next year the competition can build right across the street, spend more millions, and probably be a little more up to date. But, thankfully, it takes more than money to update service, and service is our business. *Service is the essence of excellence,* and we believe if you put excellence first, profits will surely follow."[3]

Four Seasons looks for employees who have an entrepreneurial sense of personal accountability, people who believe they are personally responsible for seeing that the customer's needs are fully satisfied. The result is an organization which deliberately sets out to please its customers, not because of pressure from the top but because of peer pressure and self-pride. Employees really want to excel at the service they render and no one wants to let their co-workers down. They all want to be proud of the organization they work for.

This begs some important questions you must ask yourself: What area of excellence have you developed? What is your competitive advantage as a person that sets you apart from all of your peers? What specific things do you have to offer that equate to personal excellence?

These are not easy questions to answer. We all want to be exceptional at something. We all want to look in the mirror each morning and be able to say, "I'm excellent at what I do." This is the key to high self-liking and high self-esteem. True self-esteem rests on knowing you are competent at what you do. People who think they are not particularly good at anything can only feel inferior and insecure around others who think more highly of themselves. If you believe you are not good at something, you can never really like, respect, and accept yourself as a worthy and deserving person. You will always accept your limitations, aim low in life, and try to get by with the least possible embarrassment.

"The quality of a person's life is in direct proportion to their commitment to excellence, regardless of their chosen field of endeavor," was Vince Lombardi's firm belief.

You are responsible for discovering and developing your own unique talents and abilities. No one starts life with all the necessary qualities and characteristics fully developed in order to succeed. If left to chance, you will develop some naturally en route — some sooner, some later, and some never. But it doesn't have to be this way if you choose to act. You should never leave the development of your full potential to chance.

All of the mental skills and attributes discussed in the preceding three chapters can be developed through purposeful effort for greater effectiveness in all areas of your life. Don't accept the view that they would be nice to have "someday," or that you will consider developing them when you find "sufficient" time, the "right" job, or the "perfect" opportunity. *You must live in the now, the precious present, for this is the only place happiness can be found.* Decide to make each of these skills and attributes a part of your life today, a part of your personality that contributes to your current performance.

CHAPTER 11

Superior Human Relations: Your Master Key to Success

"Treat people as if they were what they ought to be and you help them to become what they are capable of being."
—Johann von Goethe

Superior human relations are the eleventh key factor of success (FOS), and one of the most important subjects in this book. *You must think superior human relations if you want to think like a winner!* Anyone hoping to become successful must develop the ability to motivate and influence other people effectively and in positive, predictable ways. *To be able to do the things you want to do in both your personal and professional life, you need the support and cooperation of other people—a key core belief.* Few things of any significance can be accomplished without the help of other people. Superior human relations are an essential ingredient in the performance equation.

In this chapter, we will identify and highlight the various wants and needs you must satisfy in order to motivate people to act in cooperative ways on a consistent basis. We will do so in light of what we have previously learned about the self-image and self-image psychology. You will find that you already possess in great abundance many of the things other people desperately want and need. And you will find that by giving openly and freely to others the things they want, you will receive what you want in return. This is the essence of superior human relations.

To begin, it is important to realize that other people have to benefit from agreeing to work with you in any particular endeavor. You cannot expect something for nothing. If properly carried out, both parties will grow and benefit from the experience.

Persuasion Versus Force

There are basically three choices available to you when trying to influence other people. The first is to ignore people and simply hope they will act in your best interest. You probably will agree that this is not a very practical option, since the results can be neither effective nor predictable. By ignoring other people, you are giving up any hope of influencing them and thus are surrendering yourself to the whims of fate. In effect you are saying to the world, "I will leave you alone and, in return, I want you to do what I want," a naive and unrealistic expectation.

The second option is to use coercion and force to compel others to act in the specific way you desire. The use of threats and intimidation may produce results, at least in the short term. Fear-inducing tactics, however, never bring out the best in people, since people *themselves* must be the driving force behind their motivation if they are to put their hearts and souls into what they are doing. Fear forces people to operate in a survival mode. They may follow your instructions and orders to the letter, but seldom will they contribute any real energy or enthusiasm to their efforts.

The third option is to persuade people to do what you want them to do simply because *they really want to*. People will do what you want them to do willingly in direct proportion to how they see their self-interest is being served. In other words, you must convince people that they will receive very real benefits and rewards if they follow the path you are suggesting. These benefits must be something the other party understands and inherently wants, for whatever reason. In effect, you are offering a reward that is valued by others in exchange for a reward that is valued by you. The highest reward you can offer people is to provide them with opportunities to maximize their full potential.

The more enlightened the world becomes, the more people seem inclined to use persuasion in their relations with others, and the less inclined to use force. Yet few people have ever been taught the tools that enable them to do this successfully. With little knowledge and understanding of how to use a new methodology, they naturally end up falling back on what they have used before with some success — namely force.

Force is a primeval instinct in all of us. In raising children, for example, we often resort to using some kind of force to get the results we want when persuasion fails. As a last resort, have you ever forced your children to do their homework or clean up their bedroom so at least the bed became visible to the casual observer? We then rationalize our behavior by believing we did it for their own good and that later on, the children will agree we acted in their own best interests.

In the real world, there are instances when force must be considered. For example, when someone maliciously attacks you, tries to rob you, or forcefully enters your home, you may feel that friendly persuasion is not the best response to use to protect yourself. Or consider a foreign power that threatens to attack your country or undermine your form of government. Do you rely on simple words to try to dissuade it? Obviously there are occasions when you will elect not to back down and surrender, but choose to use force to defend yourself.

A central problem in dealing with people is this: we tend to use force in many situations when we should not. Often we don't treat others in ways that would persuade them to act in cooperative ways. Instead, we let our emotions overcome our intellect — we get mad — and in the process, we allow ourselves and the situation to get out of control.

For instance, we tend to use force when we are convinced we are *right* about a particular problem, or at least that we are more right than the other person. Myron Colbert sums up this tendency with these words: "In controversial moments, my perception's rather fine, I always see both points of view — the one that's wrong and mine."

And because we believe we are right, we feel *justified* in acting the way we do. We also tend to use force when we think we possess the actual or perceived *authority* to force our will on our adversaries. Usually encounters involving force are devoid of any meaningful two-way communications at all. Seldom is there any probing of the facts of the problem at hand to determine which have merit and which do not.

Force is not very civilized, yet it is used every day by many people in our society to get what they want. Since force is often misused in many situations, many well-intentioned people would like to see it completely eliminated from our homes and institutions. Opponents of coercion and force consider them to be weapons of last resort, as archaic and outdated tools to get people to do what we want.

We have progressed very far in devising and developing incredible new technologies to manage and control our physical environment.

Yet we have not progressed nearly as far in dealing with our human environment — other people. Parents still don't know what to do when their children refuse to eat dinner. Should such children be scolded, spanked, sent to their room, or deprived of TV for the evening? Or should they be bribed with double dessert with ice cream? Educators face the same dilemma in the classroom. Should children be controlled by strict rules of conduct and disciplined with corporal punishment for noncompliance, or should they be allowed unlimited freedom to express themselves and their own individuality? And if these are the two extremes, then where is the middle ground?

Many use a combination of the "carrot-and-stick" approach in dealing with people, a system of external rewards on the one hand and physical punishment on the other. Imagine a carrot dangled enticingly in front of a donkey's nose and a stick applied smartly to his behind. Through these means, he is alternately attracted and impelled forward toward fulfillment of his master's goal. In this well-known analogy, it is never made clear if the donkey ever gets to eat the carrot, but we know for certain that if he doesn't cooperate, he gets to feel the stick. In either case, we know the donkey does not move because *he inherently wants to.*

So it is in most organizations that claim to reward those who comply with the rules and punish those who do not. Often the external reward that is offered is simply an absence of any punishment, a sort of "Do as I say and you won't get hurt" approach. The result can only be mediocrity. In such a system, people do the least possible to avoid the known punishment, knowing they won't receive anything they deem significant in return for greater effort and cooperation. They naturally tend to focus on avoiding what is always emphasized more, *the threats*, rather than on what is only vaguely alluded to, *the rewards.*

In every controlled environment, whether a home, school, or place of business, there is usually some code of conduct in place, some set of rules that says you must comply or suffer the consequences. In any case, you rarely see a list of the benefits you'll receive if you do your job particularly well, or help others do well in turn. And if real benefits are offered, they seldom are aimed at generating internal or intrinsic motivation.

The challenge for each new generation is to raise the level of interpersonal relations onto a higher plane. Young men and women graduating from institutions of higher learning are often eager to work hard and get involved in their new careers. Yet seldom are they able to attract the kind of favorable recognition they expect and deserve. Unfortunately, superior human relations are not practiced freely in most work environments. Many people in business assume they are not important. But they are wrong. An essential skill for managers at all levels of an organization is the ability to deal with and influence other people consistently and effectively so that they willingly put forth their maximum effort.

Obviously, arguments will continue over the merits of persuasion versus force in our society as we struggle to resolve the multitude of human problems we face at home and abroad. Undoubtedly we will continue to make expensive and damaging mistakes in the conduct of human affairs until we learn more about the fundamentals of human behavior. The damage is particularly evident in lost productivity in the workplace at the rate of millions of dollars per day. Clearly in this setting, cooperation rather than confrontation must be fostered and encouraged. Industry must begin to show more leadership in teaching basic human skills, and realize that learning does not have to take place in a building labeled "school" any more than jogging has to be done on a track. A major investment is required in the training and development of *people skills* such that, collectively, we maximize human potential.

There are several reasons why we have been slow in developing our ability to live and work in harmony with one another. First, in the long history of human evolution, we have acted like animals in a wild environment far longer than as civilized people in a tame one. We began by living in small family and tribal groups, and survival meant coping with a harsh environment. Securing food, shelter, and protecting ourselves from predatory animals and other hostile tribes were all primary preoccupations. The species of Man that did survive was obviously able to overcome his physical hardships more successfully than those who perished. He survived not because he was able to persuade his enemies to live peacefully — they probably didn't even speak a common language — but because he could *fight more effectively*. This survival instinct continues as a powerful force to this day. Our powers of persuasion have never been fully developed as a result, and still lag far behind other skills we have mastered.

The second reason we have been slow in developing superior human relations is that we can offend someone or take advantage of another person without being aware of any serious consequences for a long time. Then, at a later date, we seldom associate any specific penalty with any specific mistake. We usually attribute another's negative behavior to his or her poor attitude, or a particular set of circumstances, never to our own past performance or inability to be persuasive. Since we explain away our own behavior in this convenient manner, we are able to go to sleep each night confident and secure in our own superiority, but somewhat dismayed about the unpredictability and uncooperative nature of others.

This leads us to the third and probably most important reason why we have not progressed very far in getting along with other people. We are possessed by a large and powerful ego that forces us to see things primarily from our own point of view. We will go to great extremes to justify our own behavior and prove that we are right even if we have a sneaking suspicion we are totally wrong. We know we cannot so easily defy the laws of our physical environment—a jump from a high building has immediate and serious consequences. Yet we naturally protect ourself from blame when another is involved in a failure. On almost every occasion, we find ways and means to prove to ourselves that we are right and the other person is wrong.

"It is a curious fact that of all the illusions that beset Mankind none is quite so curious as that tendency to suppose that we are mentally and morally superior to those who differ from us in opinion." —Elbert Hubbard (1856-1915), American writer.

Through such means as these, we avoid facing an important fact of life: most of us are not very effective in dealing with people. Our self-interest is being misplaced as a result, for there is much more to be lost than gained from poor and ineffective interpersonal skills. It serves no purpose to rationalize and hide behind our ego while opportunities for cooperation and collaboration pass us by. Whether we violate a law of our physical or human environment, a very real price is always paid.

History is replete with examples of Man's inhumanity to Man, whether on an individual or group basis. Our future survival now centers on Man's understanding of his fellow Man, on the many benefits that successful human relations can render in our homes, offices and factories, in our community, and in our conduct of international affairs.

We are certainly capable of rising up to this challenge. We are rational, thinking beings capable of changing our ideas and beliefs when our desires are stimulated or our survival is threatened. We have proven over and over again that we have a heart and soul full of love and compassion that can inspire magnificent expressions of self-sacrifice and human service.

We are at a crossroad. Five billion people now inhabit planet Earth. Some are trying to overcome the hardships of the land and survive, while others are trying to overcome the hardships of the mind and excel. Whatever the objective, only tolerance, understanding, compassion, and cooperation will see us through. No longer can superior human relations be deemed a matter of being *nice*—they are a matter of being *necessary*. Of course, achieving superior human relations will require a lot of self-analysis and soul-searching. It is going to require a new approach in coping techniques in our homes and places of work. But more than this. It is only by individual example that we can overcome our prehistoric tendencies and begin to look at much higher levels of self-expression and self-sacrifice. Each of us must demonstrate and promote the very real material and spiritual rewards that can result from superior human relations. For to bring together the family of Man to work cooperatively and effectively, and to create new heights of human enlightenment and accomplishment, is surely the master key to success.

Developing Superior Human Relations

Recall that the primary objective of superior human relations is to motivate and influence other people effectively and in positive, predictable ways. It is to maximize individual human potential, to allow people to perform at their optimum and in the process, experience the positive feelings of high self-worth and high self-esteem that are associated with accomplishment.

It is largely through your dealings with other people
that you yourself become successful.

The need to feel important is a central, driving force in every individual. It is the wise and alert parent, teacher, or manager who knows how to make people feel important that succeeds. It is largely through your dealings with other people that you yourself become successful.

You must appreciate and accept the fact that other people are very, very important. We all want certain things from other people. From family members we want affection, cooperation, and support. From employees we want cooperation, loyalty, and the fruits of their labor. From employers we want encouragement, recognition, and fair compensation for our labor.

Some of the most perceptive and experienced business people will tell you that to succeed at any job, you must have three main qualities. First, you must want to do the job; second, you must have the knowledge and ability to do the job; and third, you must be able to get along with people. Of these three, most consider the capacity to get along with people the most important. There are innumerable examples of individuals who are supervisors, managers, or heads of large corporations, not because of their desire or ability to do a particular job, but because of their ability to get along with other people. "I will pay more for the ability to deal with people, than for any other ability under the sun," was the comment of John D. Rockefeller (1839-1937), famous American capitalist and philanthropist.

Studies show that about 85 percent of success in business can be attributed to *people skills* and only 15 percent to technical knowledge. Unfortunately, when it comes to training programs, most organizations reverse these figures. They simply assume people already know how to initiate and maintain effective human relationships—when in fact they don't. The importance of effective interpersonal skills becomes obvious when we realize that 81 percent of all new jobs being created in America today are in the service sector.

Consider the human relations factor in any organizational setting. A common explanation of why people who are competent at one level often fail when promoted to a higher level is Dr. Laurence Peter's famous *Peter Principle* as described in his book by the same name. It suggests that because the higher level of responsibility demands different skills, people fail due to their lack of these new skills. The reason they fail, according to Dr. Peter, is because they have been promoted to their level of incompetence.

Here is one possible explanation for this phenomenon. When people are promoted in an organization, they become responsible, often for the first time, for supervising other people and monitoring their contribution to the organization's goals. But it cannot be assumed that a salesperson promoted to manager due to his or her superior sales skills will know automatically how to manage and motivate a whole salesforce. Thus we see that as people progress higher and higher, superior human relations become more and more important because their influence has a greater impact on the whole organization. Simply put, the higher you rise, the more people you affect.

Only the use of key interpersonal skills resulting in superior human relations can negate the effects of the Peter Principle. We find a new phenomenon now evolving that pertains to enlightened professional managers: *those who consistently demonstrate an ability to achieve results with and through other people tend to be promoted to a level commensurate with their proven competence.* This, obviously, is the Peter Principle in reverse.

As we proceed, recall our previous discussion describing the direct correlation between the level of your self-esteem and your ability to get along with other people. The degree to which you like yourself is always the key determinant of the quality of all your relationships, of your ability to like and work effectively with others. And as you establish and develop superior human relations with others, you allow them to show value and liking back to you. The result is a synergetic, mutually advantageous exchange: as you build others up, you allow them to build you up in turn.

There are three principal ways to develop key interpersonal skills that lead to superior human relations. The first involves adding value to other people through recognition; the second is seeing things from another's point of view; and the third is effective listening skills.

Adding Value Through Recognition

In essence, superior human relations involve *adding value to other people because they, like you, deserve it.* It is giving people something they want — recognition, in return for something you want — their cooperation. When you increase the self-esteem of others, you are showing them respect and that you expect the best from them, thereby helping them perform at their maximum.

It's interesting to realize that each of us is potentially a millionaire, at least in what we have to give to others. We all possess valuable, intangible assets that others desperately want. We all have acceptance, approval, appreciation, respect, and encouragement in unlimited quantity — to give! It is in this way that we acknowledge the importance of other people. They don't cost us anything and they can never be all used up. We all have this fortune to share.

Unfortunately, few people appreciate the fact that you have to give in order to receive. We tend to hoard what we desperately seek. We hang on to these assets as though they were a finite resource. At the same time, we go around purposely collecting and accumulating these same assets from others as much as we can in order to satisfy our own unquenchable thirst. Everyone is hungry for recognition.

Here are some things you should know about giving:

- The desire to receive is a natural instinct, whereas the desire to give is something that has to be learned.

- It is not a question of "givers" being the good guys and "takers" being the bad guys. It is a matter of being effective.

- True givers do not purposely go about "getting" anything, yet they do receive in great abundance.

Many discount the concept of giving as being altruistic and impractical. But it really isn't. You always receive in direct proportion to how much you give. In other words, people will give you what you want to the degree you give them what they want first. If you show others respect and acknowledge their importance, they usually will do the same for you. If you show disrespect and contempt, again, they usually will do the same for you. People always reflect back to you the behavior you display toward them. There is nothing altruistic about wanting others to cooperate with you and show respect for who and what you are.

Basically, there are three kinds of givers in this world:

- The first kind gives only on condition that he or she receives in the exact same proportion on each occasion. In fact, such a person is not a giver at all, but a trader.

- The second gives only occasionally, expecting that he or she will receive in return sometime in the future. But such a person is really an investor, someone who keeps track of all the IOUs he or she is accumulating.

* The third is an unconditional giver, a person who gives freely of himself or herself on all occasions, and does not expect anything in return — ever! Well, let's just say not in this life!

"Socrates, many years ago, said 'Know thyself;' Cicero said, 'Control thyself;' and the Savior said, 'Give thyself.' " — Paul H. Dunn, American religious writer.

Recognition is the deepest craving in human nature. It is the acknowledgment of the importance of people. You are who you think you are, but you are also a function of what other people think of you. If everyone around you began to treat you like a nobody and totally ignored you, soon you'd begin to wonder just who and what you really were. On the other hand, if people treat you as worthy and important, and like to be around you, this only helps confirm what you already want to believe and accept about yourself.

There are many ways to help other people feel important. Being courteous, polite, and helpful is a good beginning. Here are some additional suggestions:

1. *Be alert.* Always be on the lookout for opportunities to praise an act or accomplishment of others. The ever-vigilant and perceptive person will always find a reason to compliment or commend another. As the authors of *The One Minute Manager* suggest, catch someone doing something right!

2. *Be alive.* Always show enthusiasm in your dealings with others. Show that you are happy to meet them with your handshake, your smile, and your words.

Recall the story about three bricklayers. When asked, "What are you doing?" the first bricklayer replied, "Laying bricks." The second answered, "Making $12.50 an hour." And the third bricklayer exclaimed, "Why, I'm building the most beautiful cathedral in the world!" Now, if someone can be this excited about simple bricks, no doubt you can be as excited about meeting other people.

3. *Be available.* Always show an interest in what others are doing. Offer to help in some way if you can. Encourage them in their pursuits. A word of support can sometimes make all the difference in the world.

4. *Be attentive.*   Ask others about their families and their favorite hobbies. Find out what others are contributing to their community and applaud their efforts. Also find out where they are hurting and may need some assistance.

5. *Be appreciative.*   To "appreciate" literally means to raise in value, just as "depreciate" means to lower in value. People crave appreciation for who they are and what they represent. By adding value to others, you are adding value to the world.

B.C. Forbes once wrote in *Forbes* magazine: "No human being can be genuinely happy unless he or she stands well in the esteem of fellow mortals. He who would deal successfully with us must never forget that we possess and are possessed by this ego. A word of appreciation often can accomplish what nothing else could accomplish."

6. *Be approving.*   Everyone wants others to voice support for their efforts and endeavors, often in the face of adversity. By approving their deeds, you are approving who they are and what they stand for. There is always something positive you can approve and admire in others. As Abraham Lincoln once commented, "Everyone likes a compliment."

7. *Show affection.*   Radiate a sincere warmth for other people and they will do the same for you. Affection helps people relax and be themselves. It solidifies a relationship and makes people feel good about themselves. A soft touch communicates a strong message—that you care.

8. *Be accepting.*   Accept people as they are. Let them be themselves, and voice their own ideas and opinions freely and openly. It is through acceptance that we give others the strength and courage to change for the better.

9. *Be affirming.*   Be laudatory in your praise and silent in your criticism. Positive, affirmative statements build others up and help them aim higher in life. Always give credit where credit is due.

I like the example of the speaker who asks his audience to raise their right hand high in the air. Next, he asks them to move it down behind their head and pat themselves three times on the back. He concludes by saying, "Now, you and I both know you deserved that. It's just that we can't recall all the reasons why!"

10. *Be a friend.*   As Emerson said, "To have a friend, you must first be a friend." No one is a nobody who has friends.

"Giving And Receiving," the title of the following poem, is the ultimate expression of self-acceptance and self-love.[1]

I launched a smile; far out it sailed
On life's wide troubled sea.
And many more than I could count
Came sailing back to me.

I clasped a hand while whispering,
"The clouds will melt away."
I felt my life was very blessed
All through the hours that day.

I sent a thought of happiness
Where it was needed sore,
And very soon thereafter, found
Joy adding to my store.

I wisely shared my slender hoard,
Toil-earned coins of gold;
But presently it flowed right back.
Increased a hundredfold.

I helped another climb a hill,
A little thing to do:
And yet it brought a rich reward,
A friendship that was new.

I think each morning when I rise,
Of how I may achieve,
I know by serving I advance,
By giving I receive.

Thomas Gaines

Seeing the Other Side

Empathy has been described as walking in another's shoes for a hundred miles. It is understanding another person from his or her point of view. Seeing the other side is an essential interpersonal skill. Without it, you cannot hope to get along with people.

Many in today's fast-paced society believe a simple two-step process is sufficient to persuade others to adopt their particular point of view:

1.   Be sure you are "right" about the subject at hand.

2.   Bombard your opponent long and hard with as many "facts" as you can to support your position.

This "closed mind" approach can lead only to confrontation, argument, and a hardening of positions, since the other person thinks in his head and feels in his heart that he is right. And of course, from his own perspective, he is. In this scenario, you are giving the other person only two choices: surrender or use force in return. Neither results in a "win-win" situation.

It shouldn't be surprising that this approach is seldom successful, for "a mind convinced against its will is of the same opinion still." No matter how right you may be and no matter how many facts you may have at your disposal to prove your case, others simply will not leap up and embrace you if they have strong opinions and beliefs of their own that you are not willing to consider.

The reality is that everyone wants to be right, at least a little bit right about what he or she believes. People want to be accepted and recognized for their basic intelligence, ideas, and opinions. And it is seldom the case that one person is totally right about something and another person is totally wrong.

The point to realize is that people who believe they are right are never going to accept the fact that you are right until you find something that is right about *their point of view*. In other words, people will maintain a closed mind until you demonstrate that you understand something about their position. You give. They give. When you help other people to be right about some aspect of the problem, you are opening up your own mind a bit and putting yourself in their position to better understand why they believe what they do. When you do this and are sincere about it, other people are more likely to open up their mind a little as well and begin to consider the merits of your arguments. In the process, you both learn something about one another and why you each think and act the way you do. Unfortunately, most people don't communicate effectively with each other. They just take turns talking.

When two people open up their mind to the other's views, they are well on their way to coming to mutual agreement. Alternately, two people with closed minds are likely to continue to argue forever and never get to agree on anything.

Any good salesperson knows that even if she is 100 percent right and her prospect is 100 percent wrong, this in no way assures her of an order. She knows from experience that winning an argument is the surest way of losing a sale! Any chance of success will come only by thinking from the prospect's point of view and helping him or her to be right. If there is a key to getting people to agree with you, it is to find something positive to say about them. You can start at their shoes and work your way up if you want. The key is to make people feel important. There is always something good you can say about anyone if you take the time to do a fair and proper evaluation.

Day in and day out, you see people with closed minds going around finding something negative to say to everyone they come into contact with, and others with open minds finding something positive. It is people who are always trying to appear 100 percent right—and to prove that others are always 100 percent wrong—that cause much of the trouble in this world. People with closed minds and little respect for others have no prospect for success and happiness that can come from superior human relations.

As Robert West remarked, "Nothing is easier than fault-finding; no talent, no self-denial, no brains, no character are required to set up in the grumbling business." If you could devise a credo to reflect a positive philosophy of life, it might well go something like this:

> Compliments are welcome in our midst. Criticism of any kind
> should find another place to make itself at home. Only coopera-
> tion and understanding will get us where we want to go.

In the final analysis, many people would be devoid of any personality at all if you took away all their pet peeves and favorite hates. They're at their best only when they are putting someone else down. They believe the most important thing in the world is to be right. Unfortunately, they are wrong. This is the least productive way of gaining the respect and cooperation of other people.

Henry Ford offered this bit of advice on successful human relations: "If there is any one secret of success, it lies in the ability to get the other person's point of view and see things from his angle as well as your own."

By putting yourself in the other person's place and "seeing things from his angle as well as your own," you are creating an atmosphere of mutual self-respect. You are demonstrating a willingness to solve problems cooperatively and, in the process, create a "win-win" situation.

It is by first adopting the attitude and behavior you want others to adopt that you most influence their actions and behavior. Simply stated, others want you to recognize that they are important, that their point of view is worthy of your consideration. It should be no surprise that others want you to acknowledge their importance. You surely want them to acknowledge the same thing about you.

Successful human relations is really the art of making other people feel good about themselves.

Successful human relations is really the art of making other people feel good about themselves. It involves a process of sharing ego-related wants and needs. When people feel important, they like themselves more. And only people who genuinely like themselves can be generous and cooperative in their dealings with you.

Whoever designed the way people relate to one another obviously knew what he was doing. As we have seen, people who build others up are built up a little bit themselves in the process. Emerson commented on this principle in his remark, "It is one of the most beautiful compensations of this life that no man can sincerely try to help another without helping himself."

Can you imagine a world where it was the other way around, a world where you could build yourself up by tearing other people down? Fortunately, people who have nothing good to say about other people usually have nothing good said about them. Keep this in mind the next time you feel the urge to be critical of someone else.

Benjamin Franklin discovered as a young man that he had to change his ways if he wanted to get along with people. His secret: "I will speak ill of no man, and speak all the good I know of everybody."

Effective Listening

Effective listening is the third and final interpersonal skill leading to superior human relations. Effective listening is an active rather than passive mental skill. It requires keen concentration and attention to what other people are saying.

When you listen intently to others, you are paying them a sincere compliment. You are demonstrating that you consider them and what they have to say as important and worthy of your consideration. Effective listening adds value to other people and builds up their level of self-esteem.

Active listening takes self-discipline and effort on the part of the listener, since you can think much faster than others can talk. Most people speak at the rate of about 125 words per minute, whereas the mind functions at between 450 to 500 words per minute. This allows you to think about other things for about two-thirds of the time that others are talking to you. Your mind naturally tends to wander when it is not being used to its full capacity. When you try to listen and think simultaneously, you end up doing neither one very well. The trick is to use the spare time you have to concentrate more closely on what the other person is saying.

Ralph G. Nichols, a professor in the University of Minnesota's Department of Rhetoric, has dedicated his career to effective listening and has carried out many studies on the subject. He reports that students tested for listening ability did well when they made good use of their spare time while listening. He found effective listeners had the following four characteristics in common:

1. The listener thought ahead of the speaker. He or she tried to guess what the speaker was leading up to and considered what conclusions could be drawn from what was being said.

2. The listener continually assessed the verbal evidence as it was being presented to determine whether the speaker's points were supported by the evidence.

3. At convenient intervals, the listener would mentally sum up what the speaker had said so far.

4. While listening, the listener "read between the lines" in search of additional information and meaning the speaker may have inadvertently missed.

Dr. Nichols points out that the greater speed at which your mind functions easily allows you plenty of time to carry on all four of these activities.

Verbal communications is a major way we learn from others. Teachers in elementary and high school spend more than half their time talking to students. College students spend more than 80 percent of their class time listening to lectures or participating in group discussions. Research on retention, however, reveals that college students can recall only about 50 percent of what was said immediately after a ten-minute lecture, and no more than 25 percent two weeks later.

Students, parents, and professionals alike have difficulty listening with a high degree of efficiency. One survey found that managers spend a minimum of 40 percent of their time listening, yet a majority have only 25 percent efficiency in concentrating on what they hear.

Here are some additional ideas to facilitate effective listening:

1. *Be intensely interested* in the topic being discussed. You may think you know all there is to know about a given subject, but this is seldom the case. If you really think the subject is boring and of no interest to you, then pretend you are interested, and after a few minutes, you'll find that you will be. Even if the speaker lacks proper speaking skills and mumbles his words, ignore these shortcomings and instead focus on the words as they are being spoken.

2. *Be patient* and not in a hurry to form fixed opinions about the topic. All too often we jump to conclusions before people have stated their position fully. If you make up your mind prematurely about what a person is saying and mentally begin to refute his arguments, you are destined to frustrate his efforts to communicate with you effectively. Many listeners preoccupy themselves with thinking about how they intend to respond, and thereby miss out on much of what is being said.

3. *Pause before replying* to collect your thoughts and ensure the speaker has finished what he wanted to say. People want to be allowed

adequate time to express themselves fully before having to respond to questions and criticism about what others think their views are.

4. *Be open-minded* and empathize with the speaker from his point of view. Everyone deserves to have his say. You may not like the particular person or what he represents, but nothing is gained if ideas cannot be communicated. A person's physical appearance, dress, or use of certain words may offend you. For some of these same reasons, you may offend the other person. With an open mind and a sincere interest in the other person, each has some chance of learning from the other.

Now that you have learned how to develop superior human relations, begin today to practice the three techniques just discussed. You have plenty of people all around you to experiment with. All the research material you could ever need is within the sound of your voice and the touch of your hand. You have the tools and the power within you to motivate and influence other people effectively and in positive, predictable ways. *Superior human relations are your master key to success.*

CHAPTER 12

Leadership: Strategies for Increasing Productivity

"An organization is only as great as the people in it, and the people are only as great as the organization allows them to be."
— Anonymous

We have now arrived at the twelfth and final key factor of success (FOS), the one that brings together all of the other key factors that have the potential to have a major impact on people and the organizations where they work. *You must think leadership if you want to think like a winner!*

Leadership in the Workplace

First, let's take a look at the quality of leadership in the workplace today. Warren Bennis and Burt Nanus report in their insightful book *Leaders: The Strategies for Taking Charge* that the quality of U.S. leadership is in a sorry state of affairs. They refer to a major survey conducted in 1983 of the American workforce by the Public Agenda Foundation that cites the following results:

- Less than 25 percent of jobholders say they are currently working at their full potential.
- Fifty percent say they put only enough effort into their job in order to keep it.
- Fully 75 percent say they could be significantly more effective than they presently are.

- Almost 60 percent of American workers believe they "do not work as hard as they used to."

The responsibility for this situation, which appears to be getting only worse, rests squarely on the shoulders of corporate management. Consider once again the epigram above ". . . *people are only as great as the organization allows them to be.*" Managers must assume the key role of facilitators and catalysts to ensure that employees feel part of the organization, and that they can contribute and make a difference. In this respect, every manager must be a leader, someone who helps the organization as a unit "self-actualize," and get a little closer to its main goals and reason for being.

As an individual, you can move the organization ahead only as fast as the weakest link in the leadership allows you to.

Have you ever noticed that as you drive along the highway, you can travel only as fast as the slowest car in front of you? The same holds true in an organization. As an individual, you can move the organization ahead only as fast as the weakest link in the leadership allows you to. The obstacle may be your immediate supervisor, his or her manager, or others above them. It is not so important where the blockage is—only if it exists—and whether there are ways the organization allows employees with good ideas to get around it.

Consider a situation in the army where, as a private, there is a sergeant, lieutenant, captain, major, lieutenant-colonel, and colonel, all between you and the general (not to mention all of their secretaries!). Assume you need the general's approval for an improved procedure to catalogue and safeguard the medical records of all the people in your detachment. Isn't it true that the weakest link in this chain of command can block this or any other good idea you may have?

This bottleneck phenomenon, which serves only to cripple individual performance and the organization's effectiveness, is one of the major roadblocks holding American industry back today. It can be stated as a principle, called the *Staples Principle*, as follows:

*****
An organization is only as strong
as the weakest link in its chain of command.
*****

Clearly, if an organization is to benefit from the valued input of employees, managers at all levels need to be progressive and receptive to employee suggestions for improvement and change.

Unlocking the full potential of employees is critical to the continued success and well-being of any organization. John W. Gardner emphasizes this point in his new book *On Leadership* when he comments: "Perhaps the most promising trend in our thinking about leadership is the growing conviction that the purposes of the group are best served when the leader helps followers to develop their own initiative, strengthening them in the use of their own judgment, and enables them to grow and *to become better contributors*" [emphasis added].

Employee suggestions do save money and increase worker productivity and sense of satisfaction. Previously, we cited Toyota's success in this regard. The National Association of Suggestion Systems in the U.S. reported recently on data they collected in 1988 from more than 900 companies and agencies that had suggestion systems in place. It was found that more than one million suggestions were submitted to management, with nearly 300,000 being adopted. The average net savings to companies per suggestion adopted: fully $7,663.00!

Don Dewar, President of the Quality Circle Institute in California, reports in the *Quality Digest* that employees in Japan are more encouraged and much more involved in submitting suggestions to management. On his last trip to Japan, he found that *each employee* at Pioneer Electronics averaged 60 suggestions per year; at Cannon, 70 per year; and at Mitsubishi, over 100 suggestions per year. In the best companies in America, employees average only 3 suggestions each per year, with the U.S. average being an abysmal 0.14 per employee per year. He believes that American firms can't hope to compete in a global marketplace until they incorporate the ingenuity and creativity inherent in every employee into the operations of the enterprise.

Under the subtitle *Service* in Chapter 10, we listed eight specific attributes characteristic of excellent companies that recognized the importance of employee input. In Chapter 11, three proven ways to foster superior human relations were discussed. We'll continue here to explore other ideas to motivate and influence people to perform in positive, predictable ways, and help organizations derive the maximum benefit from their most valuable asset—their people resources.

Professor Peter Koestenbaum, resident corporate philosopher at Ford Motor Company, observes that *work* is the most important thing people do in their lives, and so it must be related to the *human condition*. He believes organizations that want to prosper in an increasingly competitive world must develop the full abilities of their managers and employees. He explains that executives who show him all their fancy compensation schemes don't understand that these are useless unless they are accompanied by pride, loyalty, inspiration, and ethical behavior. "To get people to work together goes beyond creating strategies, introducing or designing compensation packages . . . you have to go to the human core," he says.

"To be a leader, an executive must first *develop himself and then help develop those for whom he is responsible*" [emphasis added], Koestenbaum continues. "Then he will truly add value to the organization. If you do that, miracles will happen."

His advice boils down to treating people with respect and creating an atmosphere in which they can take pride and are motivated to contribute. "It's a simple principle," he asserts. *"When people grow, profits grow!"* [emphasis added].

Cooperation Versus Competition

To make the case for leadership strategies that effectively motivate people in the workplace and increase productivity, we begin by comparing the merits of cooperation with those of competition, and try to dispel the notion that competition brings out the best in people.

Free-market economies historically have shown the need for and value of open competition among firms active in the production of goods and services. For example, having five or six top-rated automobile manufacturers all competing for the consumer's dollar invariably leads to a superior product being offered to the public at the lowest possible price.

But what factors foster excellence *within* an organization, one that is competing in the marketplace to provide a product or service at a profit? The question is one of competitive advantage: who can find the most effective means and methods to allow people to work together and cooperate in order to maximize both individual and group potential, and organizational effectiveness?

We witness daily open competition in every aspect of human activity. Everyone is striving to be a winner in the key areas of his or her life. Elliott Aronson, a noted social psychologist, has observed that "the American mind in particular has been trained to equate success with victory, to equate doing well with beating someone." The assumption is that only competition can lead to achievement, that only the individual who puts his or her self-interest first can become successful.

A close look at the available evidence refutes this contention. Instead, individual and group performance is usually higher when people cooperate with one another rather than compete against one another. The effect of competition is to make one person's success dependent on another person's failure, and naturally this is disruptive and counterproductive.

This finding and others are reported in Alfie Kohn's excellent book *No Contest: The Case Against Competition.* Kohn cites a study in 1954 by Peter Blau of Columbia University regarding competition and cooperation in traditional work settings, and the effect each has on productivity. Blau studied two groups of interviewers in an employment agency who were competing against each other to fill the most job vacancies. The first group was made up of people who were very ambitious and preoccupied with their own individual performance. As a result, they concealed job notifications and kept names of qualified prospects to themselves. In contrast, members of the second group routinely cooperated among themselves by sharing this critical information. As a consequence, they outperformed their rivals.

Kohn goes on to describe seven other studies carried out during the 1980s by Dr. Robert Helmreich, a psychologist at the University of Texas. All show that competition lowers performance.

In one study, Helmreich sought to determine the relationship between achievement and such personality traits as orientation toward work, mastery (defined as a preference for challenging tasks), and competitiveness. In a sample of 103 male scientists, it was found that those with the most citations from colleagues for their work scored high on orientation and mastery but low on competitiveness.

Similar research considered academic psychologists, undergraduate students, fifth- and sixth-graders, airline pilots, airline reservation agents, and business people. In each case, it was found that competitiveness has an inverse relationship with achievement.

Of all his studies, Helmreich was most excited with the one involving businesspeople because it called into question the widely accepted belief that people in business had to be highly competitive in order to be successful. His research clearly shows that individual salaries in business go up as competitiveness goes down.

Other research described in Kohn's book shows that competitiveness ingrained in an individual is not alone in impairing performance. A structure that imposes competition on its members also tends to produce similar results. In an experiment measuring artistic creativity, psychologist Teresa Amabile of Brandeis University found that one group of girls aged seven to eleven who were competing for valuable prizes produced significantly fewer creative collages than another group that was not. The collages of the noncompeting children were judged independently to be more spontaneous, novel, varied, and complex.

Kohn points to the field of journalism where it could be argued that competition lowers the quality and accuracy of reporting. He cites the 1985 hijacking of a TWA jetliner by Shiite Moslems as a prime example of competing TV networks "hyping" their stories in an effort to outdo their colleagues. He quotes Fred Friendly, former head of CBS News, as saying, "Too many [news] decisions are made on the basis of beating the competition rather than deciding how to react responsibly."

Extensive research in the field of education cited by Kohn provides further evidence that shows competition lowers performance. David and Roger Johnson, professors at the University of Minnesota, analyzed 122 studies carried out between 1924 and 1981 that collected student performance data produced in competitive, cooperative, and individual learning environments. Their findings concluded that sixty-five studies showed cooperation promotes higher achievement than competition, eight showed the opposite, and thirty-six had no statistically significant difference.

Kohn points out that many of these studies defined achievement in quantitative terms such as speed or units of production. As this inherently favors the competitive approach, it is remarkable that cooperation scored so high in the results. Some early experiments in the 1920s indicated that workers produced more when they were competing against each other than when they were not, but this higher output was also associated with poorer quality. When quality of performance factors were measured in two studies, Kohn reports the Johnsons found that "the discussion process in cooperative groups promotes the discovery and development of higher cognitive strategies for learning than does the individual reasoning found in competitive and individualistic learning situations."

Kohn comes to certain conclusions about why cooperation outperforms competition in the majority of the studies he reviewed. He believes competitive "win-lose" situations increase stress and anxiety in people. This emotional state is fed by the real possibility they will lose the contest, a concern that understandably interferes with the learning process.

He also concludes that cooperation allows the pooling of individual skills and resources to create a synergetic effect. In other words, the collective wisdom of a group working together is usually greater than the total of individual members working alone. In a cooperative environment, people willingly work together to help each other succeed; in a competitive situation, they work just as hard individually to see that their colleagues fail.

Finally, Kohn surmises that in a competitive environment trying to outdo colleagues becomes more important than trying to do well as a group. When the focus is on individual performance, group performance necessarily loses out. In fact, both group and individual performance are hindered when each person is concerned only with his or her own performance.

It also seems that competition and cooperation focus on totally different tasks and activities. Competition's primary objective is to maximize individual output at the expense of quality of work and group cohesiveness. On the other hand, cooperation's primary objective is to organize and pool mutual resources effectively and efficiently, since this tends to increase both the quality and quantity of the group's performance.

Robert Blatchford comments on cooperation versus competition in *Elbert Hubbard's Scrap Book:*

> We are taught, many of us, from our youth onwards, that competition is essential to the health and progress of the race. Or, as Herbert Spencer puts it, "Society flourishes by the antagonism of its atoms." But the obvious golden rule is that cooperation is good and competition bad, and that society flourishes by the mutual

aid of human beings. I say that is obvious, and so it is. And it is
so well known that in all great military or commercial enterprises,
individualism has to be subordinated to collective action. We do
not believe that a house divided against itself shall stand; we believe it shall fall. We know that a State divided by internal feuds
and torn by faction fighting can not hold its own against a united
people. We know that in a cricket or football team, a regiment,
a ship's crew, a school, the "antagonism of the atoms" would
mean defeat and failure. We know that a society composed of an-
tagonistic atoms would not be a society at all, and could not exist
as a society. We know that if men are to found and govern cities,
to build bridges and make roads, to establish universities, to sail
ships and sink mines, and create educational systems, and policies
and religions, they must work together and not against one another. Surely these things are as obvious as the fact that there
could be no hive unless the bees worked as a colony and on the
lines of mutual aid.[1]

Looking at the football team example a little closer, we know that
not everyone can hope to carry the ball into the end-zone for a touch-
down. Someone must snap the ball, a quarterback must hand it off,
and several others must block opposing players out of the way. On any
team, it is not an individual player who wins or loses. **It is the team
as a unit.** In fact, a player who tries to prove himself superior to his
teammates only disrupts its overall effectiveness. Any player whose
main goal is to excel at the expense of his colleagues wins or loses on
this basis alone, and he is bound to lose more often than he wins. But
even in winning, he loses, since he has not learned how to function
cooperatively. For it is only through cooperation with his teammates
that he will excel both individually and as a member of a larger group.

A Theory of Motivation

Every motivational study ever conducted has arrived at the same
conclusion: *people perform best at tasks they themselves are motivated to perform.* Why is this the case? It appears motivation is a mystery to most people. While it has often been written about, it remains
little understood.

Motivation is most commonly associated with business, but in fact
it affects human relationships in any organization or group, whether
a family, a school, or the corner store. It is as important to the Girl or
Boy Scouts as it is to the armed forces or IBM. Anyone who is respon-

sible for the results of other people's efforts must attempt to instill intrinsic motivation in them if he or she wants to be successful.

Motivation is a contraction of the phrase "motive-in-action." It is the personification of a goal being strived for, the pursuit of something deemed desirable and worthwhile.

Motivation is brought about by furnishing another person with one or more motives to do as you ask. Take a robber who holds a gun to your head and growls, "Your money or your life!" Instantly he has furnished you with a motive to do what he wants you to do—your desire to stay alive. At another level, imagine being asked by a prestigious citizen's group to head the national United Way campaign whose honorary chairperson is the president of the United States. As before, the group is providing you with one or more motives to do as it asks, in this case, your desire to receive recognition from people you respect, and to serve others in some meaningful way.

The "carrot-and-stick" approach is traditionally associated with what is called "economic man," a term coined by classical economists looking for a simplistic way to explain human behavior. The philosopher Alfred North Whitehead once wistfully wrote, "The beauty of the economic man was that we knew exactly what he was after." He was portrayed as being a fearful, timid creature who worked only because he had to survive, while at the same time he was considered greedy and opportunistic, always eager to acquire more of the material benefits the world had to offer.

Peter Drucker, hailed today as the father of modern management, published a book in 1939 titled *The End of Economic Man*. In it, he refuted the contention that economic self-interest was the mighty force in human dynamics that the classical economists claimed. "We know nothing about motivation. All we can do is write books about it," he said. His view may be a bit harsh, but it does make its point: the modern man and woman are driven by motives much more mysterious and complex than originally thought.

Clearly the modern worker is motivated by more than the lure of money and security or the threat of discipline and dismissal. Money is not the only thing people want. Otherwise, rich people would be the happiest people on earth. But at the same time, there is no evidence the average person has stopped wanting it or the things it can buy. As well, people naturally try to avoid trouble and confrontation, and prefer the comfort and security of a steady job.

Management theorists have come to classify such things as job and financial security as low-level motivators that produce nothing more than low-level performance. "To get people to do mediocre work, one need only *drive them*, using coercive and reward power in a manipulative way," writes James J. Cribben in his book *Effective Managerial Leadership*. "To elicit their top performance," he continues, "one must get them to *drive themselves*" [emphasis added].

The modern manager must understand that it is his or her primary responsibility to help employees perform at their very best. This means creating and maintaining the proper psychological climate and designing work packages such that people are able to perform at the peak of their abilities.

Leadership aims to allow people to motivate themselves to move in the desired direction because they want to.

The process of influencing people to do their utmost for the organization is necessarily one of good leadership. Leadership aims to allow people to motivate themselves to move in the desired direction, to feel compelled to perform at a high level, because *they want to.* The opposite of good leadership is a form of dictatorship, where an unwilling effort is forced out of people by the crude application of power. The objective should always be to instill people with high-level motivation, since it alone produces high-level results.

There have been many theories about how managers should go about motivating people, but only one thing seems certain: if the motivation is to come from within an individual, it must be because *the needs and wants that dwell deep within the human psyche are being satisfied.* In other words, the work environment and job packages must be such that people thoroughly enjoy what they are doing, and are deriving high-level psychological benefits and rewards as a result of their efforts.

The most accepted theory on inherent needs and wants was formulated by Abraham Maslow in his classic work *Motivation and Person-*

ality. Maslow divided the needs and desires of healthy people into five broad catagories that represent the sum total of their personality, their innermost motivations and aspirations as shown in Figure 6, Chapter 6. It is much easier to understand human behavior once you realize that people do and say the things they do because they have specific needs and desires that are looking for fulfillment. These needs and desires include *physiological needs* such as food, air, rest, sex, shelter, other bodily functions, and protection from the elements. These drives result from the body's automatic efforts to maintain itself in a state of health and harmony. The bloodstream, for example, must maintain a constant temperature and a specific level of water, salt, sugar, protein, fat, and oxygen at all times.

Physiological drives are the most basic of all human motivations. If a person is lacking food, safety, social acceptance, and self-respect all at the same time, his or her need to satisfy the hunger drive would predominate. This is not to say the other drives cease to exist. They merely fade into the background temporarily until lower-level motivators have been satisfied. For example, a very hungry person will always be obsessed with finding food until this basic need has been satisfied. Until it is, he or she is able to concentrate on little else.

So what happens after a person has been satisfied at the basic physiological level, when his or her belly is full and all the other physiological needs and desires have been met? Simply enough, other needs emerge at the next higher level of motivation, and they begin to dominate a person's behavior.

The second tier of needs and wants are referred to as the *safety needs,* and they include freedom from fear and protection against danger, threat, and deprivation. People in our society want to live in a safe, organized world that assures them of an orderly, predictable way of life. This involves a safe environment that ensures protection against physical and psychological harm. Just as a hungry person is calmed and appeased with food, so a fearful person is made to feel safe and secure when provided with protection.

We see the face of protection all around us in our society. Physical protection is provided by the Neighborhood Watch, the local and state police, the National Guard, and the armed forces. Health protection is provided by professionally trained doctors and nurses, and the clinics and hospitals where they work. Financial security is provided in the form of medical, unemployment, and disability insurance, and government-backed home loans and mortgages. Protection is a major preoccupation of our society and must be provided if people are to aspire to higher levels of satisfaction and personal achievement.

After needs at both the physiological and safety levels have been satisfied, *social needs* such as love, acceptance, and affiliation emerge and begin to dominate a person's behavior. At this third level, a person wants to have close friends and loved ones, and the affection this generates. Association with friends, family, and other groups is very important. Social needs are met when you are accepted by friends, family, and other people for who you are and what you represent. The key to satisfying these mid-level motivators is being able to both give and receive love and affection, and to accept and be accepted by others.

These first three levels of motivation are easy enough to understand. People naturally want the basic necessities of life. They want sufficient food, water, air, sleep, and protection from the elements; they want to be safe and secure from external threats and danger; and they want to be able to exchange love and affection with others. Needs at the *ego* and *self-actualization* levels are more complex and difficult to understand.

Once a healthy, well-adjusted person has satisfied basic needs at the first three levels, he or she has a natural desire to feel esteemed and respected, and a compulsive need for high self-worth. The individual wants to exhibit a degree of mastery and competence, and seeks out prestige, status, and opportunities to demonstrate high achievement. A person operating at the ego level has an ongoing, burning desire for recognition of his or her own value. In a word, people want confirmation and acknowledgment of their *self-importance* from others.

The satisfying of ego-related wants and needs affects a person's self-image and feelings of self-worth in a positive way. On the other hand, denial of these same wants and needs detracts from the self-image and the way a person feels. It is important to realize that the craving for self-liking and self-esteem can never be satisfied once and for all. It is like the craving for food that comes and goes, day in and day out, but never goes away completely. Just as you cannot eat once and for all, neither can your desire for self-esteem be satisfied once and for all. It continually reappears and reasserts itself, forever looking for replenishment.

True self-esteem cannot be based solely on the offered opinions of others, from so-called extrinsic sources. Rather it must come from within, from intrinsic, self-generated sources as a result of personal effort to accomplish things that are deemed to be useful. All too often external fame and adoration have been sought to replace an inner craving for self-liking and self-respect, and in each case, this has proven insufficient and unsuccessful. For example, you can be admired by others for a variety of reasons and still regard yourself as undeserving. You can win every honor, yet believe you have accomplished little of importance. And you can be adored by millions, but wake up each morning with the haunting feeling of being afraid and insecure. Ultimately, all your behavior is shaped and controlled by who and what *you think* you are.

We come to the fifth and highest level of motivation, the *self-actualization* level. It is one relatively few people reach only because so few actually possess genuine, high self-esteem. Self-actualization needs call for challenges to one's highest abilities, for opportunities to demonstrate unique competence and creativity, and a desire for a degree of personal autonomy. They represent the ultimate ego gratification of living up to one's highest image of oneself, and becoming everything one is capable of becoming.

The drive toward self-actualization can best be summed up by the statement, "What you believe you can be, you must be." If you believe you can write, you must write. If you believe you can sing, you must sing. If you believe you can excel at something and be successful, you must make the attempt. This inner desire will not go away. It must find a way to be acted upon and actualized.

No one has the same set of wants and needs to the same degree or in the exact same order. One person may desire financial rewards more than love and affection, for example. A person's particular mix of motivations is very much a result of individual upbringing and background. Needs also vary according to time and circumstance. Young people, for instance, usually are less concerned with health and security until they are older. Any attempt to motivate another person to perform well, therefore, requires knowing something about that person's particular personality and makeup, and meeting his or her individual needs.

Recent attitude surveys of employees show that the factors that led to high morale and satisfaction a generation ago—creature comfort and security needs—no longer apply to the same extent. Present-day workers tend to place greater emphasis on challenging work, recognition for a job well done, individual responsibility, and opportunities for personal growth, professional development, and advancement.

This is to say what motivated employees and made them happy and function at their optimum in the 1950s and 1960s has changed. The need levels have moved more in the direction of ego and self-actualization needs, a natural progression toward greater development of human potential. At the same time, the desire to be happy hasn't changed at all. It is still the ultimate goal of most people.

William James identified this universal trait long ago when he wrote, "If we were to ask the question, 'What is life's chief concern?' one of the answers we should receive would be: 'It is happiness.' How to gain, how to keep, how to recover happiness is in fact the secret motive of all we do, and all we are willing to endure." And William Butler Yeats (1865-1939), Irish essayist and poet, added his comment that "Happiness is neither virtue nor pleasure nor this thing nor that, but simple growth. *We are happy when we are growing*" [emphasis added].

Various approaches and techniques have been developed and tried over the years to instill more intrinsic motivation in people, all aiming for greater productivity. Two approaches have consistently proven effective. They represent a small beginning in understanding a subject we know very little about, a subject that is still surrounded more with fiction than with fact, more with speculation than with specificity.

First, we'll consider the research carried out by Frederick Herzberg, currently distinguished professor of management at the University of Utah, whose writings include the book *Work and the Nature of Man*. He also wrote a landmark article that appeared in the January-February 1968 issue of the *Harvard Business Review* titled "One More Time: How Do You Motivate Employees?"[2] The article has sold more reprints than any other ever published by this prestigious magazine. Herzberg's findings regarding what he calls *motivation and maintenance factors* provide a fascinating approach and in-depth understanding of what is required to motivate employees on a consistent basis.

Second, we will review the *quality circle* approach to management, a technique pioneered in the late 1940s by W. Edwards Deming, an American engineer. Deming lectured widely in post-World War II Japan on statistical methods for quality control. He stressed the need for production workers and managers to work cooperatively together to ensure consistently high quality. The Japanese took Deming's ideas and combined them with their own belief in bringing people together in small groups to solve work-related problems. At the core of the Japanese approach is a conviction that production workers are in the best position to identify and correct quality-related problems, and that management had to tap this essential resource if quality, design, and productivity improvements were to be achieved.

Herzberg's Motivation/ Maintenance Theory

Herzberg's contribution to understanding motivation in the workplace is unique. His research shattered many long-standing American myths concerning ways to motivate employees effectively.

Have you ever sat down and really analyzed why motivation is so important? Employees with motivational problems cost organizations thousands, even millions, of dollars each year. Research indicates that only 20 percent of employees can cause 100 percent of the grievances, 45 percent of the absences, 52 percent of the garnishments, 38 percent of the medical claims, and 40 percent of all sick leave.

To return to the carrot-and-stick analogy, Herzberg explains that a push from behind with a stick or a pull from the front with a carrot has nothing to do with internal, intrinsic motivation. The only result of either of these tactics is that the donkey "moves," *but not of his own free will.* He moves only so long as he is forced or enticed to do so by external motivators. This is like having to regularly recharge an employee's battery each and every day he or she comes to work instead of the battery being recharged of its own accord. If an individual is truly self-motivated, his or her battery is always being recharged internally and the individual doesn't need continuous encouragement from outside sources. A self-motivated person functions at a high level automatically, and needs only occasional guidance and support to keep him or her headed in the right direction.

American companies have experimented with a great many approaches to get more and better quality effort out of people. Salary, stock options, and profit-sharing schemes abound; employee salary and benefit packages increase annually without any direct relationship to productivity; and expensive training and personal development programs of every kind and description have been conducted to teach employees and managers alike new and more effective coping techniques. Whether the objective has been improved communications skills, sensitivity training, or employee counseling, all have been aimed at instilling more motivation in employees and improving productivity in the workplace.

Herzberg believes that all these approaches, on balance, have failed to achieve what is intended. His motivation-maintenance theory regarding job attitudes was developed initially based on an examination of events in the job-related experiences of several hundred engineers and accountants. His research was later expanded to include numerous workers and professionals, including lower-level supervisors, professional women, agricultural administrators, imminent management retirees, hospital maintenance personnel, manufacturing supervisors, and nurses. All of these studies came to the same general conclusion.

Herzberg found the factors that led to job satisfaction and motivation are different from the factors that led to job dissatisfaction. He explains that job satisfaction and job dissatisfaction are not necessarily diametrically opposite. The opposite of job satisfaction can be NO job satisfaction, just as the opposite of job dissatisfaction can be NO job dissatisfaction.

Herzberg reached some interesting conclusions. He found that factors relating to the job's general environment were primarily job dissatisfiers. In other words, failure to improve these factors led to dissatisfaction on the job, while their improvement led only to no job dissatisfaction—*but not job satisfaction.* These factors extrinsic to the work itself included company policy and administration, supervision, interpersonal relations, working conditions, salary, status, and security.

Alternatively, he found that factors relating directly to the job itself were primarily job satisfiers. Failure to improve these factors simply led to no job satisfaction, while their improvement led to *greater job satisfaction and intrinsic motivation.* These factors included opportunities for personal growth and advancement, amount of responsibility, the challenging nature of the work, personal recognition, and sense of accomplishment.

The evidence indicates that most job dissatisfiers are more closely related to lower-level motivators, while most job satisfiers are more closely related to higher-level motivators as defined by Maslow in his hierarchy of human needs and wants. For example, dissatisfiers include the job environment and the security and protection, or lack of it, that is provided. Satisfiers include factors relating directly to personal growth and achievement, and the psychological benefits and rewards they produce.

Here is a summary of his findings:

POSITIVE FACTORS LEADING PRIMARILY TO JOB SATISFACTION

achievement, recognition, work itself, responsibility,
advancement, and growth

POSITIVE FACTORS LEADING PRIMARILY
TO NO JOB DISSATISFACTION

company policy and administration, supervision, relationship
with supervisor, work conditions, personal life, status, and security

Herzberg uses the results he obtained to promote the case for job content as being central to generating intrinsic motivation as opposed to the case for environmental factors. For example, of all the factors found to contribute to job satisfaction, 81 percent were job-related; of all the factors contributing to job dissatisfaction, 69 percent were found to be environment-related. His recommendation to managers to bring about higher productivity and better personnel utilization is to enrich job packages. This could involve such things as assigning more specialized and difficult tasks to capable individuals, allowing them more authority and scope in their work packages, and making employees more accountable for their own performance.

With greater authority, accountability, and scope in their work, employees naturally derive a greater sense of accomplishment in their lives. They feel they are growing and improving, that they have more responsibility and control, and that they are receiving recognition commensurate with their performance. Clearly, self-motivation results from receiving high-level rewards and benefits that naturally accrue from doing interesting and challenging work.

Herzberg's message is as relevant and important today as when he first proposed it. Employers cannot hope to increase productivity by simply spending more money on employees. Higher wages and better fringe benefits do not automatically increase employee satisfaction and motivation. Yet this seems to be the trend we are witnessing at the present time. It can result in people earning more even while working less, which a University of Michigan survey shows is actually happening. At the same time, fringe benefit packages are expanding proportionately faster than salaries. Not only is this approach less productive, it contributes to greater employee malaise and a false sense of security. Industries that cannot compete in a world economy are not going to survive. Employees who demand and receive excessive wage and fringe benefit increases in the short term are only going to bring about their demise in the long term, if not sooner. Recall Chrysler Corporation's near collapse in the 1970s as an example.

Job enrichment as an option to increase employee satisfaction is particularly effective in situations where employees have reached a plateau in their career and prospects for future promotion are unlikely. Employees in such situations often feel caught in a rut, that their competence is not being fully utilized or recognized. There are probably millions of people in blue- and white-collar positions today who have little or no hope of progressing above their current level.

All too often job packages have remained static for years, and have not kept pace with changes either in the nature of the work or in new technology available to deal with it. Nor have they generally kept pace with the higher expectations of the workforce and their higher level of education and training. Too many managers have overlooked job packages as a motivational tool, believing that other means had to be found to stimulate people.

The argument for job enrichment can be put in these terms: if you have good people, provide them with interesting and challenging work. Increase their level of responsibility whenever possible and recognize their efforts. Allow them to feel a real sense of accomplishment and grow as people. Otherwise, you will have serious motivational problems on your hands that can result only in needless waste and expense in both monetary and human terms.

Quality Circles

Another practical way to enrich jobs and get more out of people is to increase employee participation in workplace decisions through quality circles. Quality circles, commonly called QC's, expose employees to areas of activity beyond the scope of their own usual input. In this way, employees are able to see the bigger picture and how their own efforts help contribute to a complete unit of work. The goal of QC's is to help enrich an employee's experience, and expand his or her involvement and overall commitment. It is to make each person feel part of an overall team effort and allow him or her to identify more closely with the company's success.

QC's are based firmly on the theories and research already discussed concerning human motivation and behavior, particularly those of Abraham Maslow and Frederick Herzberg. Their findings indicate that employees are more motivated and productive when the jobs they perform meet their needs for personal growth and sense of accomplishment.

After World War II, QC's in Japan became part of a collaborative government and industry effort to modernize the country's industrial base and improve the quality of its manufactured goods. It took about thirty years, but by the mid-1970s, the words MADE IN JAPAN had changed from being something that detracted from a product to something that helped distinguish it, especially regarding its quality.

While Japan was rapidly moving ahead by using QC's to tap individual creative and productive abilities, U.S. industry was stagnating. The traditional view of American management was that all the typical worker had to do was work at his or her particular area of specialization and perform only a few well-defined tasks that he or she was specifically trained to do. It assumed workers were motivated primarily by economic factors and that they were indifferent to the intrinsic benefits that challenging and interesting work could offer. With this archaic attitude widely prevailing in the minds of U.S. managers, it is no surprise QC's were slow to be introduced here.

All this began to change in the late 1970s. The effects of the U.S. recession and the infusion of higher-quality Japanese products into the lucrative U.S. market combined to force American managers to seek out newer, more effective ways to increase worker productivity and reduce labor costs. They began to experiment with QC's because they seemed to be among the easiest of the more successful Japanese management techniques to implement.

Experience has shown that quality circles are most effective when they are used for specific purposes. For example, they could be used to gather employee ideas and suggestions on such things as paper flow and decision-making. They are also ideally suited for special projects that deal with unexpected or multidimensional problems such as quality, inventory control, or scheduling. As well, QC's are an ideal tool to experiment with more involved participative management techniques aimed at frontline workers. Generally, QC's represent a low-risk way to begin greater employee involvement in a firm's day-to-day activities, since they do not require any major change in organizational structure or management style.

Patrick Townsend, author of the book *Commit to Quality*, refined and expanded the QC concept into the quality team, or QT concept. Many American firms saw merit in this approach, and began using QT's in such critical areas as new product development. Both Ford Motor Company in its Taurus program and General Motors in its Saturn project opted for the team concept to allow maximum creativity and risk-taking in the design of new models. The teams were composed of people from all the key functional areas, and were allowed complete autonomy from the rest of the company to carry out their mission. In this way, team members were protected from more conservative elements in the company and from interdepartmental rivalries that always exist over who has ultimate control and the final say.

If quality circles are to become a more effective management tool to involve workers in key decision-making, participants will have to be given wider scope and more responsibility in their application. This will require worker participation in every facet of any problem resolution. These involve problem identification and analysis, solution generation, management evaluation and decision-making, trial implementation, monitoring and feedback, modification, and final implementation.

Today, QC's are widely accepted in America as a useful employee participation technique to improve worker productivity and organizational effectiveness. But it must be remembered that they represent only a limited first step toward meaningful employee involvement. If QC's are to have a much greater impact, more significant changes will have to take place, especially in the attitude of managers toward employees and the importance of their contributions, and in the way organizations are structured.

One manager let his employees know just how valuable each one was by writing the following memorandum, as reported in the *Pasadena Weekly Journal of Business*. It clearly demonstrates how *each person* is a critical part of any team or organization, and must do his or her part to ensure that the group works together and succeeds as a unit. Consider the effect on the *quality* of the work produced when only one person (or key) is not functioning properly.

XVXRY PXRSON IS IMPORTANT

Xvxn though my typxwritxr is an old modxl, it works vxry wxll — xxcxpt for onx kxy. You would think that with all thx othxr kxys functioning propxrly, onx kxy not working would hardly bx noticxd; but just onx kxy out of whack sxxms to ruin thx wholx xffort.

You may say to yoursxlf — Wxll, I'm only onx pxrson. No onx will noticx if I don't do my bxst. But it doxs makx a diffxrxncx bxcausx to bx xffxctivx an organization nxxds activx participation by xvxry onx to thx bxst of his or hxr ability.

So thx nxxt timx you think you arx not important, rxmxmbxr my old typxwritxr. *You arx a kxy pxrson* [emphasis added].

The last few years have seen a virtual explosion in QC's, particularly in the U.S. In a national survey by the New York Stock Exchange in 1982, it was found that 44 percent of all companies with more than five hundred employees had QC programs in place. There are now approximately seven thousand members in the Association for Quality and Participation, a group that had only one hundred members in 1978. QC's are now being applied to disciplines other than just quality control. They include financial management, marketing, personnel administration, research and development, crisis management, and strategic planning. There is probably no facet of an organization that cannot benefit from QC's and greater employee involvement in its operations.

All of the evidence we have seen in this chapter supports various leadership strategies that can make a significant difference in increasing the productivity of people in the workplace. The fact that some of the research originated many years ago only underscores the fact that we have a lot more to learn about people and how to influence and motivate them effectively, and in positive, predictable ways.

In the end, we are left with this ultimate challenge: how to maximize the human potential we possess and that of the people around us.

The Formula: A Last Look

Recall Mike, our peak-performing salesperson described at length in Chapter 1, who earned commissions that were five times higher than the average of his peers.

What enabled Mike to perform at such a high level? Physically, Mike was no different from all the others. It was only *the quality of his internal representations* that set him apart. He had exceptional "picture-images" rather than average "picture-images" dominating his subconscious reality. This is the principal difference between people who achieve average results and those who achieve exceptional results in their lives.

From what we have learned in this book, we can put everything together and take a final look at our performance equation

$$P = SIF \times (HW + FOS), \text{ where}$$

- *P* is a particular level of performance for a particular activity;
- *HW* is your hardware, the single constant factor that represents your basic equipment, the physical mind and body you were born with; and
- *SIF*, your self-image factor, and *FOS*, various key factors of success, are the two variable factors a person contributes to the process. When combined, these two factors, both personal and unique to you, represent your particular manner of thinking when processed through your mental and physical assets.

Thus Mike's ability to perform well at selling (P) is primarily a function of the two variable factors, SIF, the way he sees himself as a salesperson, and FOS, the twelve key factors of success as applied to his particular profession. In other words, if Mike *thinks like a winner* and diligently applies all twelve key factors of success in his chosen work, then he *will be a winner!*

You need only substitute maximum point scores for SIF and FOS into the performance equation in order to see how to get maximum performance out of it.

$$P = \text{(a very high self-image)}$$

times

$$(HW + \text{the twelve key factors of success}).$$

In other words, **P = PEAK PERFORMANCE!!!**

Conclusion

"The first and best victory is to conquer self; to be conquered by self is of all things, the most shameful and vile."
— Plato

You Control Your Life

The central theme of this book is that you can control your life through the thinking you engage in. As Marcus Aurelius observed, "A man's life is what his thoughts make of it." After all, what is life but a series of thoughts and experiences? Thoughts represent the substance of life and create the world as you know and accept it to be. It follows it is through your thoughts that you are empowered to change your life and the world you live in, and change them for the better if you choose.

We have seen how control over your life is possible from our discussion of *the five great wonders of the mind*. As you'll recall, they are:

First, you have the ability to control what you think about from minute to minute and day to day.

Second, you have the ability to creatively imagine your future in the precise way you want it to evolve.

Third, you have the ability to access information from a source beyond your conscious self.

Fourth, you have the ability to eliminate negative thoughts and emotions from your life.

Fifth, you have the ability to act the part of the person you most want to be, with the abilities and characteristics you most want to have.

All five wonders of the mind demonstrate one key fact: *you create your own reality.*

All causation is mental. Everything that is happening to you in your life today is determined by the contents of your mind, by the mental images you hold and cling to. It is through your thoughts that you live and experience life, and it is through your thoughts that you can change your life.

We have embarked upon a new era of great discovery and technological change. We have moved from the shining knight on horseback to a screaming fighter jet traveling at Mach 2.5. A microchip can store 100,000 bits of information on the head of a pin. A supercomputer can carry out 10 million arithmetic calculations in a millisecond with ease.

But as incredible as all of this seems, technology has only advanced the way we *already think* to new heights. It has not improved our thinking in any way, since only humans, not machines, can think.

Take the fact that a personal computer can print out the text of this book on a laser printer in less than one hour, far faster than any typist could perform the same task. Yet the computer is not able to improve on the *thinking* that is represented by the text itself. Technological progress has only provided us with more efficient means to move either *forward or backward.*

So it remains for us to enter the era of self-discovery, to uncover and unfold our full human potential. There can be no greater challenge for individuals than to make the most of their natural talents and abilities. Life is an unending process of self-discovery and self-awareness.

Change Is Inevitable

The world is changing at a pace never before witnessed by Mankind. Some people don't seem to know this is happening, others are casually watching it happen, while a few are helping to make it happen. Have you seriously considered what you can contribute to this process? Do you want to effect change in your personal and professional life . . . or have change affect you?

The following are examples of changes currently taking place in the business world that you should know about:

- A trend away from strict supervision toward teamwork.

- A trend away from specialization toward multi-skilling.

- A trend away from traditional management toward general management by all employees.

- A trend away from selective information sharing toward general information sharing.

- A trend away from limited rewards programs toward extensive rewards programs.

- A trend away from vertical hierarchies toward horizontal networks.

- A trend away from isolated on-the-job training toward extensive, continuous retraining.

- A trend away from higher productivity for only blue-collar workers toward higher productivity for white-collar workers as well.

All of these trends are directed toward humanizing organizational structures and processes, and maximizing individual human potential. Organizations do not survive on technology alone. They survive on people and their ability *to effect change* to meet new challenges and opportunities. "Human freedom never means the freedom to escape the fundamental trends of an epoch," are the wise words of American author Langdon Gilkey.

The Purpose of Life

We all wonder at some point why we have been put on earth and what the purpose of life is. Of course, there are various views on this subject, and we'll address only three possibilities.

The first is the humanistic view, which holds that you should do everything possible to reach your full potential, that you should strive to be the best that you can be. Second, fundamentalists hold that Man's ultimate purpose and reason for living is to glorify his Creator. The third, as many great leaders throughout history have taught and shown by their example, is to serve your fellow human beings. Jesus of Nazareth, Buddha, Mohammed, Mother Teresa, and Albert Schweitzer are all examples of people who committed their whole lives to the service of others.

Whatever view you are most comfortable with, there is a great deal of synergy and consistency in all of these approaches. It could be argued that to serve others is the greatest challenge to individual talents and abilities. It also helps to glorify our Creator by working together and helping each other rise above common poverty, despair, and human failing so prevalent in today's world.

Whether you believe your purpose in life is to reach your full potential, glorify our Creator, or serve others, it can only be achieved through personal sacrifice, persistent effort, and cooperative dealings with others. You must find something bigger and grander than yourself, a cause that stirs your emotions like no other. Each of us should strive to make this world a better place than we first found it. And it remains with each of us to decide what contributions we are able to make.

A Philosophy of Life

The noted Austrian-born psychiatrist and educator, Rudolf Dreikurs (1897-1972), has formulated what he calls "The Ten Premises for a Philosophy of Life." These premises, more than anything else I have discovered, encapsulate and embody the essence of what has been presented in this book. Please read them over carefully, think about them, and imagine a world in which they are accepted and practiced by a majority of the people.

1. Man is inherently neither good nor bad. His social usefulness and personal efficiency depend on his individual training and development, on his own interpretation of his early experiences, and on the life situations with which he is confronted.

2. Man is not aware of his individual strength and powers. He has intellectual, moral, and creative capacities which he does not recognize and, therefore, cannot fully utilize.

3. Man can control his own actions. Emotions are not his master but his tools. He is motivated by his convictions, his attitudes, and his goals which he sets for himself, although he often may not be aware of them, nor realize their fallacies.

4. Man influences his own destiny without knowing it; he is aware more of what is done to him than what he does to others.

5. Man's greatest obstacle to full social participation and co-operation is an underestimation of his own strength and value. Educational methods and training procedures tend to instill false concepts and attitudes about oneself in comparison with others, and cultural patterns fortify them.

6. Man's greatest evil is fear. Courage and belief in his own ability are the basis for all his virtues. Through his realization of his own value he can feel a sense of belonging, and be interested in others.

7. The basis of harmonious human relationships is respect for one's own dignity, combined with respect for the rights and dignity of others. It precludes a settlement of human conflicts through force and appeasement. Social equilibrium is obtainable only through free agreement of equals in the spirit of democracy.

8. Man is the ruler in democracy; therefore, every member of society is entitled to the same dignity and respect which is accorded to a sovereign. Fundamental human equality is not affected by any individual incidental characteristic like race, color, religion, sex, age, social and economic position, education, physical or mental health and beauty, moral or intellectual development, skill, or personal achievement. Any assumption of superiority or inferiority on the basis of such incidental factors is arbitrary and fallacious.

9. Peace of mind and peace on *earth* can be achieved when man will abolish the superiority of one man over the other, when each person's value will be firmly established in his own mind as well as in the minds of his fellow men, and when no compensatory desire for prestige or power will set man against his fellow man.

10. We need each other's constant help to maintain our vision of what we each could be, to fortify our good intentions and noble aspirations, and to counteract the discouraging and demoralizing experiences to which we are all exposed in our daily living.[1]

Consider for a moment this old and insightful quatrain regarding the way you may want to effect change in your life:

> What kind of world
> would this world be,
> If everyone in it
> were just like me?

Now substitute the words "home," "school," "church," "company," "community," and "nation" for "world" to round out your personal self-improvement program. The attitude and behavior you demonstrate have a direct and lasting effect, either positive or negative, on the personality and behavior of other groups and the people in them.

The way you think and act has a very real impact on the world around you, and on the way it treats you in turn. All renewal must begin with the self. As Pope Jean-Paul II said, "Before renewing the systems, the institutions, and the methods, one must seek renewal at the heart of man first."

The Ultimate Secret of Success

The only thing in the world you and you alone can control is what you are thinking about *at this very instant.* This is your own territory, your private domain. To most, this doesn't seem very significant or even worth doing, *yet it is the secret to all happiness and success in life.* For the way you think determines who you are, and who you are determines your contribution to the groups and organizations of which you are necessarily a part.

As Walt Whitman (1819-1892), the American poet, put it: "The whole theory of the universe is directed unerringly to one single individual—*namely to you*" [emphasis added].

In a fast-paced, chaotic world, it is easy for the average person to feel insignificant. After all, there are more than five billion people on earth all wondering what the future holds for them and the rest of humankind. Yet it is individual thought that collectively shapes and determines the course of human history. Men and women neither more nor less important than you or I have made and continue to make large and small contributions to help the world become a better place to live in. And so can you. Some of their names have been mentioned in this book. All are average people except for the quality of their thinking.

You are unique. Your particular footprint has never walked on the face of the earth before and never will again. Nor will another voice sing out encouragement and praise to people with the particular sound and characteristics of the voice you possess. All of the contributions you leave behind will be unique as well—the things you have said, the acts you have performed, and the people you have touched. *It remains for you to DREAM what you dare to dream, DO what you dare to do, and BE what you dare to be!*

"Fear not that thy life shall come to an end, but rather fear that it shall never have a beginning," was the sage advice of Cardinal John Henry Newman (1801-1890), English theologian and writer.

To the hopeful of this world, your life is at a crossroad. Two voices are calling. One is from the depths of selfishness and despair, where all success means failure. The other is from the heights of human service and enlightenment, where even failure means success. Both these lights shine brightly over all humankind. One leads to self-indulgence and servitude, while the other leads to inner peace and prosperity. Let us resolve to replace the sad sobbings of the downhearted with the glad tidings of human dignity through the realization of human potential.

It is through your thoughts that you can enrich your life and control your destiny. You can rise to any height, and find peace, happiness, and unlimited power within you. ***You can become all that you want and deserve to be.*** Ultimately, it all depends on your particular manner of thinking.

Now that you know how to think like a winner, you can begin ***to be a winner!*** You can break through the "success" barrier simply by selecting your target and pursuing it with all your talents and abilities, and all the energy at your command. It is a journey like no other you can hope to have. I, your fellow traveler, wish you well on your quest into self-discovery.

THE BEGINNING

About the Author

Dr. Walter Staples has written four books on personal and professional development. He is a certified practitioner of Neuro-Linguistic Programming (NLP).

He has lived in many parts of the United States, Europe and Canada. It was while living in Los Angeles that he met many of the leaders in the field of personal development, including Anthony Robbins, Brian Tracy, Ken Blanchard and Jim Rohn—all of whom took an active interest in his work.

Think Like A Winner is currently available in bookstores throughout North America and in over 25 other countries around the world. It has been translated into Japanese, French, Spanish, German, Portuguese and Afrikaan.

The endorsements for his many books read like a *Who's Who* in the field of motivation, including Dr. Norman Vincent Peale, Art Linkletter, Denis Waitley and Dr. Robert Schuller. His books and articles have been featured in many prominent national magazines, including *Entrepreneur, Readers Digest, USAir Magazine* and *AmericaWest Airlines Magazine.*

Dr. Staples has been interviewed on over 100 radio and television programs in the U.S. and Canada. He is one of America's most highly acclaimed authors on the subject of leadership, motivation and human potential.

He is president of Peak Performance Learning Systems and is a speaker, consultant and trainer for many of America's most successful corporations.

Notes

CHAPTER ONE

1.   Definition of the verb "to think." By permission. From *Webster's Ninth New Collegiate Dictionary.* Copyright © by Merriam-Webster, Inc., publisher of the Merriam-Webster dictionaries, 47 Federal Street, P.O. Box 281, Springfield, MA 01102.

*2.   Poem titled "Thoughts Are Things" by Henry Van Dyke. Copyright holder unknown.

CHAPTER TWO

1.   Quote from *Possibilities* magazine by John Marks Templeton. By permission. Copyright © 1986 The Robert Schuller Ministries, 4201 W. Chapman Ave., Orange, CA 92668.

2.   Poem titled "Beliefs." Anonymous.

CHAPTER THREE

1.   Quote from *Advanced Psycho Cybernetics and Pyschofeedback* by Paul Thomas. By permission. Copyright © 1985 by Paul Thomas. Reprinted by permission of Classic Publishers, 150 S. Barrington Avenue, Los Angeles, CA 90049.

2.   Poem titled "Equipment" from *Collected Verse of Edgar A. Guest.* By permission. Copyright © 1934 by Edgar A. Guest. Contemporary Books, Inc., 298 Fifth Avenue, New York, N.Y. 10001.

CHAPTER FOUR

1.   Quote from *The Art of Thinking* by Allen F. Harrison and Robert M. Bramson, Ph.D. By permission. Copyright © 1984 by Allen F. Harrison and Robert M. Bramson, Ph.D. Anchor Press, Doubleday & Co., Inc., 245 Park Avenue, New York, N.Y. 10017.

2.   Quote from *Beyond Biofeedback* by Elmer & Alyce Green. By permission. Copyright © 1977 by Elmer & Alyce Green c/o The Menninger Clinic, Box 829, Topeka, KS 66601-0829.

3.   Poem titled "Yes I Can." Anonymous.

CHAPTER FIVE

1.   Quote from *Self-Consistency: A Theory of Personality* by Prescott Lecky. Copyright © by Prescott Lecky. The Island Press, New York, N.Y.

2.   Quote from *Psycho-Cybernetics* by Maxwell Maltz. By permission. Copyright © 1960 by Maxwell Maltz. Prentice-Hall, Inc., Englewood Cliffs, N.J. 07632.

3.   Quote from *Your Child's Self-Esteem* by Dorothy Corkille Briggs. By permission. Copyright © 1970 by Dorothy Corkille Briggs. Doubleday, a division of Bantam, Doubleday, Dell Publishing Group, Inc., 245 Park Avenue, New York, N.Y. 10017.

CHAPTER SIX

1.   Inherent drives as found in *Motivation and Personality* by Abraham Maslow. By permission. Copyright © 1954 by Abraham Maslow. Harper & Row, Publisher, Inc., 10 East 53rd Street, New York, N.Y. 10022.

2.   Quote from *Language in Thought and Action*, Third Edition, by S.I. Hayakawa. By permission. Copyright © 1972 by S.I. Hayakawa. Harcourt Brace Jovanovich, Inc., 6277 Sea Harbor Drive, Eighth Floor, Orlando, FL 32821.

CHAPTER EIGHT

1.   Quote titled "Attitude" by Charles Swindoll.

2.   Poem titled "Believe in Yourself." Anonymous.

CHAPTER NINE

1.   Interview with Jack LaLanne by Shelby Loosch. By permission. Copyright © 1988 Globe International, Inc, 5401 N. W. Broken Sound Blvd., Boca Raton, FL 33431.

2.   Quote from *Medical Self-Care* by Tom Ferguson. By permission. Copyright © 1980 by Tom Ferguson. Summit Books, 1230 Avenue of the Americas, New York, N.Y. 10020.

3. Quote from *Love, Medicine and Miracles* by Bernard Siegal. By permission. Copyright © 1986 by Harper & Row, Publisher, 10 East 53rd Street, New York, N.Y. 10022.

4. Quote from *Minding the Body, Mending the Mind* by Joan Borysenko. By permission. Copyright © by Addison-Wesley Publishing Company, Route 128, Reading, MA 01867.

5. Quote from *Healing from Within* by Dennis Jaffee. By permission. Copyright © 1988 by Dennis Jaffe. Alfred A. Knopf, 201 East 50th Street, New York, N.Y. 10022.

6. The Holmes-Rahe scale of stress ratings. Printed by permission from *The Journal of Psychosomatic Research,* vol. II: T.H. Holmes and R. H. Rahe, Social Readjustment Rating Scale. Copyright © 1967 by Pergamon Press, Inc., Maxwell House, Fairview Park, Elmsford, N.Y. 10523.

CHAPTER TEN

1. Poem titled "Life For A Penny." Jessie Rittenhouse.

2. Quote from *Excellence* by John W. Gardner. By permission. Copyright © 1984 and 1961 by W. W. Norton & Company, Inc., 500 Fifth Ave., New York, N.Y. 10110.

3. Quote from speech by Isadore Sharp, Chairman, President, and CEO of Four Seasons Hotels, Toronto, Canada.

CHAPTER ELEVEN

*1. Poem titled "Giving and Receiving" by Thomas Gaines. Copyright holder unknown.

CHAPTER TWELVE

1. Quote from *Elbert Hubbard's Scrap Book* by Robert Blatchford. Copyright © 1923 by The Roycrofters.

2. "One More Time: How Do You Motivate Employees?" by Frederick Herzberg. Copyright © 1968 *Harvard Business Review.* By permission. For persons interested in the full article (*Harvard Business Review* September-October 1987), published as an HBR Classic, reprints are available from Harvard Business School Publishing Division, telephone (617) 495-6192.

CONCLUSION

*1.   Quote "The Ten Premises for A Philosophy of Life" by Rudolf Dreikurs. Copyright holder unknown.

---

*A serious effort has been made to locate sources and obtain permissions to quote when required. Instances of unintentional errors or omissions, or inability to find copyright holders, are sincerely regretted. Corrections will be gladly incorporated in future editions.

Bibliography

Allen, James. *As a Man Thinketh*. New York: Gosset and Dunlap, Inc., 1959.

Bennis, Warren and Nanus, Burt. *Leaders: The Strategies for Taking Charge*. New York: Harper and Row Publishers, 1985.

Blanchard, Kenneth and Johnson, Spencer. *The One Minute Manager*. New York: Morrow, 1982.

Borysenko, Joan. *Minding the Body, Mending the Mind*. New York: Addison-Wesley, 1987.

Brande, Dorothea. *Wake Up and Live*. New York: Simon and Schuster, 1936.

Briggs, Dorothy. *Your Child's Self-Esteem: The Key to his Life*. New York: Doubleday, 1970.

Bristol, Claude. *The Magic of Believing*. New York: Prentice-Hall, 1948.

Carnegie, Dale. *How to Win Friends and Influence People*. New York: Simon and Schuster, 1936.

Cousins, Norman. *Anatomy of an Illness As Perceived by the Patient: Reflections on Healing and Regeneration*. New York: Norton, 1979.

Cox, Allan. *The Cox Report on the American Corporation*. New York: Delacorte Press, 1982.

Cribben, James A. *Effective Managerial Leadership*. American Management Association, 1971.

Drucker, Peter. *The End of Economic Man*. 1936.

Dyer, Wayne. *Your Erroneous Zones*. New York: Harper and Row Publishers, 1976.

Dyer, Wayne. *Pulling Your Own Strings*. New York: Harper and Row Publishers, 1978.

Edwards, Betty. *Drawing on the Right Side of the Brain*. Jeremy P. Tarcher, 1979.

Ferguson, Tom. *Medical Self-Care: Access to Health Tools.* New York: Summit Books, 1980.

Fixx, James F. *The Complete Book of Running.* New York: Random House, 1977.

Friedman, Meyer and Rosenman, Ray H. *Type A Behavior and Your Heart.* New York: Knopf, 1981.

Gardner, John W. *Excellence.* New York: Norton, 1961.

Gardner, John W. *Self-Renewal: The Individual and the Innovative Society.* New York: Harper and Row Publishers, 1963.

Green, Elmer and Alyce. *Beyond Biofeedback.* New York: Delacorte Press/S. Lawrence, 1977.

Hayakawa, S. I. *Language In Thought and Action.* New York: Harcourt Brace Javanovich, 1972.

Harrison, Allen F. and Bramson, Robert M. *The Art of Thinking.* New York: Berkley, 1984.

Hertzberg, Frederick. *Work and the Nature of Man.* World, 1966.

Hill, Napoleon. *Think and Grow Rich.* New York: Fawcett, 1983.

Hubbard, Elbert. *Elbert Hubbard's Scrap Book.* New York: William H. Wise & Co., 1923.

Jaffe, Dennis. *Healing from Within.* New York: Alfred A. Knopf, Inc., 1988.

James, William. *Principles of Psychology.* Dover, 1950

Kosslyn, Stephen M. *Human Abilities.* W. H. Freeman and Co., 1985.

Koestenbaum, Peter. *The Heart of Business.* Dallas: Saybrook Publishing Co., 1987.

Kohn, Alfie. *No Contest: The Case Against Competition.* New York: Houghton-Mifflin, 1986.

Lecky, Prescott. *Self-Consistency: A Theory of Personality.* New York, The Island Press.

Lorayne, Harry and Lucas, Jerry. *The Memory Book.* New York: Random House, 1974.

Maltz, Maxwell, *Psycho-Cybernetics.* New York: Prentice-Hall, 1960.

Maslow, Abraham. *Motivation and Personality.* New York: Harper and Row Publishers, 1954.

Nesbitt, John. *Megatrends: Ten New Directions Transforming Our Lives.* New York: Warner Books, 1982.

Newman, James. *Release Your Brakes!* New York: Warner Books, 1978.

Osborn, Alex F. *Applied Imagination*. New York: Scribner's, 1953.

Peale, Norman Vincent. *The Power of Positive Thinking*. New York: Prentice-Hall, 1952.

Peter, Laurence J. and Hull, Raymond. *The Peter Principle: Why Things Always Go Wrong*. New York: Morrow, 1969.

Peters, Thomas J. and Waterman, Jr., Robert H. *In Search of Excellence: Lessons from America's Best Run Companies*. New York: Harper and Row, 1982.

Robbins, Anthony. *Unlimited Power*. New York: Fawcett, 1986.

Schuller, Robert H. *Tough Times Never Last, But Tough People Do!* Nashville, TN: Thomas Nelson, Inc., 1983.

Schuller, Robert H. *The Be-Happy Attitudes*. Waco, Texas: Word Books, 1985.

Schultz, Johannes H. and Luthe, Wolfgang. *Autogenic Therapy*. Grune, 1969.

Schwartz, David, J. *The Magic of Thinking Big*. Englewood Cliffs, N.J.: Prentice-Hall, 1959.

Schinn, George. *The Miracle of Motivation*. Wheaton, Ill.: Tyndale House, 1981.

Siegel, Bernie. *Love, Medicine and Miracles*. New York: Harper and Row Publishers, 1986.

Stone, W. Clement. *Success Through A Positive Mental Attitude*. Englewood Cliffs, N.J.: Prentice-Hall, 1960.

Stone, W. Clement. *The Success System That Never Fails*. Englewood Cliffs, N.J.: Prentice-Hall, 1962.

Thomas, Paul. *Advanced Psycho Cybernetics and Psychofeedback*. Los Angeles: Classic Publishers, 1985.

Waitley, Denis. *The Psychology of Winning*. New York: Berkley, 1979.

Waitley, Denis. *Seeds of Greatness*. Old Tappan, N.J.: Fleming H. Revell Company, 1983.

Yankelovich, Daniel & Associates. *Work and Human Values*. New York: Public Agenda Foundation, 1983.

Zdenek, Marilee. *The Right-Brain Experience*. New York: McGraw-Hill, 1983.

Ziglar, Zig. *See You at the Top*. Gretna, La.: Pelican Publishing, 1974.

Index

Treat Yourself to This Fun, Inspirational Book and Discover How to
Find Happiness and Serenity . . . No Matter What Life Dishes Out

The Dragon Slayer
With a Heavy Heart

*This new book by bestselling author Marcia Powers promises to be
one of the most important you will ever read—and one of the most
entertaining, uplifting, and memorable.*

*It brings the Serenity Prayer—which for years has been the guiding
light of 12-step programs worldwide—to everyone . . . and teaches
both new and longtime devotees how to apply it most effectively to
their lives.*

Sometimes things happen we wish hadn't. Sometimes things *don't*
happen we wish *would*. In the course of living, problems arise, both
big and small. We might wish our past had been different or that *we*
could be different. We struggle through disappointments and
frustrations, losses and other painful experiences.

As hard as we may try to be strong, to have a good attitude, not to
let things get us down, we don't always succeed. We get upset. We
worry. We feel stressed. We get depressed. We get angry. We do the
best we can and wait for things to *get* better so we can *feel* better. In
the meantime, our hearts may grow heavy . . . perhaps very heavy.

That's what happened to Duke the Dragon Slayer. In fact, *his*
heart grew *so* heavy with all that was wrong, with all that was not the
way it should be, with all that was unfair, that he became desperate to
lighten it—and set forth on the Path of Serenity to find out how.

Accompany Duke on this life-changing adventure. His guides will
be your guides. His answers will be your answers. His tools will be
your tools. His success will be your success. And by the time he is
heading home, both Duke and you will know how to take life's inevitable lumps and bumps in stride—and find happiness and serenity
anytime . . . even when you really, REALLY wish some things were
different.

"A BEAUTIFUL, EXCEPTIONALLY WELL-WRITTEN STORY THAT CAN HELP
EVERYONE TO BECOME EMOTIONALLY STRONGER AND BETTER ABLE TO
COPE WITH ADVERSITY."
                                                    Albert Ellis, Ph.D.
                                        President, Albert Ellis Institute
                                    Author of *A Guide to Rational Living*

Available wherever books are sold or send $12.00 (CA res. $12.99) plus $3.00 S/H
to Wilshire Book Co., 9731 Variel Avenue, Chatsworth, CA 91311-4315.

For our complete catalog, visit our Web site at www.mpowers.com.

I invite you to meet an extraordinary princess and accompany her on an enlightening journey. You will laugh with her and cry with her, learn with her and grow with her . . . and she will become a dear friend you will never forget.

Marcia Grad Powers

1 MILLION COPIES SOLD WORLDWIDE

The Princess Who Believed in Fairy Tales

"Here is a very special book that will guide you lovingly into a new way of thinking about yourself and your life so that the future will be filled with hope and love and song."

OG MANDINO
Author, *The Greatest Salesman in the World*

The Princess Who Believed in Fairy Tales by Marcia Grad is a personal growth book of the rarest kind. It's a delightful, humor-filled story you will experience so deeply that it can literally change your feelings about yourself, your relationships, and your life.

The princess's journey of self-discovery on the Path of Truth is an eye-opening, inspiring, empowering psychological and spiritual journey that symbolizes the one we all take through life as we separate illusion from reality, come to terms with our childhood dreams and pain, and discover who we really are and how life works.

If you have struggled with childhood pain, with feelings of not being good enough, with the loss of your dreams, or if you have been disappointed in your relationships, this book will prove to you that happy endings—and new beginnings—are always possible. Or, if you simply wish to get closer to your own truth, the princess will guide you.

The universal appeal of this book has resulted in its translation into numerous languages.

Excerpts from Readers' Heartfelt Letters

"*The Princess* is truly a gem! Though I've read a zillion self-help and spiritual books, I got more out of this one than from any other one I've ever read. It is just too illuminating and full of wisdom to ever be able to thank you enough. The friends and family I've given copies to have raved about it."

"*The Princess* is powerful, insightful, and beautifully written. I am seventy years old and have seldom encountered greater wisdom. I've been waiting to read this book my entire life. You are a psychologist, a guru, a saint, and an angel all wrapped up into one. I thank you with all my heart."

Available wherever books are sold or send $12.00 (CA res. $12.99) plus $3.00 S/H to Wilshire Book Co., 9731 Variel Avenue, Chatsworth, California 91311-4315

For our complete catalog, visit our Web site at www.mpowers.com.

How You Can Have Confidence and Power in Dealing with People

A major key to success in your business and personal life is knowing how to deal with people. In fact, studies have shown that knowing how to deal with people is 85 to 90 percent of business and professional success, and 90 to 95 percent of personal happiness.

Now here's some great news. Dealing effectively with people is a skill you can learn, just as you learned to ride a bicycle, drive an automobile, or play the piano.

Discover how you can get what you want and be the way you want to be by tapping into your hidden assets. Assets you may not even realize you have. Assets that can transform an ordinary person into an extraordinary one. Assets that can give you more confidence and personal power than you ever thought possible.

Find out how to

- Feel confident in any business or social situation
- Win others to your way of thinking
- Understand and get along with people
- Make it easy for people to like you
- Create a positive and lasting impression
- Help others feel comfortable and friendly — instantly
- Make new friends and keep them
- Find love and build relationships that work

The way you lived yesterday determined your today. But the way you live today will determine your tomorrow. Every day is a new opportunity to become the way you want to be and to have your life become what you want it to be.

Take the first step toward becoming all you're capable of being. Read Marcia Grad's book *Charisma*, which teaches a proven step-by-step plan to help anyone develop the ultimate in personal power. Then get ready for an incredible adventure that will change you and your life forever.

HYPNOSIS

WHAT IT IS

HOW TO USE IT

LEWIS R. WOLBERG, M.D.

Books by Albert Ellis, Ph.D.

A GUIDE TO RATIONAL LIVING
1.5 Million Copies Sold

1. How Far Can You Go with Self-Therapy? 2. You Largely Feel the Way You Think 3. Feeling Well by Thinking Straight 4. How You Create Your Feelings 5. Thinking Yourself Out of Emotional Disturbances 6. Recognizing and Reducing Neurotic Behavior 7. Overcoming the Influences of the Past 8. Is Reason Always Reasonable? 9. Refusing to Feel Desperately Unhappy 10. Tackling Your Dire Need for Approval 11. Reducing Your Dire Fears of Failure 12. How to Start Blaming and Start Living 13. How to Feel Frustrated but Not Depressed or Enraged 14. Controlling Your Own Emotional Destiny 15. Conquering Anxiety and Panic 16. Acquiring Self-Discipline 17. Rewriting Your Personal History 18. Accepting and Coping with the Grim Facts of Life 19. Overcoming Inertia and Getting Creatively Absorbed   304 Pages . . . $15.00

A GUIDE TO PERSONAL HAPPINESS

1. Why Search for Personal Happiness? 2. ABC's of Personal Happiness 3. Main Blocks to Personal Happiness 4. Disputing and Uprooting Emotional Disturbance 5. Emotive Methods of Achieving Personal Happiness 6. Behavioral Methods of Achieving Personal Happiness 7. Ten Rules for Achieving Personal Happiness 8. Overcoming Shyness and Feelings of Inadequacy 9. Overcoming Feelings of Guilt 10. Coping with Depression and Low Frustration Tolerance 11. Coping with Anger and with Mating Problems 12. Overcoming Sex Problems 13. Coping with Work Problems 14. Summing Up: Eliminating Your Self-Created Roadblocks to Personal Happiness 15. Upward and Onward to Self-Actualizing and Joy
                                                            144 Pages . . . $10.00

HOW TO LIVE WITH A NEUROTIC

1. The Possibility of Helping Troubled People 2. How to Recognize a Person with Emotional Disturbance 3. How Emotional Disturbances Originate 4. Some Basic Factors in Emotional Upsets 5. How to Help a Neurotic Overcome Disturbance 6. How to Live with a Person Who Remains Neurotic 7. How to Live with Yourself Though You Fail to Help a Neurotic   160 Pages . . . $10.00

HOW TO RAISE AN EMOTIONALLY HEALTHY, HAPPY CHILD

1. Neurotics Are Born as Well as Made 2. What Is a Neurotic Child? 3. Helping Children Overcome Fears and Anxieties 4. Helping Children with Problems of Achievement 5. Helping Children Overcome Hostility 6. Helping Children Become Self-Disciplined 7. Helping Children with Sex Problems 8. Helping Children with Conduct Problems 9. Helping Children with Personal Behavior Problems 10. How to Live with a Neurotic Child and Like It   256 Pages . . . $10.00

A GUIDE TO SUCCESSFUL MARRIAGE

1. Modern Marriage: Hotbed of Neurosis 2. Factors Causing Marital Disturbance 3. Gauging Marital Compatibility 4. Problem Solving in Marriage 5. Can We Be Intelligent About Marriage? 6. Love or Infatuation? 7. To Marry or Not to Marry 8. Sexual Preparation for Marriage 9. Impotence in the Male 10. Frigidity in the Female 11. Sex Excess 12. Controlling Sex Impulses 13. Non-monogamous Desires 14. Communication in Marriage 15. Children 16. In-Laws 17. Marital Incompatibility Versus Neurosis 18. Divorce 19. Succeeding in Marriage
                                                            304 Pages . . . $10.00